Outsiders in 19th-Century
Press History

Outsiders in 19th-Century Press History:
Multicultural Perspectives

edited by

Frankie Hutton
and
Barbara Straus Reed

Bowling Green State University Popular Press
Bowling Green, OH 43403

Permission is gratefully acknowledged for use of the following copyrighted material:

Portions of Chapter 1: "In the Spirit of Democracy," in *The Early Black Press in America, 1827–1860*, written by Frankie Hutton, Greenwood Press, an imprint of Greenwood Publishing Group, Inc., Westport, CT, 1993.

Portions of Chapter 2: "The Antebellum Jewish Press: Origins, Problems, Functions," written by Barbara Straus Reed, *Journalism Monographs*, no. 139, published June 1993.

Portions of Chapter 7: "Explaining the Little Bighorn: Race and Progress in the Native Press," written by John M. Coward, *Journalism Quarterly* 71, no. 3, (autumn 1994).

Portions of Chapter 8: "Historiography: A New Direction for Research on the Woman's Rights Press," written by Catherine C. Mitchell, *Journalism History* 19 (summer 1993): 59–63.

Portions of Chapter 9: "Woman Suffrage Papers of the West, 1869–1900," written by Sherilyn C. Bennion, *American Journalism* 3 (1986): 129–41.

Cover design by Dumm Art

Library of Congress Cataloging-in-Publication Data

Outsiders in 19th-century press history : multicultural perspectives / edited by
    Frankie Hutton and Barbara Straus Reed.
        p.   cm.
    Includes index.
    ISBN 0-87972-687-3. -- ISBN 0-87972-688-1 (pbk.)
    1. Ethnic press--United States--History--19th century. 2. American newspapers--Foreign language press--History--19th century. 3. American periodicals--Foreign language press--History--19th century. 4. Dissenters--United States. 5. u-us.
I. Reed, Barbara Straus.
PN4882.087 1995
071'.3'08693--dc20   95-30628
                                              CIP

Contents

Introduction   1
   Barbara Straus Reed and *Frankie Hutton*

1. Democratic Idealism in the Black Press   5
   Frankie Hutton

2. Pioneer Jewish Journalism   21
   Barbara Straus Reed

3. Spanish-Language Newspapers in California   55
   Victoria Goff

4. Chinese-American Newspapers   71
   William E. Huntzicker

5. Newspaper Representation of China and Chinese Americans   93
   William E. Huntzicker

6. Elias Boudinot and "Indian Removal"   115
   Barbara F. Luebke

7. Explaining the Little Bighorn   145
   John M. Coward

8. Historiography on the Woman's Rights Press   159
   Catherine C. Mitchell

9. The Woman Suffrage Press of the West   169
   Sherilyn Cox Bennion

10. The "Mormon Problem" and the Press   187
   David A. Copeland

11. The Peace Advocacy Press   209
   Nancy L. Roberts

Contributors   239

Index   243

Introduction

American society has historically been characterized by the marginalization of various sociocultural and religious groups and, by extension, their media. When ignored by the mainstream press, some of these groups established their own newspapers and periodicals. Throughout the 19th century, other groups were severely victimized in the press through misinformation, racist ridicule and overall unfair coverage. One result of this grossly inadequate treatment by the press is that Americans historically have had little understanding of the full extent of the outsider experience. The most essential, widely circulated avenues of communication then in existence offered little or nothing of the ethos or of the significant nation-building contributions of significant groups of people in American society. This mainstream press also failed to deal adequately with the violence and worse that some of these people were forced to endure. In an attempt to help fill this void and to make sense of the present, it is crucial to have some understanding of the fragmented nature of our nation's press history.

Insightful scholarly works such as *Up From the Footnote: A History of Women Journalists* by Marion T. Marzolf (1977); *Cherokee Editor: The Writings of Elias Boudinot* edited by Theda Perdue (1983); *The Dissident Press* by Lauren Kessler (1986); *Minorities and Media: Diversity and the End of Mass Communication* by Clint Wilson and Félix Gutiérrez (1985); *The Early Black Press in America, 1827-1860* by Frankie Hutton (1993); and *Raising Her Voice: African American Women Journalists Who Changed History* by Rodger Streitmatter (1994) have done much to establish the importance of diversity in the historical study of the American press. There is still much research to be done. This collection of articles is what we hope will be part of a long-overdue continuum on multicultural aspects of American press history.

The press is and always has been an essential window through which to view various aspects of American history. Nevertheless, the concept of diversity in the historical study of the press has been slow to find its way to the scholarly agenda of departments of history, journalism, mass communication, and other social sciences throughout the nation's colleges and universities. As student bodies on college campuses have changed to become more representative of the diverse cultures comprising America, whole new courses and redesigns of old

1

courses have been sought to respond to the needs of this new constituency as educators have to be more intellectually and socially responsible in their research, course preparation, and teaching. It is clear that higher education is in the midst of a sometimes-tortured debate over the cultural biases of the American college curriculum.

Fittingly then, this volume of essays and articles points to some of the diverse groups that were, for a variety of xenophobic, racist, and other, not-so-clear reasons, considered intolerable and were unappreciated by the mainstream, general circulation American press of the past century. This rebuff by the press of certain groups is a fact of history although American culture has been more colorful, more cosmopolitan, more diverse than any other. Indeed, cultural diversity has been one of the hallmarks of American civilization. In this collection we have endeavored to treat cultural diversity from a uniquely 19th-century perspective as journalism history literature suggests that little attention has been paid to the establishment of the presses that were outside the general circulation or "majority" framework. Nor have journalism histories been judicious in their assessments of majority newspapers that have ridiculed or unfairly covered certain cultural and religious groups. Accordingly, a couple of the chapters included here document the lack of fair treatment afforded these beleaguered groups in mainstream, general circulation newspapers. The majority of other chapters focus on the diversity in American journalism that existed outside the mainstream press as some groups felt compelled to began their own newspapers.

Each chapter in this collection stands on its own merit and needs little introduction except the knowledge that none of the groups presented here received the kind of fair, responsible, or balanced coverage they deserved in the 19th-century mainstream press. The tragic irony is that in their acquiescence to status quo rapacity and destructiveness, those who controlled mainstream journalism of the 19th century seemed content to destroy the self-respect of whole groups of the human race. Former newspaper editor John Lofton, in *The Press As Guardian of the First Amendment* (1980), explained the proclivity toward unfair coverage and the lack of adequate coverage of diverse groups in American journalism: "General circulation newspapers have tended to go along with efforts to suppress deviations from the prevailing political and social orthodoxies of their time and place rather than to support the right to dissent."[1]

While as compilers-editors we have not attempted to create a book with a single point of view, there is clearly one focus to this volume: outsiders in 19th-century American press history. Inherent in this "outsider" focus is the fact that all the groups represented here were outside of the mainstream of American society of the 19th century. None of them were accepted or considered acceptable by those who wielded the sociopolitical and economic power. Their reactions to the outsider status bestowed on them were mixed and usually commendable, given the circumstances.

Chapter 1 focuses on one of the largest minorities in America that was locked outside the mainstream of society and of the general circulation press. In response, this group of would-be African-Americans founded their own press in 1827 in New York City. In doing so, forward-looking black editors espoused democratic idealism and kept the real spirit of democracy alive in their columns though their people were haunted with charges of inferiority, chattel slavery, and negative images in popular culture and in every other aspect of society. Chapter 2 shows how the Jewish press in America was developed as a defense against the evangelization of the Jews. Jewish editors then broadened their mission to include agenda items that defined and built an American Jewish community. Chapter 3 is concerned with California's Spanish-language newspapers and shows that this press was not strictly a Mexican-American press. These newspapers pointed the way to a biculturalization of Spanish-speaking people in California who became Americanized while still clinging to Hispanic culture, language, and values. Chapters 4 and 5 focus on the Chinese as perhaps the most ridiculed and scorned group in the mainstream 19th-century American publications while suffering tremendous violence in their attempts to help build and expand the nation. The first Chinese-language newspapers were begun by Western missionaries with strong merchant support in San Francisco.

Chapter 6 spotlights Elias Boudinot and the *Cherokee Phoenix* as the only Native American newspaper in Georgia to protest Indian removal. Boudinot, known as the father of Native American journalism, was initially an outspoken removal opponent and later a removal proponent. Chapter 7 surveys the response of two important Native American newspapers in Oklahoma to Custer's Last Stand, the most famous Indian fight of the 19th century. This article shows how the Sioux and Cheyenne victory over Custer threatened the promotion of education and advancement and put Indian editors in a precarious position. Chapter 8 explores the literature of the women's rights press and counsels historians to investigate more thoroughly the issues of class, race and ethnicity within the woman suffrage campaign. Chapter 9 explores the woman suffrage press to show how a group of plucky Western female activists kept the hope of women's voting rights alive. Chapter 10 focuses on the Mormons, another group that was ridiculed in the past century's newspapers. The article highlights reactions to the landmark *Reynolds v. United States* decision which quelled polygamy among the Mormons and an important tenet of the First Amendment to the United States Constitution which provided for freedom of religion. Chapter 11 profiles the peace advocacy press whose members adopted moral and ideological positions that placed them at odds with the country. Peace advocacy periodicals and newspapers reinforced the importance of journalism as a form of activism and power to change public opinion.

Undoubtedly this collection on the multicultural aspects of 19th-century American journalism is in some way a long overdue response to a report from an Ad Hoc Coordinating Committee on Minority Education, which subsequently became the Minorities and Communication Division of the Association for Education in Journalism and Mass Communication. At the 1969 association convention in Berkeley, California, Dr. Lionel C. Barrow, of Howard University, put the mission of educators succinctly. The mission Barrow envisioned in 1969 applies now. He said:

We are attempting to educate reporters, newscasters, researchers, etc., for work in the 1970s and beyond. This is a world of urban and international problems, where whiteness is no longer considered by the non-white to be a sign of superiority. We do our students—black and white—a disservice by teaching them a rural, lily-white journalism that pays little attention to the influence of our prejudices on what we perceive and what we report. Our texts and our courses need changing.

Barrow not only pointed to a new world, but he also suggested the direction of journalism for the next century. When each of us has access to our own historical and cultural tradition and mass media, we develop pride in our own progeny, not as an end in itself but as a road which we travel to meet others, moving from learning the story of one's ancestors to learning the story of others. We must build a framework for fostering mutual respect, which becomes so necessary for the well being of all. It is perhaps the challenge of our lifetime. The mainstream press of the 19th century failed to create bridges between cultures; nor did it adequately reflect the diversity of American society.

Barbara Straus Reed and Frankie Hutton

Note

1. John Lofton, *The Press As Guardian of the First Amendment* (Columbia: University of South Carolina Press, 1980).

1

Democratic Idealism
in the Black Press

Frankie Hutton

The ideological foundations of the 19th-century black press in America are not easily discernible. What skews assessments of this idealistic ethnic press is that it began during the pre-Civil War period—a tumultuous time that was absolutely implausible for most blacks whether they were enslaved or "free." Beleaguered people of color were never really citizens from white America's perspective, and this was made clear through a number of ineluctable legal and social proscriptions from the time the black press began in 1827 with *Freedom's Journal* in New York City up to the end of the century. Not the least of these proscriptions was the United States Supreme Court's piercing Dred Scott decision in 1857 which said that not even so called "free" blacks were citizens.

After the Civil War, the abolition of slavery, and the ensuing years of racist intolerance and control typified in the black codes of southern states, a distinct system of segregationist Jim Crow laws and practices replaced the peculiar institution. These oppressive laws and practices menaced and haunted blacks until well after the middle of the 20th century.

Social proscriptions continued to be just as harsh as the legal, despite the pride of blacks about their military service in defense of the fledgling nation and despite the hard labor demanded of them to help build and expand the country. Moreover, negative images of blacks were pervasive in establishment newspapers, in other forms of popular culture and in daily social contacts as well.[1] Contemporary social scientists Jannette Dates and William Barlow have shown that theater, music, and literature during the pre-Civil War years could be uncomplimentary and even cruel toward blacks. In their recent study, Dates and Barlow noted that in popular culture, blackface minstrelsy by the 1840s was a formalized entertainment genre that gave particularly "damaging" characterizations of black Americans:

African-Americans living in the cities were invariably portrayed as urban dandies and dummies who futilely aped white manners. Plantation slaves were depicted as childlike, comical, and contented with their lot. With the slavery issue increasingly preoccupying the nation, such representations tended to reinforce the ideology of racism, especially in the minds of white working-class males, the major audience of minstrel shows.[2]

Understandably then, past and recent scholars have had differing views of the philosophical underpinning of the 19th-century black press because it was so far outside the mainstream of the majority white-owned press and because blacks themselves were put down and scorned with such a vengeance. More than any other form of black popular culture, the black press before and after the Civil War was used continually in an attempt to quell negative images of people of color. It is also the case that when the black press began, it did not fit the negative molds cast by widely used journalism histories of that period. In other words, the 25 or so pre-Civil War newspapers—such as *Freedom's Journal* from 1827 to 1829 and the *Colored American* from 1837 to 1841—that made up the pre-Civil War black press, were not part of the Penny Press, nor were they politically partisan or steeped in what one historian has called "vile innuendoes" and character assassinations that were typical of some of the mainstream newspapers.[3]

After the Civil War the black press continued to take the high road in its editorial practices—that is, the newspapers avoided scandal and hectoring. Black press historian Armistead Pride has shown that approximately 1,000 black newspapers were established nationwide during the years after the Civil War up to the turn of the century, albeit with slim survival rates.[4] These mostly weekly and monthly newspapers continued as before the Civil War to be peddled by a cadre of widely recruited, dedicated subscription agents and were largely free of external commercial controls. The newspapers were also distributed on a personal, shared-copy basis, a pattern that continued well into the 20th century.

The purpose of this chapter is to show the somewhat remarkable connection of democratic idealism to the development and growth of the black press in the 19th century—when people of color were very much outside the sociopolitical and economic mainstream of America. The endeavor here is to plumb the messages of some of the leading editors and their key associates with the democratic ideological origins of the young nation and to explore the literature in this regard.

Although the black press was also very much outside the mainstream of American journalism during its formative years, it ironically strove to be an insider in its espousal of republican ideals and democracy. The abolition of slavery was just one aspect of what this essential ethnic group sought when the black press began. As led by the editors, people of color worked toward the illusive goal of democracy in every regard: economic, educational, social, and legal. Before and after the Civil War the real unremitting work toward making the nation's democratic ideals a reality for blacks was forged by a cadre of self-selected leaders such as editors Samuel Cornish, Frederick Douglass, and Timothy Thomas Fortune, the literati of the race. Devotion to the ideals of democracy such as fairness and equality characterized the attitude of the newspapers and was an integral part of the press throughout the 19th century.

During the hurly-burly years just preceding the Civil War, some of the editors wavered and some were more consistently idealistic than others. This is exemplified in the first black editorial partnership of Samuel Cornish, who held steadfastly to the nation's democratic ideals, and John Russwurm, who eventually expatriated himself to Liberia, West Africa. Put simply, Russwurm left America never to return after losing faith that the democratic ideals could ever become a reality for blacks. Although a few black leaders like Russwurm gave up on America's ability to live up to her espoused principles, the spirit of democracy continued to be manifest in black press editorial commentary and is typified in this missive written by *Colored American* associate editor Samuel Cornish in March 1837:

Many would gladly rob us of the endeared name "Americans," a distinction more emphatically belonging to us than five-sixths of this nation and one that we will never yield. In complexion, in blood and in nativity, we are decidedly more exclusively "American" than our White brethren; hence the propriety of the name of our paper, *Colored American*, and of identifying the name with all our institutions, in spite of our enemies who would rob us of our nationality and reproach us as exotics.[5]

It is apparent from the content of early black newspapers that this fledgling press was influenced by the ideals of the American Revolution. These ideals were nowhere better laid out than in revered documents such as the Declaration of Independence and the United States Constitution to which the first black newspapers paid allegiance. Echoing the spirit of democracy and republicanism in his weekly moral reform journal, the *National Reformer*, black editor William Whipper explained the connection of the nation's people of color to the ideals of the Revolution this way: "Let us rest our cause on the republican standards of our revolutionary fathers, while we knock at the door of the Constitution...If we are asked what evidence we bring to sustain our qualifications for citizenship, we will offer certificates of our Birth and Nativity."[6]

The notion that the democratic ideals of early America influenced forward-thinking black leaders and their relationship to the young nation is not novel. It has been suggested by several historians including Bernard Bailyn, author of the award-winning work *The Ideological Origins of the American Revolution*, who explained that the cause of freedom for blacks naturally "followed from the principles of the Revolution."[7] Historian Ira Berlin noted further that the Revolutionary era was so important to black life that it, more than the Reconstruction period, "laid the foundation for modern Afro-American life."[8] Writing more recently, historian Clarence Walker also linked people of color to the spirit of democracy emanating from the Revolution. Walker explained that even though blacks were outsiders and treated as aliens in pre-Civil War America, they "embodied without reservation the ideals embodied in the Constitution and the Declaration of Independence."[9]

Belief in republicanism and in the ideals of the Revolution was indeed contagious and through several generations never left the minds and hearts of conscientious blacks involved in journalism. Coupled with belief in the ideals of the Revolution, the belief of the editors that self-elevation, morality, and social responsibility were the panaceas for black upward mobility and acceptance in America, underpinned the messages of black newspapers. The put-downs and charges of inferiority in the major white-owned, mainstream newspapers were repelled by middle-class blacks whose newspapers reported regular self-help activities, individual successes, and benevolence designed to show responsibility and progress in the race. This apparently strategic response in the press was a form of protest against charges that blacks were inferior. The democratic spirit of black newspapers likewise had the effect of magnifying the tremendous flaws in America's socio-political processes.

The editors seemed also to believe that America's ideals of democracy could become realities for the free elite and would eventually lead to the abolition of slavery and then on to a democratic reality for blacks. These somewhat idealistic leaders saw beyond the goal of mere integration. They worked toward acceptance of people of color in America, although in hindsight this was an unrealistic goal given the arrant racism and attendant social and legal proscriptions against the race. Clearly, before and to a large extent after the Civil War, black newspapers usually avoided lurid news of the exploitation of blacks, their degradation, and the violence which often haunted them, and instead flaunted the good deeds and positive contributions of the nation's people of color. These newspapers showcased the poetry, literature, educational pursuits, charity, and community involvements of people who were doggedly in pursuit of acceptance in America. Black editors of the pre-Civil War period did not use their papers to convey the fear and the anger that were sure to have been poignant outgrowths of the continued oppression and violence heaped on the race. Nor did these newspapers assume the sole posture of often reminding the race after the Civil War that it was still essentially powerless or that it was largely scorned and rebuked by the mainstream press.

Ironically the people who made the initial strides in American black journalism were often more steadfast and humanitarian in attempts to advance the precepts of democracy for all than those who actually set the foundation for the democratic experiment. While most of the 19th-century black papers appear to have been published in an idealistic spirit and quest for a nonracist democracy, an editorial in the *Aliened American*, the pre-Civil War Cleveland weekly, edited by an association of William Howard Day, Samuel Ringgold Ward, and J.W.C. Pennington serves as a reminder that pro-democratic idealism still existed in the black press right up through the progressively turbulent 1850s. "Our humble advocacy rests not upon accident of color" an editorial in the *Aliened American* read in April 1853. "We claim for all and especially for all Americans, equal justice before American Law; and are willing to stand or fall by its just application, under the Constitution of our common country."[10]

That such a statement referring to "equal justice" and to "the Constitution of our common country" could be published by a group of essentially powerless black editors during the tumultuous decade leading up to the Civil War was as boldly idealistic as it was pitifully ironic, considering that people of color were more shunned during this period than ever. A former fugitive slave and licensed minister who eventually led a white congregation in Cortland, New York, Samuel Ringgold Ward understood well the precarious nature of life for blacks in America. Though he found it necessary to flee to Canada just before the Civil War, his personal correspondence at various times reflects both his frustration with the predicament of blacks and his belief in democracy. Like other leading blacks who fled to Canada West, Ward apparently began to question whether democracy could ever work for his people. But in a letter to an official of the Liberty Party regarding the suffrage fight for African-Americans, Ward had insisted on "the equality of the whole brotherhood of the human race" and the "doctrine of inalienable rights of all men."[11] Obviously, his insistence was to no avail. Without tangible results, black editors like Ward continued to insist that America should hold true to its democratic tenets for everybody.

As evidenced by the continuance of slavery, the toughened Fugitive Slave Law and the stubbornness of the colonization movement to rid the country of free blacks, the race was put down with renewed vengeance and violent vigor during this period just before the Civil War. And although middle-class blacks, such as those who headed the press, made some personal, economic, and educational gains in their own small segregated communities, the overall situation for the race was pitiable in the larger scheme of things. As one contemporary historian, Page Smith, commented about the situation for the free elite during this period: "Discrimination in the North was constant and galling, especially for those blacks of superior education and intelligence."[12] Even white abolitionists, those northerners of influence and means who agitated so gallantly against slavery, generally preferred not to socialize with fellow black abolitionists, a number of whom were editors and the upper class of their race.

Merle Curti, a pioneer historian of American patriotism, paid only scant attention to people of color in his book *The Roots of American Loyalty*. However, Curti's comment about articulate blacks being difficult to assess regarding their loyalty to America is curious given the group's voluntary military service in every war and their dogged belief in the ideal of a democratic nation. Curti concluded that assessing the black attitude toward America in view of the slavery experience was "one of the most difficult in American historiography."[13] Undoubtedly, editors of the antebellum period fall into the category of the articulate free black to whom Curti referred. The evidence shows that the sentiments of most free blacks before the Civil War—and especially the articulate—were clear: they wanted to be accepted in America and they rejected attempts and notions to colonize them inside or outside the United States. From a group of 500,000 or so free blacks in the 1840s came the most articulate of a woefully small number of middle-class blacks in the nation. But more than in what they articulated in favor of America, the generally positive tone and uplifting spirit of their newspapers is indicative that black editors sanctioned the nation's democratic ideals while they loathed the prevalent racist practices and attendant hegemonic legalities which kept people of color repressed. Essentially, the editors thought that blacks had as much right to be full-fledged American citizens as whites, for they, like whites, had grown up with the nation and had suffered greatly to underpin its mercantile interests.

Most of the editors, with the notable exception of John Brown Russwurm, mentioned earlier as an expatriate, subscribed to the belief that America's democratic ideals could embrace people of color. That all of the editors were frustrated in their attempts to follow and believe in America's democratic ideals has already been noted in the cogent example of Russwurm while he was co-editor of *Freedom's Journal,* the nation's first black newspaper. Just months before the young editor left the nation as one of the few elite converts to the slaveholder-inspired American Colonization Society's movement to rid the nation of free blacks, Russwurm emphasized his belief in the nation's democratic ideals in the renewal prospectus for *Freedom's Journal.* "In the discussion of political subjects," the young editor wrote in 1828, "we shall ever regard the constitution of the United States as our polar star."[14]

Probably because he was then under the influence of assimilation-minded Samuel Cornish or perhaps because he really wanted to believe that blacks could fit into the young nation, Russwurm had made it clear that *Freedom's Journal* would be pro-Constitution and pro-American, and it was throughout its two-year existence. Russwurm eventually gave up his hope and work toward democracy for blacks in America. But even after Russwurm left the country, his partner, Samuel Cornish, kept the spirit of republicanism and hope for democracy alive in other weeklies, including the sequel to *Freedom's Journal,* a short-lived newspaper known as the *Rights of All.* The *Weekly Advocate* and the *Colored American,* for which Cornish was also editor and co-publisher, were also steeped in democratic idealism as these weeklies showcased the best of the black race in New York City and surrounding areas. It appears that at times some of the editors were somewhat victimized by benign deception—that is, belief that America's sacred democratic institutions and documents could embrace people of color.

Concerning the idealism of antebellum black leaders, historian Frederick Cooper explained that they "did not fully understand the situation they sought to remedy because they never fully realized they faced a race problem."[15] Cooper concluded that black leaders simply "did not realize that whites might not want to live and work with proper, abstentious blacks any more than with black drunkards."[16] As leaders, as premiere thinkers among their people, the editors apparently thought that to write uplifting and encouraging messages, and to verbalize optimistic, though sometimes chiding missives about the nation, was a way to help make their prophecy of liberty and democracy for their people come true. In this sense the editors' belief in democracy—in the ideals of the Declaration of Independence and the Constitution—inspired them and propelled the positive spirit and editorial makeup of their papers.

While optimism about the precepts of democracy was apparent in various news and feature columns of the black press, it was not unusual for some of the editors to give testimony to their faith in America. Samuel Cornish, an educated, well-spoken assimilationist and Presbyterian minister born in Delaware, was apparently the leading editor in this regard. He led the weeklies with which he was connected with incredible benevolence, good will, and high spirit. One could read in the *Colored American* in 1837, for instance, that blacks would not always be a "downtrodden people" and that black youth could be "as eligible to the Presidency of the United States as any other portion of the community."[17] The *Colored American*, the premiere black-owned New York City weekly of its time was eventually published by a committee headed by Charles Ray and Philip Bell. The paper's editors and publishing committee also vowed to help give youth of color "ample qualifications" to aspire to the United States Presidency.

From miles west of the Hudson River, near Philadelphia, the *National Reformer* as edited by William Whipper and backed by the American Moral Reform Society, continued to be no less optimistic than Cornish that the niche for blacks was America. Whipper's monthly journal was backed by the American Moral Reform Society from 1837 to 1839. Whipper believed that free blacks had a responsibility to help those in bondage and this was reason enough for staying in America. Also a staunch integrationist and Underground Railroad operative, Whipper summarized his resolute belief in America: "we believe and affirm that the duty we owe to the land of our birth and the interest of our suffering brethren" necessitates that blacks "remain on our soil."[18]

In practically the same period that Cornish and Whipper published their idealistic editorial views in the *Colored American* and the *National Reformer* respectively, across the Atlantic Ocean in Glasgow, Scotland, James McCune Smith, a young black medical student from New York City, lauded the positive attitude of his people toward America. Smith, who was eventually to become editorial associate of several black newspapers including the *Weekly Anglo-African* and the *North Star* and one of New York's most illustrious antebellum physicians, assured his antislavery audience that blacks would defend America whenever they had to. Speaking on March 15, 1837, in Glasgow, Smith said that "if at this moment any warlike armament were to invade the United States...the men who would strike first, and would struggle longest in defense of the American coast would be the 800,000 free people of color."[19] Smith further assured his foreign audience that blacks were "Americans by birth, Americans in principle, and [had] proved themselves in many a field of fight, as well as by present sufferings."

Blacks were, according to Smith, "ardent lovers of the American soil."[20] If Smith's speech sounded strange coming from a black man who had been forced to go abroad to earn a medical degree because of blacks' limited access to medical schooling in America, stranger still was his continued faith after he returned to America to set up a segregated medical practice in New York and to write for several black journals and newspapers. Smith's progressive views can be read in the *North Star* published in Rochester, New York, from 1847 to 1851, in the *Weekly Anglo-African* from 1859 to 1860, and in the *Anglo-African Magazine* from 1859 to 1861, both published in New York City. Smith's notions about the rightness of black people's place being America appear not to have subsided as he worked in a variety of self-improvement and reform organizations to aid his people, particularly in the New York City area.

Henry Highland Garnet's exasperation over the republican ideals he saw quelled have been well noted. Prior to becoming a Presbyterian minister and editor of two Troy, New York, 1840s ephemeral weeklies, the *National Watchman* and the *Clarion*, Garnet had experienced two poignant episodes of racism. As a young man he had briefly attended the integrated Noyes Academy in New Hampshire, but was made to leave when it was demolished by racist whites and never rebuilt. Later his family life was disrupted by the intrusion of slave hunters in the family home in New York City. Moreover, Garnet's background and experiences never paralleled the privilege of black press associate James McCune Smith, who had successfully studied medicine at the University of Glasgow and interned in Paris. And yet, early in his career Garnet let it be known early on in a published discourse on the state and plight of blacks that he too subscribed to democratic ideals and favored living in America rather than elsewhere. Garnet has been noted for his own personal achievements in the face of horrific odds, including the amputation of one of his legs. In an 1848 privately published discourse on the past and present condition of blacks, Garnet lamented that young black men were "brutalized in intellect" and their energies "chilled by the frosts of slavery."[21] Garnet tempered a portion of his screed about the nation that had repeatedly repelled him. "America is my home, my country and I have no other," he said incisively.[22]

That Frederick Douglass, a premiere abolitionist, the most illustrious of the 19th-century black editors, and a reform-minded humanitarian, was pro-American and a democratic idealist has been well documented by several historians and is not surprising. A recent intellectual assessment of Douglass's attitudes toward America found him to be an assimilationist, bourgeois in his values, and foremost among free blacks in his belief in democratic ideals. Contemporary historian Waldo Martin described Douglass as a "democratic as well as Christian idealist."[23] Martin said Douglass "gloried in the democratic idealism and achievements of the American, French, Haitian, and 1848 European revolutions."[24] Frustrated in his attempts to bring people of color to their rightful status in America, as an editor, Douglass fretted over America's limited, selective democracy and racist ways in his newspapers in both satire and disgust. Douglass rather obviously wanted to be, and worked to be, part of the country's mainstream. His reasoning in this regard, like that of James McCune Smith, was simple: blacks had "grown up" with the country and had a right to be in America. He explained the natural fit: "we have watered your soil with our tears, nourished it with our blood, tilled it with our hard hands. Why should we not stay here?"[25] Douglass wanted to know why any black man or woman would consider leaving America. "We came when it was a wilderness, and were the pioneers of civilization on this continent," he reasoned.[26]

Added to his belief that America should be the niche for blacks, Frederick Douglass's initial ambiguity and eventual reasoned support of the United States Constitution is legendary. His view that the Constitution was not proslavery not only helped to solidify the break with his abolitionist mentor William Lloyd Garrison who believed the Constitution permitted slavery, but it also led to a fair amount of discussion in the columns of his newspaper. Douglass presented his views to readers in a March 1849 issue of the *North Star*. According to him, the Constitution "standing alone, and construed only in the light of the letter, without reference to the opinion of the men who framed and adopted it, or to the nation under it, from the time of its adoption until now, is not a pro-slavery instrument."[27]

Almost five years later, Douglass still continued his support of the United States Constitution. According to an account in *Frederick Douglass' Paper*, Douglass attended an 1851 meeting of the American Anti-Slavery Society at which his paper was criticized because it was thought to be too pro-union, unlike Garrison's newspaper, the *Liberator*, and several other abolitionist newspapers which were more critical of the Constitution and the continued union with slaveholding states. An editorial in *Frederick Douglass' Paper* explained that the weekly was "opposed generally" at the convention because it was not a disunion paper, but advocated voting under the Constitution of the United States. Douglass hereupon announced that he now believed in and advocated voting under the Constitution for the abolition of slavery, and hence, if such sentiments were obnoxious his paper was would stand true to his beliefs.[28]

Douglass was willing to isolate his newspaper from other abolition newspapers and the American Anti-Slavery Society if the alternative meant disavowing the union. For his pro-Constitution views, Douglass was accused of making "the success of his paper paramount to principle."[29] Nevertheless, from this point on, Douglass appears not to have wavered in his support of the United States Constitution.

In essence, Douglass felt blacks were entitled to all the privileges and benefits of being American citizens. They had earned the title "American," and early black editors, like Douglass, Garnet, Cornish and Whipper, though sometimes in disagreement over strategies, were in unison on the matter of uplifting of their people through the vehicles of education, temperance, prudence, continued morality, and a closely knit, genteel social life.

There is no doubt that all of the editors were aware of the rancorous racism that kept the vast majority of blacks downtrodden. Although there were a few, modest sociopolitical and economic advances after the Civil War, most blacks still worked in the most menial jobs for the lowest possible wages when they could find work at all. The masses of blacks should have been as enervated as they were impoverished, yet they seemed to take solace and rejoice in the spirit of freedom as they hoped for the best after the Thirteenth, Fourteenth and Fifteenth Amendments were ratified. Eric Foner, a leading historian of the Reconstruction period and after has explained that the black community's religious, social, and political mobilization was in the face of "a wave of violence that raged almost unchecked in large parts of the post war South."[30]

During the Civil War era, the patriotism of blacks and their willingness to fight for the Union were underscored by the very few black newspapers managing to survive. Typifying the patriotism exhibited by blacks during this time is the brief account in a May 1861 issue of the *Weekly Anglo-African* about a black fraternal organization parading with drum and fife in New York City with the American flag. The parade was dispersed by a crowd of racist, anti-Civil War whites who ridiculed the blacks, called them derogatory names and took their flag away.[31] In another region of the country, *L'Union* in New Orleans, a black-inspired French-language newspaper begun in 1862, was preoccupied with patriotism and the Union troop effort. Published triweekly, on Tuesday, Thursday, and Saturdays, *L'Union* was directed toward politics, literature, and progression of the race. In October 1862, *L'Union* assured its readers in a front page commentary entitled "Patriotisme" that the United States would not perish and the Confederate rebellion would be crushed.[32] *L'Union*'s view was prescient. During the Civil War, *L'Union*'s news feature about the New Orleans Reverend Cure Lemaitre's celebratory church service in honor of the

Emancipation Proclamation declared that "nations, like individuals are subject to mistakes; they sin like individuals and they must make amends."[33] According to *L'Union*, the Reverend Lemaitre made his remarks to a standing-room-only crowd and an estimated 1,000 spirited celebrants outside.

There is no doubt that all of the editors were aware of the rancorous racism and hegemonic legalities, prejudice, and hatred that kept the majority of blacks at the bottom of America's ethnic heap. Prejudice and intolerance toward these people remained rampant among whites of every echelon throughout the 19th-century sociopolitical and economic advances just after the Civil War. Commentary in one midwestern black newspaper complained in 1878 that prejudice so "opposed the progress of the colored people as to render it well-nigh impossible for them to make any headway at all."[34] The unattributed commentary had described the situation very mildly, considering the growing violence and lynchings of blacks in the post-Civil War South.

It should be reiterated that pointing to instances of democratic idealism and patriotism in black newspapers is not intended to suggest that the editors were unmindful of the horrific circumstances confronting them and their people in America, even after slavery ended. Such editorial content and feature in the papers has been suggested earlier to have been a clever strategy waged to shame America about her undemocratic ways. At the same time democratic idealism in the papers must have been used to prod skeptical blacks so that they would continue to believe in America and to act as though they had a stake in the young nation.

In various post-Civil War black newspapers, there continued to be calls for an ideal time, as described in the *Colored Patriot* in 1882, when "all men shall be free and equal—equal under the law, equal in every condition, equal in every avenue and walk."[35] Following this pattern of democratic idealism, a leading late-19th-century black weekly, the *New York Age*, edited by the erudite Timothy Thomas Fortune, often featured political news and features as though people of color were real movers and shakers in the nation's political arena. Fortune eventually supported Marcus Garvey's back-to-Africa movement; but in 1887 he urged blacks "to use peaceful methods of agitation" and not to "run away from violence."[36] Despite his nationalist stance, Fortune did not cease to use his newspaper in support of patriotism and democratic ideals. Two well-placed, lengthy front-page stories illustrate this point. In November 1891, for instance, Fortune featured a story about a lecture at St. Mark's Church, in New York City, commemorating the work of the Massachusetts 54th, a regiment made up of the most well-known of the

Civil War's black troops.[37] In 1892, a substantial portion of the front page of Fortune's newspaper was devoted to various celebrations and programs in honor of former United States President Abraham Lincoln. At Lyric Hall in New York City, a group of 300 well-dressed blacks was reported to have danced and been entertained by a large orchestra, all in patriotic honor of the man who was credited with freeing the slaves.[38]

When the editors used their columns expressly to expose the efforts of self-elevation and patriotism of the race, they naturally brought some of the positive social advances of their people to the fore as they helped to quell notions of inferiority. Likewise, when black editors continued to offer editorial encouragement about the ideals of true republicanism, they strategically reminded America's leaders that the country's democracy was very badly flawed.

Obviously the methods and efficacy of the 19th-century black press are debatable. It could be argued that the more effective editorial policy would have been persistent fulminations about the deplorable undemocratic situation for blacks. Yet it could also be argued that such an editorial posture would have elicited even harsher repression from white-run 19th-century governments than already existed. From a practical perspective, it is conceivable that the optimistic tone selected by the editors actually helped keep alive the hopeful spirit necessary for the survival and uplift and continued socialization of an already resilient group of free blacks. It was after the turn of the century that black journalism became less idealistic and much more restive about America's perverted democracy. The editors were then compelled to denounce Jim Crow laws and, as led by Ida B. Wells, the escalating lynchings of blacks in the South.[39] They were forced to take stands on other pressing issues such as the mass migration of blacks from the South in the face of sociopolitical postures of accommodation versus nationalism.

Notes

1. See the author's *The Early Black Press in America, 1827–1860*, 58-59, for an example of how blacks were socially ostracized at every level. This example from an original source provides an account of a scene in a boarding house when an Englishman visiting America was advised to disassociate himself from black women.

2. Jannette L. Dates and William Barlow, eds. *Split Image: African Americans in the Mass Media* (Washington, D.C.: Howard University Press, 1990), 7.

3. For a classic history of American journalism which encompasses the antebellum period see Frank Luther Mott's assessment in *American Journalism: A History 1690-1960* (New York: Macmillan, 1953), which describes both the Penny Press of the 1830s and the political newspapers of the era. Mott describes the period from 1801 to 1833 as the "Dark Ages of Partisan Journalism." He also discusses the use of "vile innuendo," which typified the periods newspapers, 168. For a more recent assessment of American journalistic practices of this period, see Edwin Emery and Michael Emery, *The Press and America: An Interpretive History of Mass Media*, 5th ed. (Englewood Cliffs, N.J.: Prentice-Hall, 1984), describing the Penny Press as too often willing to "lower standards," 142.

4. This figure is suggested in Armistead Pride's "A Register and History of Negro Newspapers in the United States 1827-1950" (Ph.D. diss., Northwestern University, 1950). Some select "personals" appeared in classified advertisement format in the early black newspapers and there was scant commercial advertising in some of the papers, but it is evident that this was not sufficient to financially sustain the newspapers. To help the newspapers stay afloat, which was difficult, all sorts of fund-raising efforts were made by free blacks in various communities. Advanced paid subscriptions also appear to have been an important source of revenue for the newspapers. Subscription agents and shared copies were essential aspects of the circulation of early black newspapers.

5. *Colored American* (New York, N.Y.), 4 March 1837.

6. See William Whipper's comments in *The National Reformer* (Philadelphia), December 1839, 180.

7. Bernard Bailyn, *The Ideological Origins of the American Revolution* (Cambridge, Mass.: Belknap Press of Harvard University Press, 1967), 236.

8. See Ira Berlin's article "The Revolution in Black Life" in *The American Revolution*, ed. Alfred F. Young (DeKalb: Northern Illinois University Press, 1976), 351-82.

9. Clarence E. Walker, "The American Negro as Historical Outsider, 1836-1935," *Canadian Review of American Studies* 7 (summer 1986): 138. For a more recent perspective on how democracy evolved in America without making a place for African-Americans, see Eli Ginsberg and Alfred S. Eichner, *Troublesome Presence: Democracy and Black Americans* (New Brunswick, N.J.: Transaction Publishers, 1993).

10. *Aliened American* (Cleveland, Ohio), 9 April 1853.

11. As quoted in C. Peter Ripley, ed. *Witness for Freedom: African American Voices on Race, Slavery and Emancipation* (Chapel Hill: University of North Carolina Press, 1993), 144.

12. Page Smith, *The Nation Comes of Age: A People's History of the Antebellum Years* (New York: Penguin, 1981), 641.

13. Merle Curti, *The Roots of American Loyalty* (New York: Atheneum, 1968), 87.

14. *Freedom's Journal* (New York, N.Y.), 25 April 1828.

15. Frederick Cooper, "Elevating the Race: The Social Thought of Black Leaders, 1827-1850," *American Quarterly* 24 (December 1972), 624.

16. Cooper, "Elevating the Race," 624.

17. *Colored American* (New York), 1 July 1837.

18. *National Reformer,* September 1839, 181.

19. Read Smith's speech in *The Black Abolitionist Papers*, vol. 1, *The British Isles, 1830-1865*, ed. C. Peter Ripley (Chapel Hill: University of North Carolina Press, 1985), 66. Note that Smith's estimate of the number of free blacks in America at that time (800,000) is a bit high when compared to contemporary historians' estimate of about 500,000.

20. Smith, *Black Abolitionist Papers*, 1:66.

21. See Henry Highland Garnet's *The Past and Present Condition and the Destiny of the Colored Race: A Discourse* (Washington, D.C.: Moreland Foundation, 1848, 29; reprint, Miami: Mnemosyne Publishing, 1969, 15).

22. Garnet, *Past and Present Condition*, 29, reprint, 15.

23. Waldo E. Martin, Jr., *The Mind of Frederick Douglass* (Chapel Hill: University of North Carolina, 1984), 49.

24. Martin, *Mind of Frederick Douglass*, 49.

25. John W. Blassingame, ed. *The Frederick Douglass Papers*, series 1, vol. 2. 1847-54 (New Haven: Yale University Press, 1982), 304.

26. Blassingame, *Frederick Douglass Papers*, 2:304.

27. *North Star* (Rochester, N.Y.), 16 March 1849.

28. *Frederick Douglass' Paper* (Rochester, N.Y.), 13 January 1854.

29. *Frederick Douglass' Paper*, 13 January 1954.

30. Eric Foner, Reconstruction: America's Unfinished Revolution, 1863-1877 (New York: Harper & Row, 1988), 119.

31. *Weekly Anglo African* (New York, N.Y.), 4 May 1891.

32. *L'Union* (New Orleans, La.), 8 October 1862.

33. *L'Union* (New Orleans, La.), 2 May 1863.

34. As quoted from the *Colored Citizen*, Fort Scott, Kans., 23 November 1878, in Martin E. Dann, ed. *The Black Press 1827-1890: The Quest for National Identity* (New York: Putnam's, 1971), 196.

35. As quoted from the *Colored Patriot*, Topeka, Kans., 20 April 1882, in Martin E. Dann, ed., *The Black Press 1827-1890*, 353.

36. Quoted in *The Black Press 1827-1890*, 375.

37. *New York Age* (New York, N.Y.), 21 November 1891.

38. *New York Age* (New York, N.Y.), 21 November 1891.

39. With regard to antilynching, muckraking journalism of the post Civil War era, Ida B. Wells was the leading journalist to call for a stop to the horrible practice. See her autobiography, edited by her daughter Alfreda M. Duster,

Crusade for Justice: The Autobiography of Ida B. Wells (Chicago: University of Chicago Press, 1970). Also of interest is Mildred Thompson's biography, *Ida B. Wells-Barnett: An Exploratory Study of an American Black Woman, 1893-1930* (Brooklyn: Carlson Publishing, 1990).

2

Pioneer Jewish Journalism

Barbara Straus Reed

The outsider theme applies to the birth of Jewish journalism in America. Many publications established in the pre-Jacksonian and Jacksonian periods came from the need to respond to the activities of others.[1] The pioneer publications were concerned with the theme of defense, as a reaction to external religious pressures. Under the impact of community growth, the press became a community builder, covering internal social values, general politics and international affairs affecting Jews. The editors were concerned about their people's development, preserving their heritage as did other groups. For people who had been persecuted—and the Jews have had a long history of persecution—maintaining themselves by observing their faith was considered extremely important to the editors.

The first Jewish periodical in America was established in 1823 as a response to the Protestant evangelical efforts to convert Jews to Christianity. As David Paul Nord says, "evangelical" can be added to other terms, such as "technological" and "economic" and "political," to explain how the public's reading habits developed in the United States during the first half of the 19th century.[2] For some Christians, the Jew was an object of an evangelical commitment. Numerous associations, societies, and organizations sprang up at the end of the 18th and beginning of the 19th centuries, including the London Society for Promoting Christianity Among the Jews, the Baptist Society for Evangelization of the Jews, and the American Society for Promoting Christianity Among the Jews.[3] The most active association was the American Society for Meliorating the Condition of the Jew (ASMCJ). The ASMCJ and its organ, *Israel's Advocate*, resulted in the first regularly issued American publication by and about Jews.

Solomon Henry Jackson and the "Jew"
The Jew, Being a Defence of Judaism against all adversaries and particularly against the Insidious attacks of Israel's Advocate, the

publication's full title, can be regarded as the first Jewish periodical in America. The *Jew* began publication in March 1823. As its title suggests, it was devoted wholly to attacking the idea of Christian conversion, in particular, those urged by the ASMCJ. With some 200 branches from Maine to Georgia and affiliation with six independent sister organizations, the ASMCJ reached nearly 20,000 people through its printed vehicle, *Israel's Advocate*.[4]

Jackson had come to America from London around 1787, making his home in Pike County, Pennsylvania, where he married and fathered five children. After his wife died, Jackson moved his family to New York City around 1820.[5] As the first Jewish printer in New York, Jackson made several contributions to American Jewish life. He translated and published a Jewish prayer book in Hebrew and English in 1826, as well as the first American edition of the Passover Haggadah, or Order of the Service, in Hebrew and English in 1837.[6]

Jackson moved his office frequently—every year from 1824 to 1831.[7] He listed his occupation as editor until 1829–30, then chose printer. Jackson died probably on February 13, 1846.[8]

The *Jew,* measuring 5 1/4 by 8 1/2 inches, appeared on the first day of each Jewish month; it consistently ran to 20 pages. Below the nameplate Jackson used Hebrew fonts for biblical quotations, which changed monthly; Hebrew fonts were also used throughout the text.[9] Jackson lacked a cylinder press and possessed only a flat bed and Hebrew font type. His work with synagogal printing suggests that he was the only printer in New York with Hebrew fonts.[10]

Jackson bound the year's issues into one volume so that families or individuals could easily preserve them. He brought out a first set of bound issues in 1824. The second year's bound issues noted Solomon Henry Jackson had edited the volume. The *Jew* appeared from March 1823 through March 1825, as Jackson published it continually on a monthly basis except for the month of August 1824, when no issue appeared. Thus, 24 issues were produced.[11]

Content and Role

The *Jew* had as its object the combating of Christian missionary teachings. Jackson was ever-watchful of information from *Israel's Advocate*. In fact, as with other minority presses, the watchdog role was the primary purpose of the publication.

In addition to strong attacks on evangelizing efforts, articles attacked the ASMCJ directly. Each issue bore this statement: "Each number is expected, at least, to controvert one position or text in dispute; the whole to be conducted with candour, temper and moderation; the language to be always such as should not offend even our opponents; derision will never be admitted."[12] However, Jackson's attack on the ASMCJ and on *Israel's Advocate* did not live up to that promise. Jackson apparently took offense and felt abused from the appeals in the house organ, as if it were an anti-Semitic sheet. The *Jew* took the form of a theological exegesis, a continuing polemic against the Christian missionary activity of *Israel's Advocate.*

Jackson chose not to hide behind a freethinker; he openly declared his name, his identity as a Jew, and the name and address of his Jewish publisher. In an early issue he boldly proclaimed his identity:

I am…a man as yourselves, whom you have unwarrantably attacked—a Jew! a citizen of the United States! and an inhabitant of New-York who, standing on the defence of his religion, on the defence of his people and kindred, which, and whom you have, and do unfairly, wantonly, and unmanly attack, calls on you to guard.[13]

Furthermore, in terms reminiscent of the first issue of *Freedom's Journal,* the first black newspaper in America, but predating its appearance by four years, Jackson wrote:

The right of defence, when attacked, is considered a first law of nature: it is not only inherent in man, but exists with equal strength in the insect and the reptile; hence the adage, "tread on a worm and it will turn." Israel has long been a "worm, and no man"; and has borne (to call it by no harsher name) the gainsayings of the Gentiles.[14]

Jackson's stridencies bore similarity to the public religious disquisitions of the Middle Ages. He reviled the Christian Bible and Christianity's founder. He defended his faith alone. He could not praise Christianity.

Essentially the *Jew* was divided into three subject areas: There were the theological discussions disproving Christianity; an out-and-out attack on the ASMCJ, its motives and methods; and a defense of Judaism and Jews from misinformation created by innuendo or direct statement. By far the greatest amount of space was devoted to theological discussions. They described Old Testament prophets, language, critiques of the gospels of the New Testament, and special interpretations of Old Testament material.

Jackson's front page held information refuting a biblical issue or an attack on the ASMCJ. He totally ignored news of the world as well as news within the Jewish community. For example, information about the Monroe Doctrine, promulgated in 1823, did not appear, nor did news in

1824 of Jewish expulsions from Russian villages. Thus, despite important events taking place in the world as well as in America at the time of his publication, Jackson chose not to report or respond to them.

Rather, the *Jew* was conceived of basically for the purpose of defense. The 20 pages of each monthly issue constituted generally a single polemical essay framed in response to the missionizing content of the Society's house organ. Jackson's substantive discussions on theological and related matters not only set the record straight but also transmitted something of the Jewish religion and culture. In fact, Jackson tried to disseminate the ideas of Judaism through his periodical; he saw that as the primary obligation to his readers.

Indeed, in addition to Jackson's own efforts, two sets of letters continued to emphasize differences with Christianity. Dea's Letters, commencing with vol. 1, no. 5, July 1823, regularly offered a complete, orderly attack on Christianity (there were thirteen such letters in all published in the *Jew*).[15] The letters began with a disquisition about how the New Testament was not divinely inspired. Questioned were the authority and identity of those who established New Testament canon. The Old Testament remained the sole authority for both Jews and Christians, the letters proclaimed. Prophecies for restoration of the Jews as well as New Testament allegories were refuted, while extensive commentary was offered on Matthew and told how the Christian notion of prophecy was confused and thus failed. The letters commented on the changeability of Christian applications of biblical prophecies to Jesus, and noted various Old Testament prophets. These letters clearly were aimed at those well-educated theologically; the average lay reader would not have followed the ideas.[16] In printing them, Jackson addressed himself exclusively to educated Christians.

Also printed were three letters from Abraham, beginning with vol. 1, no. 7, September 1823. This columnist, lacking a surname, refuted a letter to a vice president of an ASMCJ chapter in Connecticut, wrote about the spuriousness of Jesus of Nazareth, suggesting he was not a messiah, and commented on variations of the gospels.[17] He corrected misquotation and rebutted at length the Christian interpretation of the four empires in the Book of Daniel expounded by the Society. With both sets of letters, Jackson gave no suggestion about Abraham's identity.

Jackson craved a dialogue. He wrote,

If the American Society for meliorating the condition of the Jews [*sic*] are serious in their purpose of converting the Jews, they are called on to come forward manfully. We will fairly consider all they have to say in favour of that religion they wish us to embrace, and let the world judge between us. But if they will not come forward, even to defend their own religion, the world will pronounce them to be "blind, greedy dogs, loving to slumber," while I shall accuse them of being convicted sinners, sinning against great light and knowledge.[18]

But from the first, the missionaries ignored him and his publication. Jackson even pitted his subscriber list against that of *Israel's Advocate*."THE JEW has a larger, and full as respectable a list of subscribers as Israel's Advocate; (the difference is in proportion of the mole-hill to the mountain)."[19]

Jackson offered direct assaults on the ASMCJ and its leaders, and evoked the futility of evangelical societies to the Jews in general. He charged that melioration societies were based on bribes and lies, and that members did not understand the Holy Scriptures from a Jewish point of view.

Jackson quarreled with the missionaries who termed circumcision "misery." Jews, he asserted, are not miserable because they are circumcised. He likened such "misery" to the "misery" of baptism and explained the meaning of circumcision.[20] "It [circumcision] is their [Jews'] glory, their boast," for they were chosen by God to be of service among mankind.

After the ASMCJ proposed a colony particularly for Jewish converts to Christianity, Jackson argued that Jewish converts from Europe would not accept being herded into a settlement colony in America. The ASMCJ had considered purchase of 1,500 acres for an orchard and vegetables, 300 for growing grain. At most, 200 to 300 families did not think so many apostates could be found.[21] He pointed out that the work would not suit them: "hoeing in the fields will overheat, haying will start, and the harvest will entirely dissolve them." Furthermore, the settlers would "run from the colony about as fast as new cargoes arrive from Europe." He pointed out that these "droves" of apostatized Jews would return to the city, crying "we repent, we repent...." The New York Jews would then have their benevolence taxed by missionaries who would "empty Europe of paupers and inundate our cities with them."[22]

Overall, the *Jew*, founded as a response to missionaries, took a hard line of defense and attack. The *Jew* acted as a sentry, a watchdog. It served as a teacher or transmitter of Judaism's principles and practices. Moreover, it attempted to begin a dialogue with its avowed enemies. While Jackson invited responses from the Christian community, only one person responded, the Rev. Alexander McLeod, minister of the First Reformed Presbyterian Church, New York. Jackson said the sole purpose of McLeod and the missionary societies—as well as of Christianity in general—was, "That the Jews shall amalgamate and be blended with .....ians [*sic*]; that they shall no longer be Jews; that there shall be no distinction; that Judah shall cease from being a nation.... It is the purpose of God that the Jews shall remain a distinct people as long as time continues."[23] The response attacked evangelizing efforts, such as those of the ASMCJ, and the idea of conversion stories.

Death of the "Jew"

Jackson announced he would cease publication of the periodical at the end of volume 12.[24] The publication folded after two years and 24 issues. The *Jew* was a one-person effort, and one that did not meet with much response. The ASMCJ would not react to the feisty Jewish editor, and he may have realized this was a showcase effort on his part for the community and consequently turned his attention elsewhere.

The *Jew* also may have folded for lack of support. In the final issues, Jackson noted that "subscribers in arrears ... are respectfully requested to forward the amount of their subscription." Jackson relied on subscribers to pay for the publication, which was not subsidized by a society or other organization and did not carry advertising. For the monthly periodical, the publisher paid 5 cents, and later 10 cents, for an annual postage of 60 cents, and later $1.20. This was a significant amount indeed, when the subscription price itself was but $1.50.[25]

Another reason for Jackson to discontinue the periodical was the Postal Act of March 3, 1825, which raised magazine rates. Those issued periodically continued to pay 1 1/2 cents per sheet for up to 100 miles, but the charge rose to 2 1/2 cents for those mailed greater distances. The 1825 act left newspaper rates untouched, so any periodical deemed a magazine was placed at a competitive disadvantage. Magazines styled as newspapers to take advantage of the lower rates did not fare well. Moreover, the mailability of non-newspaper publications again could be judged by the postmasters.[26] It was not clear if Jackson intended his publication to be a newspaper or magazine; it fit neither category.

Jackson ended his editorial career in March 1825 with a quote from Job (6:13). "Is it because I have no ability? or that theology is quite gone from me?" Three-fourths of the way down the final page, in all capital letters appeared THE END. *Israel's Advocate,* which was started three months ahead of Jackson's effort, died in 1826.

Why the Name?

A prime example of Jackson's feistiness was in the selection of the *Jew* as a positive, unflinching assertion in naming his publication.

Unlike other editors of Jewish publications who followed him, Jackson chose to title his publication the *Jew,* ignoring any negative or prejudicial meaning Christians wanted to infer. Some Jews named Jewish hospitals or institutions "Hebrew" or "Israelite" in an effort to win respect of the Christian community (for example, Hebrew Benevolent Society). While the word "Jew" was synonymous with the Jew of the ghetto, often hated and made fun of by Christians, "Hebrew" or "Israelite" identified Jews with those of the Bible, whom Christians respected. Jackson did not concern himself with such niceties. The *Jew* appeared for reasons of self-defense and, imperfect as Jackson was, with it he boldly staked a claim in American society for the Jewish people.

Indeed, missionary efforts had little effect upon the Judaism of the Jewish community in America, but they gave Solomon Henry Jackson an opportunity to assume a role of leadership, to become known as a spokesman for American Jewry, both to the Jewish community and to the Christian.[27]

Impact and Evaluation

Jackson claimed the right to be himself, the right to be different. This right allowed him to perceive his Jewish difference as no less real, worthy, and honorable than any other "difference." Preserving differences constituted the true measure of equality which the Declaration of Independence had set forth. Therefore, in the American tradition, retention of distinctive cultures and religions needed to be encouraged. He was not yet ready to relinquish his traditions in favor of the values of the American melting pot. He did not assimilate. He refused to conform to the white Anglo-Saxon Protestant norms of the original settlers of the country.

Thus, the birth of Jewish journalism in America came, as it did for other ethnic groups, from the need to respond to the activities of others. The pioneer publication was concerned with the theme of defense, which the editor and publisher perceived as compatible with the loyalties to America. However, despite the notice in one issue about having a Philadelphia agent, the publication must have been printed as a showcase to Jewish defense and not as a viable, widely circulated publication. Evidence of this comes from the specialized content, its depth, and the exclusion of any material that could broaden the audience.

In conclusion, the *Jew,* born in adversity, died prematurely for lack of funding and support. Nevertheless, Jackson showed indomitable spirit and courage. Here in the New World the Jews, outnumbered a thousandfold, found courage and tenacity to withstand the onslaught of Christian missionary efforts. The literary merit of the *Jew* can indeed be questioned, although its long-winded theological arguments probably paralleled those of the Christian press. However, the merit and significance of the publication is that it showed a Jew could speak up, not only to defend but also to attack aggressively those in pursuit of converting Jews. A Jewish answer to Christian missionaries, the first Jewish publication in America must have given courage and served as a specific example to others who followed later in the propagation of the Jewish press.[28]

Clearly he experienced disappointment, for to conduct a searching discussion for the truth, an avowed and oft-stated goal, more than one side of an argument had to be presented to be persuasive and interesting. When Jackson noted that the *Advocate* had changed publishers and was about to change editors, he hoped the new editor would be willing to exchange issues, to see what Christian knowledge the *Advocate* was spreading. He implored the Rev. Stephen N. Rowan, newly selected editor of *Israel's Advocate,* to "answer the numbers of THE JEW satisfactorily, and you shall stand absolved from all other former obligations you consider yourselves under to us ... this is no vision, no dream ... you shall leave the field, if you have not sufficient arguments and reasons to support your cause."[29]

But from the first, the old editor of *Israel's Advocate,* the Rev. W. Gray, disdained the invitation to open his pages to dialogue. Thus, in a small note, Jackson expressed his disgruntlement, because the fifth and sixth numbers of the missionary monthly were barren of argument and did not quote the text of a Holy Scripture which the Jewish editor would have liked to refute. "It contains, indeed, some lame attempts at misrepresentation of the Jewish religion—not worthy of a serious confutation." He took a verbal swipe at the position of editor, who received $25 per issue for his labors or $300 yearly: "For doing what? for cutting out extracts from publication, marking them, as also marking the communications, and sending them to the printer, who does all the rest (perhaps reading the proof!)."[30]

Jackson also attacked Gray as Gray was leaving for a mission to Europe and a salary of $2,000 per year, plus special advantages: "Is not this meliorating the conditions of the Jews!!!" he exclaimed.[31]

Jackson also delivered continual attacks on *Israel's Advocate,* comparing the tone of his publication with the other, noting that Jews were not being cut off from all Jewish ideas of the messiah, answering an address first printed in the *Advocate*—which he reproduced—and correcting various items in the missionaries' organ. One attack refuted an article carried in the *Jewish Expositer* of London, which confuted an article in the *Jew.* In an article correcting material in the *Advocate,*

Jackson made the preposterous statement that the real object of the ASMCJ was to make Presbyterianism the established religion in New York.[32]

The lengthiest attack appeared in the last issue, ran three full pages, and criticized the ASMCJ annual report; Jackson noted the existence of an avowed and unavowed design of the Society, a declared and undeclared object. The ASMCJ also considered purchase of 1,500 acres for an orchard and vegetables, 300 for growing grain. At most, 200 to 300 families were needed to reside on the land. Jackson did not think so many apostates could be found.[33] He pointed out the work would not suit them. Despite the meager list of subscribers to the *Jew*, the missionary society issued another publication titled *A Jew Indeed,* showing evidence of some knowledge of Jackson's publication.

What Was the "Jew"?

First of all, the *Jew* did not meet the requirements of a newspaper. A newspaper must appear weekly, at least, and print anything of interest to a general public, as contrasted with some of the religious and business publications.[34] The *Jew* did not meet these qualifications.

"Magazine" came from the French *magasin* and originally meant storehouse or repository. A number of early magazines used the term "miscellany" in the title, conveying the storehouse connotation, a collection of odds and ends designed to attract all members of the family. Therefore, a publication with a newspaper format but with a wide variety of content could be considered a magazine. Typically, the magazine of the 1820s included fiction, profiles of the famous, articles on politics, philosophy and religion, literary essays, history, and book reviews.

While magazines were used as platforms for theological arguments where the great issues of the day were debated, they also contained specialized sections or departments, news accounts, and inspirational comments. Jackson's publication, however, did not contain articles on science, politics, news, etc., but was of one subject. Hence, it does not qualify under these definitions for the label "newspaper" or "magazine."[35]

Or, Jackson's publication may be considered an independent religion magazine. After all, religion magazines have influenced Americans from before the Revolution and served as models, possibly for Jackson. The trail-blazing periodical the *Christian History, Containing Accounts of the Revival and Propagation of Religion in Great Britain & America* began as a weekly in 1743, at the time of the Great Awakening.[36] Others followed. Thus, magazines with religion as their focus were established and published in Jackson's day, and Jackson may have taken inspiration from them to begin his own publication. Yet, it was not a religion magazine either. The *Jew* should be considered a periodical, that is, a publication with a regular, fixed time between issues or a schedule of issues. It appeared monthly, in pamphlet form, but lacked the variety of material necessary to be considered a magazine.

The history of American Jewry suggests an encounter between the forces of Americanization and the traditions of the Jewish historical experience, between the forces of assimilation and the pluralism of the American Jewish community.[37] The Jewish journalism of the period recounts the record of the resultant struggles and challenges. The second publication for the American Jewish community was a magazine, the *Occident and American Jewish Advocate,* born in a time of change in the roles and expectations of American Jews.

Editor Isaac Leeser

Editor Isaac Leeser proved to be "most important and the most influential American Jewish religious leader in the antebellum period."[38] It was he who was responsible for the first American Jewish publication society, the first American rabbinical school, and the first association of congregations. Leeser translated the Hebrew Bible into English, organized Jewish parochial schools, and made the English sermon a regular feature of the Sabbath morning service. "Almost every kind of publication which is essential to Jewish survival was written, translated, or fostered by him."[39]

Yet most important, and his most lasting contribution, was his founding the first successful Jewish periodical in this country—the *Occident and American Jewish Advocate.* The magazine portrayed the number of Jewish settlements, the quality of Jewish life, and the major problems and issues facing the Jewish community in the New World. It is the only body of contemporary information about the period 1843–1849, "The years of American Jewish history from 1830 until the close of the Civil War are, in fact, the 'Age of Leeser.'"[40]

In 1824, at the age of 18, Leeser emigrated from Central Europe to Richmond, Virginia, where he frequently sought intellectual stimulation from Richmond's more learned Jews.[41] Later, he entered a private school and studied English for a few months, then learned the ways of a shopkeeper from his uncle. But the attraction of the synagogue was strong; he voluntarily assisted in conducting the services. He identified himself with leaders of the fledgling Richmond Jewish community and taught without charge the younger portion of the congregation. He read broadly and omnivorously and in four years had mastered English.[42]

Leeser and Jewish Life in America

In 1829, Leeser accepted an invitation to be lay reader or leader of services of Mikveh Israel, or Hope or Repository of Israel, a congregation in Philadelphia.

When he accepted the call to Mikveh Israel, there were almost four thousand Jews in the country, served by perhaps a dozen congregations: two per community in New York, Philadelphia, and Charleston; and one each in Baltimore, Richmond, Savannah, Cincinnati, and New Orleans. But not even one ordained rabbi lived anywhere in America.

Native-born Jews who had lived in America with their parents and even grandparents believed that Judaism could not develop in the American milieu, a conviction generally shared by recent immigrants, as well. Most early efforts to confront the problems of Jewish education and adjustment met with indifference or hostility.[43] In the United States, Judaism possessed no roots.

In the American milieu, one wide open and offering a variety of ideas and ideals, Jews chose, on their own, to commit themselves anew to their faith, to become Christians, or to become secular persons, though born into the Jewish faith.[44] However, there was in American society, where individuals could choose among a variety of identities, the continued pressure from missionary groups to convert Jews to Christianity.

Leeser did not experience much support. Infrequent synagogue attendance, violating the Sabbath, and intermarriage plagued the community. Thus, he wrote, translated, and published; he planned; he organized.[45] Leeser also devised ways to create—but did not himself create—such local institutions as Jewish hospitals, orphanages, and community-wide charity federations as well as to coordinate Jewish undertakings on the national level that resulted in schools to train rabbis and teachers. Nothing could keep him from his endeavors, perhaps because no personal distractions entered his life. He remained unmarried and worked ceaselessly, often to the point of illness.

Moreover, from the time he took the pulpit at Mikveh Israel, Leeser was not content to be a paid functionary. In 1840, unexpected events propelled him to national prominence. That year, the charge of ritual murder was brought against the Jews of Damascus at the insistence of the French consul of that city. The consul utilized the accusation for political purposes and was actively supported by the Franciscan order. Many Jews were imprisoned and tortured, and of these a number died.[46] In the United States, Leeser organized efforts and urged President Martin Van Buren to act to end the injustice and inhumanity toward the Jews of Damascus.[47]

The campaign to defend Jewish rights abroad carried great import by demonstrating what the Jewish community could do if it united. Leeser had seen what common action could do for the world Jewish community. He took a broad look at what could be done in America to promote unity. After discussion with friends, he decided to embark on a publishing effort, modeled after those in Europe. It would take the form of a magazine.

In April 1843 Leeser began publishing the monthly magazine the *Occident and American Jewish Advocate.* He could gain neither encouragement nor praise for his successful endeavors; the congregation did not like him. He served notice that he would vacate his position with the congregation when his contract expired. Then he made a complete break with the congregation which he had served for 21 years.

To take up a financial appeal face-to-face, by meeting many of his growing number of supporters who lived throughout the country, he embarked on a railroad tour. It would facilitate his promoting of his chief livelihood, the *Occident.* It became the first instrument to instill a sense of national belonging to the broadly dispersed Jews in the United States.

The "Occident"

The *Occident* came into being one year after the American Society for Meliorating the Condition of the Jew [ASMCJ] began to publish the *Jewish Chronicle,* a monthly with the avowed aim of converting Jews. Jewish immigrants and their families had settled and become visible in several places, as the Jewish community experienced enormous growth: from 4,000 in 1830 to 15,000 in 1840.[48] The growth brought with it new problems as Jews began to accommodate to their new home, and Leeser felt the need to address, on a regular basis, the issues facing the Jews in the United States and abroad. Therefore, the *Occident* was more than a response to the *Jewish Chronicle* in the way that Jackson's publication was to *Israel's Advocate.*

Leeser, who had come from Westphalia, was impressed with *Der Orient,* a Leipzig-based publication for intellectuals. It appears that Leeser, in part, fashioned his magazine after it, naming the *Occident* in juxtaposition to the *Orient.* The rest of the new magazine's title, *American Jewish Advocate*, came from what Leeser defined as his agenda. He pledged to try "to speak the truth...without malice, whenever in our humble opinion we conceive danger approaching unto the welfare of Israel."[49]

Leeser declared he would publish articles offering something instructive, resorting to translations of Hebrew, French, or German works, if necessary. He promised one sermon each month. He promised reviews of new books and controversial articles.[50] He offered to provide news of public religious meetings and to publish debates, essays, and articles on religion and Jewish history, fiction, and poetry, as well as news of American and foreign Jewish congregations.

The *Occident* prescribed new communal institutions as the best defense against missionaries. Jewish schools, hospitals, even a Jewish publication society, would guard the vulnerable and ignorant from missionary snares while building up Jewish knowledge and pride. Clearly worried about the inroad of conversion, Leeser made education, like union, a vital component of Jewish defense.[51]

Usually of 48 to 60 pages, the monthly was stitched and carried an "advertiser" section before and after the editorial matter, always on a colored stock. The pages measured 5 3/4 by 8 3/4 inches. His use of Hebrew was sparse. Indeed, the *Occident* bore most characteristics of a modern academic journal. Year by year, for 25 years, the industrious editor bound the *Occident* into leather-clad volumes, complete with indices and formal cover page.

Most new immigrants did not understand or read English at that time. The *Occident* was published for those native born, British, Dutch, and some Polish Jews. The younger generation constituted his primary target audience, for they were more conversant with English than were their parents. Also, Leeser fully intended his magazine to be read by non-Jews.

The price of the *Occident and American Jewish Advocate,* $3 per year, would be low enough "for nearly all the friends of our religion in America," he wrote.[52]

Leeser's magazine went to a national audience. Indeed, the *Occident* in 1843 reached a modest number of persons abroad. Jews everywhere relied on Leeser's *Occident* to bring them news of Jewish concerns for six years until the appearance of the *Asmonean,* the first English Jewish weekly in New York. Leeser's magazine lasted until 1869, a year following his death.

Contributors and Content

Valued contributors to the *Occident* included professors, lay leaders and "Reverend Doctors," or Jewish clergy, from the United States and Europe, the last group offering sermons for publication.

News of the American as well as worldwide community dominated the content from the beginning. Most news items lacked bylines or other attribution, but a large number came from Jewish publications from abroad. The *Occident* chronicled new American Jewish settlements, synagogue changes, new religious schools, Jewish hospitals, philanthropical efforts, and the comings and goings of prominent individuals. It covered foreign events: new rulings for Jews in various countries, rabbinical conferences, synagogue and seminary news, epidemics, Jewish rights, and information about individuals. These news items typically were of no more than one paragraph, although a few extended to cover more than a page.

A sampling of news items reveals the breadth of news offered to readers:

- New outposts in Buffalo, New York; Lynchburg and Wheeling, Virginia; Marysville, Nevada City, and San Francisco, California; Quincy, Illinois; South Bend, Indiana; and York, Harrisburg, and Lancaster, Pennsylvania.
- The need for lay leaders, butchers, and ritual circumcisers. When these services were procured, the *Occident* took note and named the individual who would take on the enormous responsibilities.
- Synagogue consecrations, when synagogues moved or were enlarged, and when lots for synagogues were purchased. New religious schools were covered by listing curricula, instructors, and examination performances.
- The need for and the establishment of hospitals for Jews, their financial reports, and a detailed annual summary of hospitals' vital statistics.
- Charity balls, the establishment of organizations to assist Jews in the Holy Land, generous philanthropical gifts of money, land, and buildings for Jewish institutions, and the establishment of various Hebrew benevolent societies.
- Visits, sermons, and lectures of prominent Jewish clergy.
- Officers elected to posts in community organizations, and resignations, retirements, and deaths of noteworthy American Jews.

Editorials ranged from preaching about Judaism to talking about changes needed in the Jewish community. Leeser began by advocating and instructing, imploring and demanding, but later simply told readers what to believe, rather than how to behave. He advocated alterations and modifications in the community, and the reader could always figure out where Leeser stood on every issue addressed.

Rights, Obligations, Expectations

The *Occident and American Jewish Advocate* reflected the aims of its editor. It projected his plans to institutionalize the Jewish community on a national level. At the same time, it defended Judaism from a variety of attacks, both inside and outside the community. It attacked missionaries, anti-Semitism, assimilation and intermarriage, the Swiss Treaty, and Reform versus traditional Judaism. It championed civil rights, philanthropy and charity, education, a Jewish foster home, a Jewish publication society, Palestine, religious observance, separation of church and state, and unity, to name some of the issues.

The most important issues on Leeser's agenda were to defend Judaism against onslaughts of missionaries as well as other forms of anti-Semitism; to champion the cause of Jews abroad; to combat intermarriage and apathy in the Jewish community, and—more generally—to secure "a place in the sun" for American Jewry. The *Occident* became an effective vehicle for the conduct of this defense.

Defense of Judaism

The movement in the 1820s of missionaries to convert Jews was renewed in the 1840s. Leeser battled in print with these groups; they were of paramount concern to him. He felt they had shameless tactics. He repeatedly told the editor and "conductors" of the ASMCJ-sponsored *Jewish Chronicle,* based in New York, that American Jews were more than "dry bones" (a simile, used by conversion groups, for tattered remnants) and that shaking them produces truth rather than the false spirit missionaries wanted to instill.[53] He also complained about their methods of reaching Jews. Some missionaries supplied tracts, New Testament Bibles and other testaments to Jews in schools, in hospitals, or even in the synagogue, in their attempt to reach students, the poor, and those hospitalized. He asked Jews not to open the doors of their homes to these proselytizers, who boasted of their successes, Leeser angrily suggested they were exaggerating the number of converts, for he believed converts to be almost nonexistent.

National Issues: "Blue" Laws,
Thanksgiving Proclamations, Anti-Semitism

The Occident railed against Sunday "blue" laws for years. It used arguments from important Christians whose views agreed with those of the Jews. Sometimes it equated Jews being subjected to the Sunday laws with undergoing baptism or forced attendance at a church. Observing Sunday closings could weaken traditional Jewish practices; some already were breaking the Jewish Sabbath to observe the Christian. Whenever a Hebrew (the term Leeser preferred to Jew) was arrested for Sabbath-breaking, Leeser wrote an impassioned article pleading his rights. The *Occident* waged this fight for many years, with many variations. To Leeser, Sabbath observance was an individual, private matter—one not to be legislated. Such laws violated the Bill of Rights with its freedom of religion clause.

Other troubles Leeser considered in print were the Thanksgiving Day proclamations whereby governors tied the holiday to Christians and Christianity. This exclusion of Hebrews from celebrating Thanksgiving violated the spirit of the Constitution, Leeser noted.

In addition, intolerance appeared in high places, such as in California in 1855. The Speaker of the California Legislature, slated for a spot on the Know-Nothing ticket for governor, slandered the Jews and suggested a special tax be levied so Jews would no longer try to settle in California. His views were given space and rebutted.[54]

Jewish Issues: Education and Unity

The furthering of Jewish education among the young and the old and the deep concern for the prevailing ignorance and apathy among American Jews were items receiving highest priority in the magazine.

The subject of indifference Leeser likened to a fatal disease, for he believed the ignorance about Judaism prevailing among American Jews would devastate the Jewish population, as surely as would a plague. Jews were not observant enough for Leeser; they did not understand what their duties were and were unsure of their religious demands.

The *Occident* spoke about religious education, and sought a Sunday school "for Religious Instruction of Israelites" as an answer to proselytizing activities on the part of Christians.[55] However, for all its promise and potential, Leeser knew the once-weekly Sunday school would never be able to abate the ignorance demonstrated among Jewish children. As a result, Leeser decided Jewish day schools needed to be established.

Another educational matter concerned language. Leeser always maintained that the vernacular of the country in which one lived was to be used. Therefore, to continue to speak German after arriving in America seemed wrong to him, and parents who insisted on having German used for instruction in the schools were wrong, too.[56]

The *Occident* also took note of another Jewish institution, the England-based Cheap Jewish Library, Dedicated to the Working Classes, and published articles encouraging the establishment of a Jewish publication society that would issue quality books for a Jewish audience.[57]

The *Occident* sought to strengthen American Jews' commitment to Judaism. Leeser worried because through the ages intermarriage had lost many Jewish children to Judaism, but in the United States the problem was exacerbated because Jewish men frequently married non-Jewish women, as a result of the paucity of young Jewish women.[58] Yet he felt no Jew should be punished for that act by being refused burial in a Jewish cemetery. He fought intermarriage not by condemning it but by suggesting measures to prevent it.

Another concern to the community dealt with religious observances of the dying. Christian authorities might convert the Jew on his deathbed and bury the person as a Christian. Thus the need for Jewish hospitals.

Moreover, there was a growing need to impart new character, new meaning, and new purpose that could be shared by the budding Jewish communities and institutions. The *Occident* began aggressively to fill those needs. The *Occident* decried "The Disjointed State of American Jews." "Too many individuals pursue private aims, neglecting matters of spiritual welfare. Geographic as well as doctrinal divisions are current." It was imperative to have a union of action.[59]

But unity on whose terms? Many of the newcomers, particularly from German-speaking areas, brought with them a new Judaism, alien and threatening to the traditional Orthodox Jew. Indeed, between Orthodoxy and Reform the fight would continue to the present. From 1843 till its demise in 1869, the *Occident* became the intellectual and spiritual arena for that fight.[60]

Reform in America referred to developments in German-speaking Central Europe as a model. Leeser looked upon progress in Judaism and Reform, as proposed by the German-speaking European rabbis at their several conferences, as destructive of Judaism. Agitation for reform soon grew into an organized movement with a formal program and militant leadership. As Jewish immigrants sought to blend in with American life, they wanted more respectable, disciplined, shorter services, with parts to be in English as well as Hebrew. They called for weekly sermons (on the Protestant model) and a dues structure for all members of a congregation. But that was only for starters.

Reform was a revolt against the unquestioning authority of the past. Congregations questioned many of the sacred precepts and basic practices of traditional Judaism, such as Sabbath observance, dietary laws, intermarriage, the belief in a personal messiah, and close identification with other Jews. Leeser felt the ranks of the American Jews were divided hopelessly because of Reform.

International Issues

When the United States, in the mid-1850s, negotiated a treaty with Switzerland that discriminated against the rights of American Jews, Leeser defended Jewish rights and campaigned vigorously, resulting in a delegation's calling on President James Buchanan.[61]

In 1858, a seven-year-old Jewish Italian child, Edgar Mortara, was taken from his parents because he had been baptized secretly in the Roman Catholic Church by his Catholic maid. The case was well publicized in the United States, where Protestants and even some Catholics, as well as the American Jewish community, protested the abduction. Petitions and appeals were sent to Washington, but both President Buchanan and his secretary of state said nothing could be done. Leeser even journeyed to Washington to meet with the secretary.

Leeser had long sought to create an institutional unity for the American Jewish community. The Mortara case had a deep effect on American Jewry, who blamed their failure to obtain the child's release on their own lack of unity. Thus, on November 22, 1859, delegates from 29 synagogue congregations and 13 cities met in New York to establish the Board of Delegates of American Israelites, the first real national organization of American Jews.

This national organization was successfully established because it concentrated on defending Jewish political rights, the issue on which American Jews were most nearly united. It could speak for American Jewry in cases where the rights of Jews were in jeopardy.[62] It fought successfully to have Jewish chaplains in the Union Army during the Civil War; it protested effectively against General Ulysses S. Grant's order expelling Jews from Tennessee. During the Civil War, Leeser served as a natural bridge between rabbis of the North and South, i.e., those of the Confederacy, and tried to occupy a position of neutrality during the entire period. He refused to discuss the slavery issue, preferring to criticize demagogues and agitators on both sides. Leeser thought the Jews should be the peacemakers and try to placate both sides.

The Board of Delegates of American Israelites also successfully fought the Presbyterian Church's proposal to make Christianity the official American religion. Most important, it served the original purpose of issuing formal statements protesting anti-Semitism wherever found.

Unfortunately to Leeser, the board never operated effectively. It never concerned itself with religious questions such as setting up uniform standards for teachers, or the establishment of a central religious authority; nor did it concern itself to any great degree with Jewish philanthropy or education on a national scale.[63] It should have been clear to Leeser that American Jews did not want such an authority and that any attempt to create one could only result in the death of the Board of Delegates itself.[64]

Impact and Evaluation

The *Occident* made a significant contribution to Jewish journalism in America. The magazine defended Judaism and the Jewish people against threats. It championed the rights of the Jews for the freedom of belief and religious practice that was the cornerstone of the American Constitution. Leeser prepared the framework for a variety of new institutions, to help preserve a separate identity for the American Jews. That separate identity was a role foreign-language and other ethnic editors encouraged in their publications as well.[65] The *Occident and American Jewish Advocate* became the instrument for fostering community identity and Jewish culture.

The magazine responded strongly to the issues developed around the broad areas of rights, obligations, and expectations. It became a leader in the fight against missionaries, for the American Society for Meliorating the Condition of the Jews, along with other missionary groups, continued to spread falsehoods about Judaism and the Jewish people that served to denigrate both in the eyes of Jews and non-Jews. In addition, the *Occident* also stood up to governors and judges who denigrated the editor's religion and people. It was a community and national beacon. Moreover, it addressed grievances to the governments of other countries when Jewish life and Jewish lives were affected.

The *Occident* became a major vehicle to propose, to ensure, and to watch the growth of community institutions. In sum, Isaac Leeser and his magazine came at a crucial time in the development of American Jewry and served the community well. It was a successful, significant publication.

The third English-language publication for the American Jewish community was a weekly newspaper, the *Asmonean,* edited and published by Robert Lyon.

During the years 1843 to 1849, the Jewish community began to increase substantially as whole families, rather than isolated individuals, began to arrive in America. It was the time when the contemporary American Jewish scene emerged and found its shape and direction. For American Jews, experimenting with new life patterns engaged their full attention. In 1849, approximately 50,000 Jews lived in the United States. Roughly 13,000 to 14,000 lived in New York, the leading community in the country, then as now.[66]

The new immigrants, mostly from Central Europe, began to find a niche for themselves economically but found the Jewish community undistinguished and divided. Many leaders were untrained and pursued their duties as religious lay readers as merely another way to make a living. Isaac Leeser, the pioneer, with his magazine, the *Occident and*

American Jewish Advocate, attempted to reach members of the far-flung Jewish communities throughout the country. Yet, his magazine, appearing only monthly, made, at most, a modest impact on Jews who needed information and inspiration. Also, he lived in Philadelphia, a large Jewish center but one which stood in the shadow of New York's 14,000, who needed their own organ. American Jews at that time possessed neither a broad general education nor even a proper Jewish one.

Two publications, weeklies, were established in 1849 to answer the needs of Jewish New Yorkers. *Israels Herold* [*sic*], the first and in German, began publication on March 30, with Isidor Bush as editor; it lasted but three months.[67] Bush's weekly was highly philosophical in tone, and therefore it failed to reach a large number of people, to form a cohesive audience. With the twelfth issue, Bush gave up.

Editor Robert Lyon

The *Asmonean,* the second Jewish weekly begun in 1849, and in English, was edited by Robert Lyon. Born January 15, 1810, he was the second son of Wolfe Lyon, a London tradesman.[68] He received an education for commerce and business, although he maintained an interest in science. In 1840, he and another Jew, Baron de Goldsmid, presented a congratulatory address to Queen Victoria on her marriage. In 1844, Lyon and his wife emigrated to New York; they had seven children.[69]

Lyon established an umbrella "manufactory" but could not make a steady living in that field. At the same time, he thought he could help the "Jewish cause" by publishing a weekly. He knew English well but lacked any kind of background in Hebrew and German, the two languages of the Jewish community of the time. Shortly after Lyon's arrival in America, Isaac Leeser, editor of the *Occident and American Jewish Advocate,* ran two of his essays and an article about uniting American Jewry.[70]

Lyon had no experience publishing a paper. Financial support would depend on circulation and advertising, although Lyon acknowledged his paper had a patron. When the *Asmonean* began, only the *Occident* served as competition. But competition it was, a fact not lost on the Philadelphia editor, Isaac Leeser. Lyon's paper was intended originally for the Jewish population of New York City but later went to places throughout the country.[71]

Lyon was active civically and politically, for the New York City Directory of 1840-1841 lists Lyon's occupation as assistant city inspector with an office at City Hall. In the Jewish community, Lyon was a vice president of the Hebrew Benevolent Society. He had connections to political figures locally and nationally. Henry Clay, General Lewis Cass, and Daniel Webster all knew him.

The "Asmonean"

The first issue of the *Asmonean* appeared on October 19, 1849, and each Friday thereafter for nearly ten years.[72] The masthead, large and elaborate, consisted of symbols: In the center was an escutcheon, displaying figures representing the tribes of Israel: a wolf of Benjamin, a bull of Menasseh, and a lion of Judah. The *Asmonean* took its name from the surname of Mattathias and his sons who led the successful revolt of the Jews against the Greeks in the second century B.C.E.[73] Subtitled "A family journal of commerce, politics, religion, and literature, devoted to the interests of the American Israelites," it ran a column of "Patronage and Support" listing the names of ministers, presiding officers of nine New York congregations, and prominent Jews from several cities. The peculiar motto, "Two are better than one, and a three-fold cord is not quickly broken," referred to uniting American Jewry and was taken from Ecclesiastes 4:9, 12. In the third volume it was simplified with the removal of the symbols and the addition of a simple slogan, "Knowledge is power."[74] The design on the first issues was copied from the *Irish-American,* which appeared only a number of months before the *Asmonean* was launched.[76] The *Asmonean* endured to become Leeser's competition and survived until Lyon's death. The typical 19th-century minority newspaper was a one-person enterprise and usually ceased publication with the demise of its publisher.[76]

The *Asmonean* appeared to be a relatively unattractive publication 10 1/2 inches wide and 15 1/4 inches long. Lyon did not believe in giving space to lead, for the columns were cramped and the layout unappealing, particularly on the inside pages. The paper used a three-column format on the first page of an issue but a four-column format on the inside pages and in the advertising sections. Few illustrations, and mostly only those connected with ads, made the editorial material a sea of gray. The paper was serious, dry, and often colorless.

In the first issue of the *Asmonean,* Lyon noted his intention to promote a congregational Union of Israelites of the United States. He also wanted to disseminate information about or relating to the Jewish people. All foreign and domestic news would receive ample coverage, "up to the latest moment prior to going to press." Lyon also promised to comment on events "temperately." But the most important reason to publish was for "a Unity of action between the learned and the philanthropic of Israel." He acknowledged his lack of experience as a journalist, but said, "We are not deficient of zeal in our desire of preserving our national integrity, and averting the curse of infidelity from our people." Unlike other Jewish publications up to this time, Lyon's printed editorial material of a non-Jewish nature; he also reprinted from all kinds of sources, both foreign and domestic.

Politics and Community News

Politics occupied a significant place in the *Asmonean,* undoubtedly as a result of Lyon's long-standing interest in politics. In the 1850s, the paper opposed Know-Nothingism and in 1856 it supported James Buchanan for the Presidency and Fernando Wood for mayor of New York.[77] When a reader wrote about Lyon's rather outspoken preference for various political offices, Lyon responded that his paper was a commercial, religious, and literary as well as a political organ. Lyon maintained that part of his duty was to inform the Jewish public of his stand on political matters.[78] It may very well be that periodic advertisements from Tammany Hall and the City of New York— including city ordinances—had much to do with the *Asmonean*'s forthright political statements and bias towards the Democrats.[79] Lyon reported on city elections, too, unlike other editors of Jewish publications. He facilitated the workings of a democratic government in the same way that a regular city paper did. His interests in politics did not stop at the state level.

Jewish communal and foreign news, or "intelligence" as it was called, was probably the main drawing card of the *Asmonean.* Additionally, some of a general nature, an occasional story, book reviews, letters to the editor, editorials, and translations and excerpts from other journals filled the reading columns.

Advertising and Circulation

Advertising grew immensely in the first two years. By the end of the second full year, the *Asmonean* was carrying six full pages of advertising, three at the beginning and three at the end of each 12-page issue.[80]

The *Asmonean* sold for $3 per year "invariably in advance"; it never raised its price.[81] Circulation always seemed to trouble Lyon, and its counterpart, advertising, tried to appeal to a large audience with many interests. Regularly the *Asmonean* ran a blurb that it represented 200,000 Jews in America and included among its subscribers "a large and increasing body of Unitarians, besides a great number of German Citizens of the United States."[82] Lyon claimed many subscribers in New York as well as out of town.[83] The paper appeared to be financially sound through most of its existence. Lyon bragged that the *Asmonean* circulated in every state, north and south.

German Supplement

From the outset, Lyon recognized the majority of the Hebrew population in America was German speaking, and therefore, a portion of the paper had to be in that language.[84] He felt impaired because he could not effectually reach a great mass of the German-speaking population. He thought he needed a German supplement, hoping to attract the large and ever-increasing number of German-speaking Jews in the city and around the country. However, he knew little German and found it necessary to hire an assistant for the task. Finally, in 1851, after repeated pledges, he issued one supplement and promptly scuttled it.[85] However, advertisements printed in German appeared in the paper frequently.[86]

Contributors and Content

Because people did not pay for their subscriptions, or money was delayed in reaching him, Lyon acknowledged that he could not afford to pay contributors. Yet he made arrangements for correspondents and sought to find them in each section of the country.

Shortly after its beginning, the *Asmonean* carried a letter from Rabbi Isaac Mayer Wise welcoming the new newspaper and offering to help "if you think it advantageous." This warm welcome was not lost on Lyon. For 18 months, beginning in September 1852, Wise contributed many scholarly articles to the *Asmonean*; they ran in a section called "Theology and Philosophy." In addition to essays and translations of various European writers, Wise also introduced rabbinical legends. Further, he instituted a department of foreign news, clipped from other publications. Gradually Wise became co-editor of the paper. His work appeared on the editorial page, and it was not uncommon for his work to take five columns of the paper. His connection to the paper, as well as Lyon's independent journalism, enabled the *Asmonean* to obtain support of those alienated from Leeser's magazine because of its uncompromising orthodoxy in tone and content. However, Wise ended his relationship with the *Asmonean* because he saw the limits of using the paper for espousing Reform views. He began his own newspaper, the *American Israelite,* in 1854.

In addition to Wise, Rabbi Max Lilienthal contributed pieces based on his personal experiences in Russia. Other learned men contributed articles to the *Asmonean* on a variety of topics. Abraham DeSola of Canada and Michael Silberstein of Germany contributed theological pieces. Another author was Marcus Heymann Breslau, also of Germany, who moved to London and answered the London Society for Promoting Christianity Among the Jews and wrote of the denial of Jews' rights in England. The Orthodox view was represented by contributions from rabbis S.M. Isaacs and Morris Raphall and others.

Lyon covered the news comprehensively. He apparently had a backlog of hard news items. He quickly learned how to use scissors, for by the second volume he had dramatically increased non-Jewish items from other sources. He covered the theatrical scene and literary life of New York. He took material from foreign and domestic publications frequently. Indeed, in time, non-Jewish news exceeded news of the local community; moreover, it predominated. As time went on, Lyon may have felt more comfortable in America and may have wanted to share material of interest to a very wide audience. Surely, if the Unitarians and Germans were reading his publication, such material would appeal to them more than the material of a strictly Jewish nature.

The Goal of Unity

Lyon from the beginning wanted to use his publication as a vehicle for establishing unity, at first among New York's diverse Jewish population and later nationally. He called for a statistical census of the Israelites in the United States by asking trustees and officers of congregations and societies throughout the country to furnish particulars about the association, names of officers, number of members, and so forth.[87]

Defense of Judaism

The *Asmonean* was always on guard to vindicate the honor of the Jew and to reply to strictures by the English-language press. The general newspapers of New York City, particularly the *Tribune* and the *Herald,* had the habit of identifying Jews in crime stories. Lyon quickly criticized such offensive practices in the secular press, and he also questioned the veracity of accounts involving Jews.

In addition to correcting the local press, Lyon castigated missionaries. He reminded his readers that the ASMCJ was not an American but an English institution, with agents in America, and exposed their "falsehoods" and "absurdities." The ASMCJ said it had seven converts. "Who are the seven, how many times, in how many countries and for how much money have they been made converts? Publish their names," Lyon demanded.[88]

National Issues: "Blue" Laws, Oaths,
and Thanksgiving Proclamations

Lyon also wrote that Jews still felt excluded and discriminated against in America. He was unhappy about the Sunday "blue" laws, especially in Pennsylvania. Moreover, he was upset with the new Maryland constitution, for it required a person to "profess Christianity" to hold office. Lyon published Thanksgiving Day messages from Jewish leaders. The custom was to open the synagogues on Thanksgiving and have a service as the Christians did. As Leeser before him, Lyon criticized the governors of surrounding states for their Thanksgiving Day messages if they made their proclamations under the name of Jesus Christ, thereby making it a Christian holiday. The governor of New York State, Hamilton Fish, came under criticism for this reason in 1849.[89] Apparently, Fish got the message, apologized, and made a contribution to the Hebrew Benevolent Society. His 1850 proclamation was in welcomed contrast to the one a year earlier and received praise from Lyon.[90] The proclamation by the governor of Rhode Island, which was issued in the name of Christ, came under strong criticism.

Jewish Issues

Lyon and others in the *Asmonean* covered the controversies between the Reformers and the Orthodox, the religiously liberal and conservative. Throughout, however, Lyon maintained strict independence. He felt discomfort and distress when others perceived him to support liberalizing Judaism. Moreover, the provoked Orthodox leaders in New York City determined they would need an editorial organ of their own, resulting in S.M. Isaacs's *Jewish Messenger,* begun in 1857.

Another important issue of the day and various problems surrounding it dealt with where the dead were to be buried. Lyon urged the establishment of a free burial ground, and a proper officer appointed to superintend the interment.[91] As for burials in cities, the *Asmonean* advocated strongly that burials not take place within the city limits. However, burial grounds were only part of the issue; another aspect dealt with removing corpses from one cemetery to another, a common practice.

The *Asmonean* advocated that a fence be added, along with shrubs, flowers, and trees, to the Jewish burial ground of the oldest New York City congregation.[92] The second oldest synagogue needed a cemetery, this one on Long Island, but the members thought they needed to apply to the city; Lyon did not think this to be the case. In another article, Lyon noted that under English law, the cost to re-inter, erect monuments, and so forth was deemed the heir's right, but Lyon said such laws did not yet exist in America.[93] Thus, while he advocated, he informed the community how the city operated and how to operate in it.

International Issues: England and Switzerland

Lyon, the Englishman, covered and commented on Jewish affairs in England. He brought up the Baron Rothschild cause, which dealt with Rothschild's not being able to sit in the House of Commons, despite his wealth, influence, and rank, despite being an acute reasoner and able mathematician. Yet in a "land of perfect liberty," no such occurrence would take place. Lyon contrasted the situation in England with the freedom in America.[94]

Another country of special concern to the community was Switzerland. During the 1850s various treaties were developed between the United States and Switzerland. The problem was that American representatives understood that American Jews in Switzerland could become citizens under the same conditions as Christians and could engage in commerce as their Christian counterparts did. However, this was not the case. As a result, Jews felt it was their duty to protect their brethren in Switzerland and petitioned the United States government with their objections to the various treaties. Lyon's newspaper and Leeser's magazine, to a lesser extent, became the instruments to promulgate Jewish reaction, helping to galvanize the community into action. Petitions asking for measures to help secure rights of American Jewish citizens in foreign countries were sent to the Senate Committee on Foreign Relations.[95] Daniel Webster, Henry Clay, and Lewis Cass all became involved. Wise issued a call to American Israelites asking for delegates elected by their congregations to meet in New York to "frame and adopt a petition to congregations, requesting our government to protest against the illegal, inhuman, and degrading laws which have been forced upon our brethren by the Pope in Rome and by the Government of Switzerland." Those who could not meet in New York should send a written copy of their views to the editor of the *Asmonean*.[96] In Switzerland, Jews were thrown out, some after being there 50 years. The Jewish position was strongly defended, but the Swiss openly rejected the notion of having Jews in their country. The situation dragged on for years.[97]

Impact and Evaluation

The general physical appearance of papers born after the *Asmonean* indicated the great influence of Lyon's paper. Lyon made a living by purveying news; he did not obtrude his personality on the *Asmonean*. He felt people would not support a "party" organ, and he probably did not have the confidence of those knowledgeable about theological matters to call attention to himself and thrust his own opinions onto his readers. Lyon appealed to a wider audience than did either Jackson or Leeser, and as a result his paper appealed to advertisers. He sought to make Jewish readers more American by acquiring knowledge about the country they now lived in and how it operated. He ran stories about reading material, books, magazines of the day. His theater reviews and reviews of dance and vocal performances frequently appeared in the publication. He also ran whole pages of market items and prices, including pork, lard, and ham.

Lyon had instruction from Mordecai Manuel Noah, a superbly successful editor and Jew.[98] Noah, editor of the *New York Enquirer,* the *New York Evening Star,* the *National Advocate,* and other newspapers, probably taught Lyon how to conduct a truly local paper, to advocate for community development, to correct instances of corruption, deception, or injustice. Thus it was Lyon's paper that led the fight for a Jewish hospital, one based on democratic practices. The *Asmonean* probably came in first for its public service. Lyon's newspaper was truly for a mass audience. The *Asmonean* reached out to readers, to provide leadership in the community, a community at once assimilating yet recognizing its special place in America.

Yet, Lyon recognized that American Jews had interests outside the American Jewish community. Therefore, he determined it was feasible to run articles dealing with business, the theater, literature, and politics. Lyon developed an excellent financial section, perhaps modeled on the "money page" of James Gordon Bennett's *Herald.* He aggressively promoted his advertisers, although some advertisements smacked of bad taste, quackery, and sensationalism. Certainly the *Asmonean* looked like the most financially successful Jewish publication of the era.

Robert Lyon suffered a stroke at work on March 10, 1858, and died hours later at home. Unfortunately his publication died with him, although for weeks after his death his widow pleaded for someone to buy into the paper or at least conduct it—to no avail. The paper folded.[99]

Conclusion

This brief look at the English-language antebellum press has examined the content, elaborated on the issues covered, as well as given some background on the individuals responsible for the publications. The time period covered can be viewed as American Jewry's early adolescence. The community's growth spurted rapidly, and it began to realize its own potentials, articulated by editors such as Jackson, Leeser, and Lyon. The economic challenges of survival in a new country coupled with the ideal of freedom promoted their success.

In America the Jewish immigrants soon discovered, as had their ancestors in other lands, a failure or unwillingness of society to grant them the full acceptance granted to other citizens. The virus of anti-Semitism spread to American shores with some unpleasant symptoms. Despite the constitutive ideologies at the state and federal levels proclaiming religious freedom and tolerance, official pronouncements from judges and governors often reminded the Jews that America was for Christians only; they were regarded as outsiders. Sunday laws discriminated against Jewish persons in business who wanted to observe the Jewish Sabbath as their own day of rest. Thanksgiving at times was proclaimed at the state level as a Christian holiday. Even the press discriminated by singling out for religious identification of criminals those who were Jewish. Most important, missionary societies, imported from Europe, sprang up on the fertile American soil and aggressively began to convert Jews, threatening the very existence of the fledgling Jewish minorities. Even when not successful in their conversion effort, the missionaries damaged the self-esteem of the Jews and their image in the minds of their fellow Americans. For the Jews, America offered a single set of laws for all citizens and the opportunity for full participation in American society, in theory at least. Such participation did not require relinquishing ethnic or religious identity. Indeed, it suggested opportunity and prosperity.

Yet the freedom of America created its own problems for the Jew, too, for each could determine his or her own identity. Exactly what Jewish ingredients of the past should enter one's own life in America became the challenge of survival of the Jewish group, and the main danger was that of assimilation. Jews wanted to belong, to fit into American society, perhaps more than other groups. The price of belonging appeared to be a divesting of past culture and tradition, that they become a new nation, accepting American culture and civilization. Many willingly entered the melting pot, to disappear as Jews and emerge as a new people.

Yet there were those who saw the new environment as conducive to genuine Jewish existence and continued practice of the Jewish heritage, the editors of the American Jewish press among others. Jews learned to be both authentically Jewish and unqualifiedly American at the same time, each part of one's identification giving the power to resist outside forces, the ability to endure—while at the same time offering a balance, a proportion, and a stability to the individual to produce even greater achievements. The glue and mortar for the structure was to be education.

Education was survival; survival was education. The pioneer Jewish publications in America did their part to strengthen identity, defend against outside forces, assist in accommodating to life in America while discussing issues troubling the community. The press served a diverse community and set the agenda for discussion. Indeed, it was the only intercommunal agency in existence before the Civil War.

Notes

1. This can be seen with other chapters of this book. Many presses came to be established because of the "tyranny of the majority," to quote Alexis de Tocqueville. See seminal studies of early ethnic presses in journalism history by such scholars as Félix Gutiérrez, Sharon Murphy, Lionel C. Barrow, and others.

2. David Paul Nord, "The Evangelical Origins of Mass Media in America, 1815-1835," *Journalism Monograph* 88 (May 1984).

3. Max David Eichhorn, *Evangelizing the American Jew* (New York: Jonathan David, 1978); see also Eichhorn's *Conversion to Judaism* (New York, Ktav, 1965). See too, Joseph L. Blau and Salo W. Baron, *The Jews of the United States, 1790-1840: A Documentary History,* 3 vols. (New York: Columbia University Press, 1963).

4. See Lee M. Friedman, "The American Society for Meliorating the Condition of the Jew and Joseph S.C. Frey," *Early American Jews* (Cambridge: Harvard University Press, 1934), 96-112.

5. See Malcolm H. Stern, *First American Jewish Families* (Cincinnati, Ohio: American Jewish Archives, 1978), and various *City Directories of New York.*

6. See Hyman B. Grinstein, *The Rise of the Jewish Community in New York: 1654-1860* (Philadelphia: Jewish Publication Society of America, 1945).

7. *City Directories of New York 1820-1847* (Boston: R.L. Polk and Co.).

8. Some sources say he died about 1847; city directories do not list him after the 1845-46 volume. Stern, *First American Jewish Families,* 130.

9. *Jew* 2, no. 2, (April 1824), 298.

10. Grinstein notes on p. 218 that he was the only one. For example, p. 271 of *The Jew* (New York: S.H. Jackson, 1825) had a translation of six paragraphs in Hebrew fonts, so his holdings were considerable.

11. An index to the publication by Mark Cartun is located at the American Jewish Archives, Cincinnati, Ohio.

12. *Jew* 1, no. 2 (April 1823), 38.

13. *Jew* 1, no. 4 (June 1823), 78.

14. Preface to the collected issues, *The Jew,* v.

15. *American Jewish Archives,* November 1965, 114. Noted as [Benjamin] Dias [Fernandes' *Series of] Letters [on the Evidences of Christianity].*

16. *Jew* 1, no. 4 (June 1823): 85-98; ibid., no. 6 (August 1823): 115-120; no. 7 (September 1823): 136-39; no. 8 (October 1823): 159-60; no. 10 (December 1823): 207-17; no. 12 (February 1823): 239-44; *Jew* 2, no. 2 (April 1824): 279-86; no. 3 (May 1824): 306-16; no. 4 (June 1824): 336-44; no. 5 (July 1824): 350-56; and no. 6 (September 1823): 364-68.

17. *Jew* 1, no. 7 (September 1823) 141-43; no. 8 (October 1823): 165-68; no. 9 (November 1823): 187-91; and no. 10 (December 1823): 217-22.

18. *Jew* 1, no. 6 (August 1823), 122.

19. *Jew* 1, no. 9 (November 1823), 193.

20. *Jew* 1, no. 3 (May 1823), 57.

21. *Jew* 2, no. 12 (March 1825), 479.

22. *Jew* 1, no. 4 (June 1823), 68.

23. *Jew* 1, no. 4 (June 1823), 64. Jackson never used the word "Christ" but instead used dots to represent the word, partially or in full.

24. *Jew* 2, no. 7 (October 1824), 397.

25. See Richard B. Kielbowicz, "News in the Mails, 1690-1863: The Technology, Policy and Politics of a Communication Channel," 2 vols. (Ph.D. diss., University of Minnesota, 1984).

26. Kielbowicz, "News in the Mails," 2:292.

27. No actual records exist to determine circulation. One must conclude, however, that some individuals read it, based on references to problems with the Post Office and its longevity. With no advertising, it would be surprising if Jackson could afford to publish it out of his own finances.

28. Other editors noted the existence of Jackson's paper.

29. *Jew* 1, no. 5 (July 1823), 78.

30. *Jew* 2, no. 6 (September 1824), 381.

31. *Jew* 2, no. 6, (September 1824), 381.

32. *Jew* 1, no. 9 (November 1823), 193; and *Jew* 2, no. 11 (February 1825). Unfortunately, no comparison can be made using both publications.

33. *Jew* 2, no. 12 (March 1825), 479.

34. Eric W. Allen, "International Origins of the Newspaper: The Establishment of Periodicity in Print," *Journalism Quarterly* 7 (December 1930), 314.

35. Tina Levitan, *Jews in American Life* (New York: Hebrew Publishing, 1969), 48-49; George L. Berlin, "Solomon Jackson's 'The Jew': An Early American Jewish Response to the Missionaries," *American Jewish History* 71 (September 1981), 100-28; Charles A. Madison, *Jewish Publishing in American: The Impact of Jewish Writing on American Culture* (New York: Sanhedrin Press, 1976), 6-7.

36. The Great Awakening was the revivalist movement that swept New England and battered at doors of the conservative church. See Alan Heimert and Perry Miller, eds., *The Great Awakening: Documents Illustrating the Crisis and Its Consequences* (Indianapolis and New York: Bobbs-Merrill, 1967), 71-354.

37. See John Higham, *Send These to Me: Jews and Other Immigrants in Urban America* (New York: Atheneum, 1975); Morris U. Schappes, ed., *A Documentary History of the Jews in the United States, 1654-1875,* 3rd. ed. (New York: Schocken Books, 1976); and Lee M. Friedman, *Pilgrims in a New Land* (Philadelphia: Jewish Publication Society of America, 1948).

38. Jacob Rader Marcus, *Memoirs of American Jews, 1775-1865,* "Isaac Leeser, American Jewish Missionary," vol. 2 (Philadelphia: Jewish Publication Society of America, 1955), 58. Data about Leeser's life include Henry Englander, "Isaac Leeser," *Yearbook, Central Conference of American Rabbis* 28 (1918), 213-52, which discusses in detail some of Leeser's convictions and beliefs; Bertram Korn, *Eventful Years and Experiences* (Cincinnati: American Jewish Archives, 1954), 151-213. Jacob Rader Marcus, *Memoirs of American Jews, 1775-1865,* 58-87, which excerpts reports of his travels to various Jewish communities; Maxwell Whiteman, "Isaac Leeser and the Jews of Philadelphia," *Publications of the American Jewish Historical Society* 48 (June 1959): 207-44; Naomi Cohen, *Encounter with Emancipation, The German Jews in the United States 1830-1914* (Philadelphia: Jewish Publication Society of America, 1984); Lance J. Sussman, "'Confidence in God': The Life and Preaching of Isaac Leeser (1806-1868)" (ordination thesis, Hebrew Union College–Jewish Institute of Religion, 1980); Lance J. Sussman, "Another Look at Isaac Leeser and the First Jewish Translation of the Bible in the United States," *Modern Judaism* 5 (May 1985): 159-90; Sussman, "Isaac Leeser and the Protestantization of American Judaism," *American Jewish Archives* 38 (April 1986): 1-21, and Mayer Sulzberger, "No Better Jew, No Purer Man: Mayer Sulzberger on Isaac Leeser," *American Jewish Archives* 21 (November 1969): 140-48.

39. Bertram Korn, "Isaac Leeser: Centennial Reflections," *American Jewish Archives* 19 (November 1967), 133.

40. Maxwell Whiteman and Edwin Wolf, *The History of the Jews of Philadelphia from Colonial Times to the Age of Jackson* (Philadelphia: Jewish Publication Society of America, 1957), 372-73.

41. Maxine Seller, "Isaac Leeser, Architect of the American Jewish Community" (Ph.D. dissertation, University of Pennsylvania, 1965).

42. Seller, "Isaac Leeser."

43. See Jonathan D. Sarna, *Jacksonian Jew: The Two Worlds of Mordecai Noah* (New York: Holmes & Meier, 1981), 128. See also, Michael A. Meyer, "German-Jewish Identity in Nineteenth-Century America," in *The American Jewish Experience,* ed. Jonathan D. Sarna (New York and London: Holmes & Meier, 1986), 45-61.

44. For a full explication, see Milton R. Konvitz, *Judaism and the American Idea* (Ithaca and London: Cornell University Press, 1978).

45. Sussman, "Another Look," 164.

46. Cyrus Adler and Aaron M. Margalith, *With Firmness in the Right, American Diplomatic Action Affecting Jews, 1840-1945* (New York: American Jewish Committee, 1946).

47. Adler and Margalith, 5. The American Minister sent a copy of the order to Washington, expressing his hope that, in the future, it would not be necessary for him to take any steps when the interests of the United States were not immediately affected.

48. Ira Rosenwaike, *On the Edge of Greatness, a Portrait of American Jewry in the Early National Period* (Cincinnati: American Jewish Archives, 1985), 17.

49. *Occident* 1, no. 7 (October 1843), 317.

50. *Occident* 1, no. 1 (April 1843), 4-5.

51. *Occident* 1, no. 1 (April 1843), 6. However, Leeser would not honor a subscription for less than a year and refused to sell copies singly.

52. *Occident* 1, no. 1 (April 1843), 43-47; *The Occident* 14, no. 6 (September 1856), 303.

53. *Occident* 1, no. 2 (May 1843), 101.

54. "Anti-Jewish Sentiments in California, 1855," *American Jewish Archives* 2 (April 1960), 15-33.

55. *Occident* 1, no. 10 (January 1844), 469-73, for Isaacs's first article on Jewish education. Also *Occident* 2, no. 11 (February 1844), 538-43, and *Occident* 6, no. 12 (March 1849), 581.

56. *Occident* 1, no. 3 (July 1843), 111.

57. *Occident* 1, no. 9 (December 1843), 409-14.

58. *Occident* 10, no. 1 (April 1852), 48.

59. *Occident* 14, no. 4 (July 1856), 200-01.

60. *Occident* 14, no. 3 (June 1843), 153; *Occident* 1, no. 6 (September 1843), 308; and *Occident* 2, no. 11 (February 1845), 518-25.

61. *Occident* 12, no. 2 (May 1854), 96; *Occident* 8, no. 12 (March 1851), 613-15; *Occident* 15, no. 7 (October 1857), 349-53, and no. 6 (September 1857), 291-97.

62. Allan Tarshish, "The Board of Delegates of American Israelites (1859-1878)," *Publications of the American Jewish Historical Society* 49 (1959), 16-22.

63. *Occident* 26, no. 3 (June 1868), 147.

64. *Occident* 23, no. 4 (July 1865), 190.

65. See, for example, Robert E. Park, *The Immigrant Press and Its Control* (New York: Harper & Brothers, 1922).

66. Ira Rosenwaike, "An Estimate and Analysis of the Jewish Population of the United States," *Publications of the American Jewish Historical Society* 50 (September 1960), 23-67.

67. The American Jewish Archives in Cincinnati has a card catalogue of the contents of Bush's paper. An excellent description of the publication is by Guido Kisch, *Historia Judaica* 2 (October 1940), 65-84.

68. Hyman Grinstein, "*The Asmonean*: The First Jewish Weekly in New York," *Journal of Jewish Bibliography* 1 (April 1939), 62-71. Fragments of Lyon's life are described in the *Asmonean* 17, no. 22 (12 March 1858), 172.

69. *Asmonean* 6, no. 23 (24 September 1852), 222. The extremely meticulous genealogist Rabbi Malcolm Stern, in his *First American Jewish Families,* noted only two male children, Gerald and Edmund Robert. However, according to the *Asmonean* of 12 March 1858, Lyon addressed his final words to his oldest son, William, age 15.

70. *Occident* 4, no. 2 (May 1846), 90-96, and no. 6 (September 1846), 293-97; *Occident* 7, no. 6 (September 1849), 320-23.

71. *Asmonean* 5, no. 10 (26 December 1851), 92; *Asmonean* 1, no. 1 (25 October 1849), 1.

72. *Asmonean* 17, no. 22 (12 March 1858), 172. Pagination is irregular; two systems prevail: first, page numbers begin with the first month of each year; second, from 16 May 1850, vol. 2, no. 4, through 25 July 1852, vol. 4, no. 14, each issue additionally sports a "Whole No."

73. *Asmonean* 1, no. 2 (1 November 1849), 13. "The last reigning princes amongst the Children of Israel were Asmoneans."

74. *Asmonean* 6, no. 18 (24 August 1852), 173.

75. Grinstein, *Rise of the Jewish Community.*

76. See, for example, Vishnu V. Oak, *The Negro Newspaper* (Westport, Conn.: Negro Universities Press, 1970).

77. Editorial endorsements of Buchanan, Breckenridge (James, for vice president) and Wood (for mayor and then governor) ran in every issue from 25 July 1856, vol. 14, no. 15, to 31 October 1856, vol. 14, no. 29, where a column was devoted to a state-by-state tally of electoral votes.

78. *Asmonean* 14, no. 18 (15 August 1856), 140.

79. In the *Asmonean* 17, no. 5 (13 November 1857), he endorsed individuals for local elections, the city and county races.

80. *Asmonean* 4, no. 26 (17 October 1851).

81. *Asmonean* 5, no. 1 (24 October 1851), 1, for example.

82. *Asmonean* 4, no. 1 (25 April 1851), 7.

83. Lyon noted that the new postage law allowed his *Asmonean* to go to any part of the Union, "California and Oregon included," for 1 cent or 6 1/4 cents per quarter or 25 cents per year if paid in advance.

84. *Asmonean* 4, no. 6 (30 May 1851), 44.

85. *Asmonean* 4, no. 10 (27 June 1851), 76-80.

86. *Asmonean* 5, no. 14 (23 January 1852), 126.

87. *Asmonean* 1, no. 8 (14 December 1849), 57.

88. *Asmonean* 6, no. 6 (28 May 1852), 44.

89. *Asmonean* 2, no. 6 (7 December 1849), 53.

90. *Asmonean* 5, no. 4 (14 November 1851), 42.

91. *Asmonean* 3, no. 13 (17 January 1851), 100.

92. *Asmonean* 6, no. 1 (23 April 1852), 4.

93. *Asmonean* 14, no. 9 (13 June 1856), 68.

94. *Asmonean* 2, no. 19 (30 August 1850), 148.

95. *Asmonean* 3, no. 20 (7 March 1851), 20.

96. *Asmonean* 6, no. 6 (28 May 1852), 44.

97. The Swiss Constitution, adopted in 1874, made the treatment of foreigners a federal matter, not one to be determined in the cantons.

98. Jonathan D. Sarna, *Jacksonian Jew*, 128. This book is the definitive treatment of Noah.

99. *Asmonean* 17, no. 23 (19 March 1858), 180; no. 24 (26 March 1858), 188; no. 25 (2 April 1858), 196; no. 26 (9 April 1858), 204; *Asmonean* 18, no. 1 (16 April 1858), 4; no. 5 (14 May 1858), 36.

3

Spanish-Language Newspapers in California

Victoria Goff

When gold was discovered in California in 1848, there was not one Mexican-owned, Spanish-language newspaper to report the news to California's native Mexican (Californio) population. Although there were strong press traditions in the capital of Mexico City and in many Mexican states, California's handful of small pueblos and scattered ranchos had never been able to support newspapers. All this changed with the arrival of Hispanic "Forty-Niners" from Spain, South America, Central America, and other parts of Mexico, especially the nearby state of Sonora. Since tradition has it that one out of four California miners of any nationality were journalists, it is not surprising that the Hispanic newcomers, along with the long-established Californios, were quick to establish a Spanish-language press in this newly acquired American territory.

Unfortunately, only a few historians and librarians thought it important to preserve examples of Spanish-language newspapers from this era or from subsequent decades. Therefore, it is quite a task for the historian to piece together a coherent history of the Spanish-language press in California during the 19th century, despite the fact that the state's Spanish-language press continued to grow throughout the second half of the 19th century and into the 20th.

Most of the 19th-century Spanish-language newspapers were concentrated in San Francisco and Los Angeles, but there were also newspapers in Monterey, Azusa, and Santa Barbara. Because of its proximity to the gold mines, San Francisco boasted the greatest number of newspapers. Since the audience of the Spanish-language press was composed of both native Californios and immigrants from other Spanish-speaking countries, California's Hispanic press has never truly been an immigrant press, making it unique among the immigrant/ethnic press in the United States.

Without adequate biographical information about the editors and publishers, it is difficult to determine whether the Californios or the new Hispanic immigrants played a greater role in the development of the press in the 19th century. In describing their readers, these Spanish-language journalists used terms such as *castillaño* (Castilian) or *la raza española* (the Spanish race) more frequently than they did *Mexicano* (Mexican). At the time of the Mexican-American War (1846–48), Mexican nationalism in many parts of Mexico, including California, was weak. After three hundred years of Spanish domination, many people continued think of themselves as Spaniards. By the time of the Treaty of Guadalupe Hidalgo (1848),[1] which ended the Mexican-American War, California had only been under Mexican rule for a little more than a quarter of a century. Mexicans from remote states like California also tended to regard themselves as citizens of their state first and then as citizens of Mexico.[2] So in all likelihood, Californios thought of themselves more as Spaniards or Californians than as Mexicans, consequently making it difficult to determine which group, the Californios or the immigrants, had more impact on the Spanish-language press just from examining words the newspaper editors chose to describe their readership.

It is thus a mistake to categorize California's Spanish-language press as strictly a Mexican-American press. A term such as "Mexican-American press" is more applicable to southwestern states during the 19th century than to California where such a term is more a phenomenon of the 20th century than it is a reflection of reality during the 19th century when immigration from Mexico was relatively modest and when immigration from other Spanish-speaking countries was high, especially during the 1850s and 1860s. For instance, *El Eco de la Patria*, which began publication on February 14, 1878, claimed to be the state's first Mexican newspaper. While this is not an accurate statement, an article in its first issue argued its case by listing Spanish-language editors and their nationality. This gives some insight into the international nature of the Spanish-language press, at least during the 1870s. According to the article, Señor don Pastor de Celis, editor of *La Crónica*, was Spanish as was the editor of *El Eco de la Raza Latina*. The editor of *El Joven*, don A. Cuyas, was a Catalan, and Federico Epson, who edited *La Sociedad*, was a German who was born in Mexico and raised in California. Felipe Fierro, editor of *La Voz del Nuevo Mundo*, was a Chilean, and the Pimentel family, who edited *El Tecolote*, was Colombian.[3]

Today, however, it is appropriate to refer to the Spanish-language press in California as a Mexican-American press. After decades of heavy

Mexican immigration, people of Mexican-American descent are California's largest minority and are expected to outnumber any other racial or ethnic group sometime in the 21st century. Many wonder whether they will lose their cultural identity by that time.

This same concern about cultural identity was one factor that spurred the development of the Spanish-language press during the second half of the 19th century, and the press played a major role in protecting and preserving Californio and Hispanic culture. Despite whatever social, economic, racial, and national differences they may have had, members of the larger Hispanic community used Spanish-language journalism to preserve those elements that *la raza española* shared in common. The press also acted as a typical immigrant press, serving the needs of the first and subsequent generations of immigrants, by reporting news of homelands and by providing a sense of community in an alien environment.

Thus the press helped Californio and immigrant readers alike adapt to this new and alien way of life.[4] As the number of Americans grew, it became extremely difficult for the Californios in particular to ignore the new Anglo culture that was being imposed on them. In early 1848 California's population had numbered only 15,000, but by the end of 1849, there were more than 100,000 people in California. As historian David Weber has described it, Californios quickly became "foreigners in their native land."[5]

Survival in this society almost dictated some kind of assimilation, but pride demanded retention of many aspects of Hispanic culture. At this point in their history, Hispanics, especially Californios, were being forced by circumstances to choose between assimilation or separation. Consciously or unconsciously, most of them opted to blend the two cultures. A careful study of the Spanish-language newspapers of the period reflects how the Spanish-speaking population was becoming Americanized while still clinging to its culture, language, religion, and values. Thus, the typical Spanish speaker evolved into someone who had one foot in each culture while belonging to neither. This split personality is evident in the pages of the newspapers.

Spanish-language journalism in 19th-century California was also an attempt to maintain the status of the native Californio middle and upper classes. These groups had seen their wealth and prestige diminish dramatically with the coming of the Yankee. This readership, sensitive about its image in the press, preferred to be pictured as sophisticated equals of Anglos,[6] and editors and publishers, who some scholars think were members of the elite, obliged these readers for the most part.[7]

The pages of the newly founded Spanish periodicals also provided an important forum for Californio and Hispanic grievances. At first the newspapers reported discrimination against Hispanic miners. Later when many unsuccessful Anglo miners turned to ranching and farming by squatting on Californio land, the Spanish-language press closely covered the decisions of the courts which were slowly settling questions of land ownership. The Californios came out on the losing end in most of these disputes. Even when they won, they often lost. The court cases, typically long and expensive, forced the Californios to mortgage their ranchos to pay for court costs. Very few were able to hold onto their land.

In addition to land disputes, the newspapers responded to the frequent assaults on the religion and culture of their readership. For example, a writer in San Francisco's *El Eco del Pacífico* encouraged his readers "as Americans and members of the noble Spanish race" to raise their voices "to denounce before the supreme tribunal of public opinion the injustices, abuses, and outrages of which our people have been and continue to be victims."[8]

Hispanics were not affected only by the dominant American culture. The Spanish-speaking press was influenced by the other ethnic and immigrant groups that had come to California from every part of the globe during the Gold Rush. California's ethnic diversity was reflected in the variety of foreign-language or ethnic newspapers that was available from the 1850s on. This ethnic and immigrant press included Afro-American, Chinese, Danish, French, German, Hawaiian, Italian, Irish, Japanese, Jewish, Portuguese, Serbo-Croatian, Slovenian, and Swedish newspapers.

Several Spanish-language newspapers were bilingual publications. The English/Spanish publications were usually owned by Anglos, who saw a potential for profit in printing laws and regulations in Spanish or in selling advertising space to merchants who specialized in goods for the Hispanic community. Six of the bilingual periodicals were in English and Spanish, one was in Spanish and French, and another in Spanish and Italian.[9] And one experimented with both French and English pages at different times.[10]

Histories of California journalism rarely allude to foreign-language newspapers. One early history, Edward C. Kemble's *History of California Newspapers, 1846-1858*, mentions only a few Spanish-language newspapers.[11] John Young, a former managing editor of the *San Francisco Chronicle* and author of *Journalism in California*, wrote his history for the *Chronicle*'s Golden Jubilee edition in 1915.[12] He mentioned only two newspapers that were written in Spanish—the state's first newspaper, the *Californian*, which was bilingual, and *La*

Crónica. The latter, which began as a bilingual publication (Spanish and Italian), became San Francisco's first newspaper written entirely in Spanish. It warranted just one sentence in Young's work. In references to the early Californios and to their lack of a press during the colonial period, his comments reflect a strong racial bias.[13]

The Spanish-language press in California has received relatively little study by modern scholars. There has been a tremendous growth in the number of studies on California's Chicano (Mexican-American) community during the past four decades. While this research has uncovered a wealth of information about Mexican-Americans and has given a forgotten people a history, not much attention has been paid to the press. However, bits and pieces of information relating to the Spanish-language press can be found in many of these Chicano studies publications.

Of the few studies that have been done on the Spanish-language press in the United States, Félix Gutiérrez's "Spanish-language Media in America: Background, Resources, History" is helpful.[14] Another article worth mentioning is Carlos E. Cortés's "The Mexican-American Press," which appears in *The Ethnic Press in the United States: A Historical Analysis and Handbook.*[15] While useful, the Cortés article, like the Gutiérrez article, focuses on the entire Southwest and only touches on California. The most important contribution of the Cortés article, for the purposes of studying Spanish-language journalism in California, is his analysis of earlier ground-breaking bibliographical work done by Herminio Ríos and Guadalupe Castillo.[16]

Ríos and Castillo identified 372 Mexican-American newspapers in Arizona, California, Colorado, New Mexico, and Texas that were established between 1848 and 1942. According to the editor of *El Grito,* the journal that published these bibliographies, these studies contributed "greatly toward the eradication of the commonly disseminated but erroneous notions of the non-literate, non-literary, and non-intellectual Mexican-American," and the newspapers themselves "will become an indispensable research tool for those Chicanos, who in the near future, will do historical research based on the firm knowledge that the Mexican-American not only had a body, but also a mind to go along with it."[17]

Of 372 newspapers identified by Ríos and Castillo, only 136 newspapers were established during the 19th century. New Mexico, with 52 newspapers, had the largest number of newspapers; it was followed by Texas with 38, California with 34, Arizona with 11, and Colorado with one. Where it was possible to determine publication frequency, Ríos and Castillo estimated that nearly 80 percent of these newspapers

were weeklies. Of the six daily newspapers they found, half were
California newspapers—*El Eco del Pacífico* (San Francisco); *El Eco
Mexicano* (Los Angeles); and *El Tecolate* (San Francisco). California
accounted for 28 percent of the Mexican-American newspapers that Ríos
and Castillo found in these five states during the 19th century.[18]

While this bibliographical work is a good place to start, its
usefulness is somewhat limited. The press itself is the best source for an
understanding of Spanish-language journalism in California. These
newspapers represent a key to the political, economic, social, and
cultural history of the Spanish-speaking population of California and
present fascinating examples of foreign-language frontier journalism.
For this study the University of California and California State
University library systems as well as the two state libraries in
Sacramento and San Francisco were thoroughly searched. The results of
this search revealed twelve more 19th-century Spanish-language
newspapers than the Ríos and Castillo bibliography. It was not always
possible to determine publishing frequency or the exact dates when
periodicals ceased publication. The following is the most current
bibliography of 19th century Spanish-language periodicals in California.

Azusa
1. *Azusa Valley News* (weekly)*	1885-95?

Los Angeles
1. *El Aguacero* (weekly)	1878-?
2. *El Amigo del Pueblo* (weekly)	1861-?
3. *El Clamor Público** (weekly)	1855-59
4. *La Crónica* (semi-weekly, weekly)	1872-92
5. *El Demócrata* (semi-weekly)	1882-?
6. *Las Dos Repúblicas* (weekly)*	1892-98
7. *El Eco de la Patria* (weekly)	1878-?
8. *El Eco de la Puerta* (weekly)	1878-?
9. *El Eco Mexicano* (daily)	1885-?
10. *La Estrella** (weekly, daily)[19]	1851-55
11. *La Fe en la Democracia* (semi-weekly)	1884-?
12. *El Joven* (semi-weekly)	1877-78
13. *El Monitor* (weekly)	1898-?
14. *El Monitor Mexicano*	1889-95
15. *La Reforma* (semi-weekly)	1877-78
16. *Revista Hispano-Americano* (weekly)	1889-95?
17. *Revista Latino-Americana* (weekly)	1892-93?
18. *La Union*	1896-1912
19. *La Voz de la Justicia*	1876-?

Monterey
1. The *Californian**	1846-48

San Francisco
1. *Anglo-Spanish Merchant** (semi-monthly)	1880-83
2. *La Bandera Mexicana* (triweekly)	1864
3. *La Correspondencia* (weekly)	1885-87
4. *El Crespusculo* (weekly)	1874
5. *La Crónica* (twice weekly)	1854-55
6. *La Cronista* (weekly)	1884-85
7. *Don Clarito* (weekly)	1879
8. *L'Echo du Pacifique** (daily)	1854
9. *El Eco de la Raza Latina* (semi-weekly)	1878
10. *El Eco del Pacífico* (daily)	1852-57
11. *El Nuevo Mundo* (weekly)	1864-68
12. *La Prensa Mexicana*	1868-?
13. *El Progreso* (semi-weekly)	1871
14. *La República* (weekly)	1879-97
15. *El Republicano* (semi-weekly)	1868-69
16. *La Sociedad* (semi-weekly, weekly)	1869-88
17. *Sud Americano*	1855
18. *El Tecolote* (daily)	1875-79
19. *El Tiempo* (semi-weekly)	1868-69
20. *La Voz de Chile*	1867-68
21. *La Voz de México* (semi-weekly)	1864-66
22. *La Voz del Nuevo Mundo*	1867-83

Santa Barbara
1. *El Barbareño* (weekly)	1895-97
2. *La Gaceta* (weekly)	1858-79
3. *Gazette**	1855

*Indicates the publication was bilingual.

This represents forty-six 19th-century Spanish-language newspapers in all, twenty-two from San Francisco and nineteen from Los Angeles. It must be remembered that during most of the 19th century Los Angeles's population was dwarfed by San Francisco's. Because of the northern gold mines, the European, South American, and North American immigration focused on Northern California. It was not until the latter part of the 19th century that Los Angeles's population exploded.

The above list also includes nine bilingual newspapers.[20] In fact, the first newspaper ever published in California was bilingual. Published in English and Spanish, the *Californian* was begun on August 15, 1846, when the Americans occupied Monterey. It is questionable whether it should be considered a Spanish-language newspaper since it was edited and published by the Reverend Walter Colton and George Semple, who were associated with the occupying force in Monterey during the Mexican-American War. This bilingual newspaper—the "first paper printed on the Pacific Coast between Oregon and the Equator"[21]—was printed on a one-page sheet 12 1/2 by 8 3/4 inches. The *Californian* was issued weekly on Saturdays, and the subscription price was $5 a year, payable in advance. It moved to San Francisco (then known as Yerba Buena) on May 22, 1847, and later merged with the *California Star* to form the *California Star and Californian.*[22]

Why weren't there any newspapers in Spanish California prior to the appearance of the *Californian*? As previously mentioned, Mexico had a firmly entrenched press by the time California was annexed by the United States. In fact, the first precursor of newspapers in *Nueva España* (New Spain) was an *hoja volante* (flying sheet) which was printed in Mexico City in 1542. *Hojas*, which were not published on a regular basis and which dealt with one news event at a time, were the dominant vehicle of news dissemination during the 16th and 17th centuries.[23] The first newspaper, *La Gaceta de México*, was not established until 1722, and the first daily, *El Diario de México*, was founded in 1805. *El Misisipí* of New Orleans, the first periodical in the United States to use the Spanish language, was started by the Anglo firm of William H. Johnson and Company in 1808.[24] In the 1810s there were Spanish-language newspapers such as *La Gaceta* and *El Mexicano* published in the area that would later become Texas.

Until Mexico's War of Independence in 1810, Mexican journalism centered in Mexico City. During the revolution, insurgent editors published their newspapers in hiding from the countryside. This marked the emergence of the provincial press, which continued its separate history from that of Mexico City.[25] By the time independence was declared in 1821, there were many provincial newspapers, but according to all accounts, there was no active press in California. There may have been some *hojas volantes* since several sources mention the existence of a printing press in California as early as 1834, but there are no extant examples of *hojas*.

While there are no extant newspapers from this period either, Augustín Zamorano, the owner of the printing press that arrived in Monterey in 1834, did issue a public notice listing his printing rates for "gentlemen who may wish to establish any periodical." While no one took advantage of his services, there was apparently an attempt to establish a newspaper in 1842. According to a 1918 University of

California master's thesis by Ralph S. Kuykendall, Governor Manuel Micheltorana tried to establish a newspaper in Monterey. Manuel Castanares, administrator of customs, and don Enrique Camburton, director of establishment of education, went so far as to draw up a plan to respond to the governor's wishes, but they were unsuccessful.[26] California remained without a newspaper until the American occupation of Monterey in 1846.

The way California was settled perhaps offers an explanation for why California never developed an independent press during the colonial and early national periods. Although Santa Fe, New Mexico, was founded in 1610, settlement of California, which was the final colonization in the northern borderlands, did not begin until Mission San Diego was founded in 1769. Missions, presidios, and pueblos were the institutions used to settle this remote part of the empire, and Spanish California was sparsely populated by Franciscan priests, soldiers, administrators, rancheros, and citizens of the pueblos. There were six main pueblos—San Diego, San Jose, Los Angeles, Santa Barbara, Monterey, and Santa Cruz.

In 1790 there were 900 inhabitants in all of California. By 1810 there were 2,000 and by the end of the Spanish era 3,500.[27] This small and scattered population, a weak economy, a high illiteracy rate, and the limited availability of paper were deterrents to the growth of a press. Beginning with the Gold Rush all that changed. As the population grew dramatically, there was enough of an economic base to support the growth of a Spanish-language press by the time California was admitted to the Union in 1850.

Although the 1850s saw the birth of newspapers in both the north and south, Los Angeles had the honor of publishing the second bilingual newspaper in the state. The *Los Angeles Star*, which was primarily an English-language newspaper, published a Spanish section, *La Estrella* (the Star), between 1851 and 1855. The *Star* itself was published until 1860 as both a weekly and a daily and was continued by the *Daily Los Angeles Star*.

The first Spanish-language newspaper in San Francisco also started as a bilingual newspaper. This time the second language was Italian. The twice weekly *La Crónica* (the Chronicle) began publication in August 1854 and ceased publication in 1855.[28] It was issued by J. Joffre and J.T. Lafuente. Its fourth page, *La Cronica Italiana* (the Italian Chronicle), was printed in Italian. The Italian department was discontinued at the end of a couple of months, and *La Crónica* became California's first all-Spanish publication.[29] In August 1855, Lafuente, along with two partners named Leguizamont and Elespura, founded a small daily Spanish paper, called the *Sud Americano* (South American), that survived only a few weeks.[30]

El Eco del Pacífico (the Pacific Echo) was another San Francisco newspaper. It evolved from a Spanish page in *L'Echo du Pacifique* (The Pacific Echo), a French publication owned and edited by a Monsieur Derbec.[31] According to Kemble's history, Derbec was the oldest newspaper proprietor in San Francisco. The French *Echo* was a triweekly from 1852 until January 1, 1856, when it was changed to a daily. It was one of the largest papers in the city—28 by 42 inches in size.[32] The fourth page of *L'Echo* was printed in Spanish under the title of *El Eco del Pacífico* until January 1856 when a separate paper was started under that title. Its editor was José Marcos Mugarrieta.

Los Angeles's first full Spanish-language newspaper was the weekly *El Clamor Público* (the Public Outcry), which was published for the first time on June 8, 1855. It ceased publication circa December 1859. *El Clamor*'s editor Francisco Ramírez, who had received his journalistic training while working as an editor for *La Estrella*, was a linguist and experimented on several occasions with pages in languages other than Spanish. He introduced English sections twice. On the second occasion he said he was running it to help Spanish-speakers learn the language. Californios, he said, had been cheated of their herds and lands because they did not understand English. He also began running several French columns in 1856 to attract the sizable French population.[33] By July 4, 1857, he ran a full French page, but it was discontinued by August 1.

In Santa Barbara, the *Gazette* was begun on May 24, 1855. Its proprietors were R. Hubbard and W.B. Keep; the editor was T. Dunlap, Jr. Neutral in politics and religion, it ran a Spanish page for seven months in the latter part of 1855. In 1858, the *Gazette* was reorganized as *La Gaceta* (the Gazette), becoming Santa Barbara's first Spanish-language newspaper. According to Kemble, the "enterprise, in the beginning, received but little encouragement from the native Californians, who constituted nineteen-twentieths of the population of the city and county of Santa Barbara. Though many subscribed, they were generally delinquent in paying their subscriptions."[34] It was published in San Francisco and distributed by mail.

The 1860s witnessed a dramatic increase in Spanish newspapers. There were ten new periodicals during this decade, one in Los Angeles and nine in San Francisco. In Los Angeles the weekly *El Amigo del Pueblo* (the Friend of the People) was published for the first time in November 1861 but only lasted six months. San Francisco had newspapers with varied life spans during the 1860s, including *El Nuevo*

Mundo (the New World), *La Voz del Nuevo Mundo* (the Voice of the New World), *El Tiempo* (Time), *La Prensa Mexicana* (the Mexican Press), *La Sociedad* (Society), *El Republicano* (the Republican), *La Bandera Mexicana* (the Mexican Flag), *La Voz de México* (the Voice of Mexico), and *La Voz de Chile y El Nuevo Mundo* (the Voice of Chile and the New World).

Articles in these newspapers during the 1860s reflected the turbulent political times. Slavery and the Civil War in the United States and the European occupation of Mexico were covered extensively.[35] Most Hispanic readers were loyal to the North, and the majority of their newspapers backed the Republican party. On the other hand, the question of the French invasion of Mexico made it clear that many Mexican-Americans were still concerned about the motherland. Other Latin American readers probably followed developments because the idea of a European power on American territory was repugnant to them. One paper in particular, *La Bandera Mexicana*, worked closely with the *Juntas Patrióticas*, which had been established in San Francisco to foster support for Benito Juárez's fight against the French.

The decade of the 1870s marked the beginning of a new cultural experience for Californios. Economic and demographic changes combined to alter California society radically, making newly arrived Anglo Americans an entrenched majority and Mexican Americans, who had lived in California for generations, foreigners in their homeland. Despite cultural dislocation and a depression which caused widespread unemployment and bank failures, there were fourteen new newspapers in the 1870s, including eight newspapers in Los Angeles and six in San Francisco. It was the first decade when there were more new Spanish-language newspapers in Los Angeles than in San Francisco.

The Los Angeles papers included the weekly *El Aguacero* (the Pouring Rain), *La Crónica* (the Chronicle), *El Eco de la Patria* (the Echo of the Country), *El Eco de la Puerta* (the Echo of the Port), *El Joven* (the Youth), *La Reforma* (Reform), *La Union*, (the Union), and *La Voz de la Justicia* (the Voice of Justice). The San Francisco papers published in the 1870s included *El Crespusculo* (the Dawn), *Don Clarito*, *El Eco de la Raza Latina* (the Echo of the Latin Race), *El Progreso* (Progress), *La República* (the Republic), and *El Tecolote* (the Owl).

In the 1880s a publicity campaign brought thousands of people to Southern California, which experienced a rapid population growth and a subsequent land boom. Again there were more new Spanish-language newspapers in Los Angeles (five) than in San Francisco (three). There was one more new paper in the Southern California area, the English-language *Azusa Valley News*, a weekly which was published from 1885 until about 1895. It periodically published a Spanish-language page. Sometimes it was as short as one column or even a half column.

Los Angeles's *El Demócrata*, established October 14, 1882, is an interesting example of a political newspaper for Spanish-speaking voters. On the front page of each issue of this short-lived election-year publication there was a list of Democratic candidates for state offices, another listing of county candidates, biographies of individual candidates (including two Hispanics), and the party platform. Although the paper carried some poetry, the majority of its coverage was political. Typical stories covered court decisions and political events throughout the state. For instance, an article, "Voto de los Cuidadanos de Color," was about "colored" voters in Oakland.[36]

There were no new newspapers in San Francisco in the 1890s, but there were three new papers in Los Angeles and one in Santa Barbara. The Los Angeles newspapers included *Las Dos Repúblicas* (the Two Republics), *El Monitor* (the Monitor), and *Revista Latino-Americana* (the Latin American Review). Santa Barbara's third newspaper, *El Barbareño* (the Santa Barbaran), a weekly, was founded in 1895 and was published until sometime in 1897.

Throughout the decades, it is clear that there had been a determination on the part of Spanish-speaking journalists to keep their communities informed, to report Mexican-American and Latin-American affairs, and to provide an outlet for Hispanic expression. The newspapers upheld Catholicism, the Spanish language, and Hispanic cultural mores and also projected a positive image of the Californio middle and upper classes.

Spanish newspapers also fostered the arts. From the birth of the first newspaper in New Spain in 1722, periodicals were transmitters of culture and published the works of Hispanic men and women of letters. The Spanish-language newspapers in California carried on this same tradition. Along with translations of English poetry and novels and translations of popular works from the continent, the works of Californio poets and writers were showcased. Culture and social criticism were sometimes combined, especially in poetry.

The newspapers also protested discrimination, pointed out the lack of public services, raised social consciousness, and urged the Spanish-speaking population to take action. *El Clamor Público* printed many impassioned editorials on lynching[37] and also vehemently denounced filibusters and squatters. Spanish-language newspapers also spread official government information about how Americans were supposed to act and socialized Spanish speakers into the American way of life.[38] For instance, Ramírez, the editor of *El Clamor Público* and a frequent critic of Anglo-Saxon society, called for his readers to "become Americanized all over—in language, in manners, in customs and habits."[39] Editor Ramírez, as noted, didn't think the American system perfect. He condemned American injustice and supported a repatriation plan to Sonora, Mexico, yet interestingly, he attributed the productivity and energy of a group of repatriates to schooling "by contact with the Saxon race."[40] The newspapers' role in Americanizing the immigrant and the Californio alike was often subtle. The first number of the Spanish section of the *Los Angeles Weekly Star* on July 2, 1853, for instance, had an article about Fourth of July celebrations,[41] and an ad in the Spanish section of the 1874 edition of the *Azusa News* invited everyone to come to a Thanksgiving turkey shoot.[42]

Newspapers also helped politicize Spanish-speaking Americans. *El Clamor Público*, for example, backed Frémont for president. Like *El Clamor,* most Spanish-language publications were Republican. However, they were independent enough to shift gears if a candidate was viewed as a threat to the Spanish-speaking community. Even though Ramírez was a Republican politician, *El Clamor Público* did not support the Republican nominee for governor in 1856 because he had favored the settlers over the Californios.

Finally, it should not be forgotten that many publications were in business to make money. Los Angeles's *El Clamor Público*, for instance, did public printing for the state and city. For the former, it occasionally printed a law in Spanish; for the latter it published many ordinances and official notices as well as a compilation of revised ordinances.[43] During 1856-57 this paper had a practical monopoly of city printing; its bid was said by the council to have halved the competing offers.[44]

Despite similarities among 19th-century periodicals, content, philosophy, and political orientation varied from newspaper to newspaper and from place to place. Nonetheless, *la raza* and its culture were maintained and protected in the pages of all the Spanish-language press. Much remains to be done before there is a definitive work on California's press and its impact on the Hispanic community. Hopefully, this study has begun this process.

Notes

1. On February 2, 1848, the American commissioner and the interim president of Mexico met at the village of Guadalupe Hidalgo and signed a

tentative treaty that was later ratified on May 30. Under the treaty, Mexico gave up all claims to Texas and lost two-fifths of her territory but less than half of one percent of her population. Sparsely settled California became part of the United States under the treaty; it became a state in 1850.

2. The various rebellions in Yucatan, Texas, and other states and the debates between federalists (states' rights) and centralists throughout Mexico during Mexico's early national period attest to this.

3. *El Eco de la Patria,* 14 February 1878, 2.

4. See *El Amigo del Pueblo,* 30 November 1861; *El Eco del Pacífico,* 23 July 1856; *La Bandera Mexicana,* 11 December 1863; *El Nuevo Mundo,* 27 March 1865; *La Voz de Chile y El Nuevo Mundo,* 28 May 1868.

5. David Weber, *Foreigners in Their Native Land: Historical Roots of the Mexican Americans* (Albuquerque: University of New Mexico Press, 1973).

6. *El Aquacero* 24-30 March 1878; *El Clamor Público,* 16 October 1855; *La Sociedad,* 24 December 1869; *La Voz de Chile y El Nuevo Mundo,* 20 June, 4, 18, 25 August 1868.

7. Félix Gutiérrez, "Spanish-Language Media in America: Background, Resources, History," *Journalism History* 4 (summer 1977), 39; Rodolfo Acuña, *Occupied America* (San Francisco: Canfield Press, 1973), 113.

8. *El Clamor Público,* 23 February 1856.

9. *L'Echo du Pacifique* had a Spanish page, and *La Crónica* (San Francisco) printed a page in Italian.

10. *El Clamor Público* ran English-language and French-language pages at different times.

11. Edward C. Kemble, *A History of California Newspapers, 1846-1858* (Los Gatos: Talisman Press, 1962). He originally wrote this piece for the *Sacramento Union.*

12. John Young, *Journalism in California* (San Francisco: San Francisco Chronicle, 1915).

13. Young, for example, in referring to colonial Californios uses the term "sluggish Spaniard," and writes that "the beneficiaries of land grants and their dependents vegetated," 3.

14. Gutiérrez, "Spanish-Language Media in America," 39-41, 65-67.

15. Carlos E. Cortés, "The Mexican-American Press," in *The Ethnic Press in the United States: A Historical Analysis and Handbook,* ed. Sally M. Miller (New York and Westport, Conn: Greenwood Press, 1987).

16. Herminio Ríos and Lupe Castillo, "Toward a True Chicano Bibliography," parts 1 and 2, *El Grito, A Journal of Contemporary Mexican-American Thought* no. 3 (summer 1970): 17-24; no. 5 (summer 1972): 40-47.

17. Ríos and Castillo, 5:39.

18. Their figures do not include other Spanish-language newspapers such as those of New York and Louisiana. They deal only with publications in southwestern states that were once Mexican.

19. *La Estrella* (the Star) was a section of the English-language *Los Angeles Star*.

20. Bilingual publications were not exclusively a California phenomenon. *L'Abeille* (the Bee), a trilingual (French, Spanish, English) daily in Louisiana ran from 1827 until 1916.

21. From the masthead of *The Californian*, 1846-48.

22. Young, *Journalism in California*, 12.

23. Victoria Goff, "*Hojas Volantes*: The Beginning of Print Journalism in the Americas" (paper presented at the American Journalism Historians Association Convention, Coeur d'Alene, Idaho, October 1990).

24. Gutiérrez, Félix. "Spanish-Language Journalism in the U.S." *Caminos* 5 (January 1984).

25. Victoria Goff, "Colonial Foundations of the Mexican Press: 1541 to 1821" (paper presented at the Association for Education in Journalism and Mass Communication Convention, Boston, August 1991).

26. Archives of California, Departmental Records 13, 43-44, and Departmental State Papers, Benecia, 3, 32-33, 36-77 (Bancroft), and a letter in the Santa Rosa *Sonoma Democrat*, 9 September 1885, in Ralph S. Kuykendall, *History of Early California Journalism* (master's thesis, University of California, 1918).

27. Albert M. Camarillo, *Chicanos in California: A History of Mexican Americans in California* (San Francisco: Boyd & Fraser, 1984), 8-11.

28. There seems to be some discrepancy regarding the dates. According to Young, the Spanish paper *La Crónica* began in 1854 and was discontinued in 1865, 37.

29. Kemble, *History of California Newspapers*, 118.

30. Kemble, *History of California Newspapers*, 120.

31. One of the two longest-running newspapers in the history of the French-language press in America was San Francisco's *L'Echo du Pacifique*. It has undergone name changes and is published today as *Le Journal Français en Amérique* (The French Journal of America). See Jacques Habert, "Historie de la Presse Française aux États-Unis," *Le Bulletin de La Société Historique Franco-Américaine* 12 (1966): 127-29.

32. Kemble, *History of California Newspapers*, 111.

33. See lists of French names in *El Clamor Público*, 5 December 1857, 9 January 1858; see also *Southern Vineyard*, 4 November 1859.

34. Kemble, *History of California Newspapers*, 110.

35. For Mexican-American responses to these conflicts, see Leonard Pitt, *The Decline of the Californios* (Berkeley and Los Angeles: University of California Press, 1970), 229-44.

36. *El Demócrata*, 21 October 1882, 3.

37. Gregg Layne, *Annals of Los Angeles* (San Francisco: 1935), 67. Also see *El Clamor Público*, 21 February 1857. For other editorials on the same subject, see *El Clamor Público*, 28 February; 7, 14 March; 11, 25 April 1857.

38. Gutiérrez, "Spanish-Language Media in America," 38-39.

39. *El Clamor Público*, 18 June 1859.

40. *El Clamor Público*, 28 August 1855.

41. *Los Angeles Star*, 2 July 1853.

42. *Azusa News*, 1874.

43. Gutiérrez argues that the dependency of some publications on local and state government contracts, along with ties with the Anglo business community and the English-language press, "most likely place journalists with 'Establishment Mexicans,'" 39.

44. For instances of state printing, see *El Clamor Público*, 15 August 1857; for bills presented to the council, see Los Angeles Council Records 3:313, 315, 319, 344, 423, 435-36.

4

Chinese-American Newspapers

William E. Huntzicker

As a frontier journalist, Mark Twain noted the failure of mainstream American newspapers to bridge the cultural gulf between Chinese and European immigrants. Twain remembered many persecutions of the Chinese in the West, including this story:

[T]he Brannan Street butchers set their dogs on a Chinaman who was quietly passing with a basket of clothes on his head; and while the dogs mutilated his flesh, a butcher increased the hilarity of the occasion by knocking some of the Chinaman's teeth down his throat with half a brick. This incident sticks in my memory with a more malevolent tenacity, perhaps, on account of the fact that I was in the employ of a San Francisco journal at the time, and was not allowed to publish it because it might offend some of the peculiar element that subscribed for the paper.[1]

Twain wrote about the Chinese in Virginia City as quiet people, free from drunkenness. "A disorderly Chinaman is rare, and a lazy one does not exist." The people who persecute them, Twain said, are not the ladies and gentlemen of society. "Only the scum of the population do it—they and their children; they, and, naturally and consistently, the policemen and politicians, likewise, for these are the dust-licking pimps and slaves of the scum, there as well as elsewhere in America."[2]

Twain was not the only white journalist sympathetic to the Chinese. C.O. Cummings, editor of the *Watsonville Pajaronian* in California published one of the rare first-person accounts of a 19th-century Chinese man in the United States. Translated by a mutual friend of the editor and the author, Chung Sun's account appeared in two issues of the Watsonville newspaper. Chung Sun's letters reflected his disillusionment after expecting to find America as a land of justice for all. Instead, he was beaten and robbed in Los Angeles, escaping death only because he spoke English and could plead with his attackers.

I left the loved and ever venerated land of my nativity to seek in [the United States] that freedom and security which I could never hope to realize in my own, and now after some months' residence in your great country, with the experience of travel, study and observation, I hope you will pardon me for expressing a painful disappointment. The ill treatment of [my] own countrymen may perhaps be excused on the grounds of race, color, language and religious, but such prejudice can only prevail among the ignorant.

The letter concludes in an optimistic tone about Chung Sun's plan to continue working because "work is more honorable than idleness." And he vows to try to treat people with kindness even though they treat him badly. In his second letter, he called the United States "a jumble of confusion and a labyrinth of contradictions." Confucian principles were reversed with the uneducated becoming rich and the learned going hungry. Americans, he said, lacked manners and "are very properly styled barbarians."[3]

Twain and Cummings stand out because they were exceptional among journalists. Typical newspapers perpetuated fears and negative stereotypes in an era which Harold Isaacs has described as an age of contempt for China and the Chinese.[4] Throughout the 19th century, politicians advocated the exclusion of Chinese—the only group systematically excluded from the United States because of race.

Many Chinese-language newspapers advanced agendas favoring the same interest groups, primarily white American missionaries and businessmen, who created the negative stereotypes in the first place. Unlike mainstream newspapers, however, Chinese-language newspapers understood the challenges facing immigrants and temporary visitors and helped them adjust to American life. Chinese-American newspapers ranged from religious publications to tabloid sensations. They advertised Chinese imported products and shipping, promoted religious ideas and values, and provided moral support to lonely men far from home.

To leave China in the 19th century, permanent emigrants defied local laws and risked decapitation, the official punishment for emigration. When they reached the United States, they faced additional persecution. Americans both exploited and ridiculed them. Attitudes toward the man's queue, which Americans derisively called a pigtail, symbolized the cultural gulf. Western Americans thought it was fun to jump a "Chinaman" and cut off his queue. To the Chinese, however, the queue symbolized loyalty to his country and his plan to return home. To return home without it would be evidence of an intention to emigrate. Loss of this lock of hair, as a result, could mean death to those who returned to their homes and families in China.

In the 19th century, the Qing (or Ch'ing) Dynasty, which had ruled China for two centuries, was in decline. Military expenditures and corruption undermined economic stability. Internal rebellions, some backed by foreign-supported secret societies, occurred throughout the 19th century. Invaders and traders on the coast challenged China's self-esteem as the Middle Kingdom to which foreigners were to defer and pay tribute. The very idea of trading as equals undermined the emperor's authority. Yet foreign merchants and missionaries debated the amount of violence appropriate to force their way into Chinese society.[5] Several missionaries even served occasionally as diplomats and editors. As temporary secretary to the U.S. Legation, the Reverend Samuel Wells Williams supported violence because the Chinese, he said, "would grant nothing unless fear stimulated their sense of justice for they are among the most craven of people, cruel and selfish as heathenism can make men, so we must be backed by force, if we wish them to listen."[6]

In the United States, most Chinese-language newspapers were founded by well-meaning white missionaries and supported by businessmen, primarily from a powerful business group known as the Six Companies. A comprehensive analysis of the relationship between these newspapers and the typical Chinese resident and sojourner will emerge as historians continue to research the social histories of Chinese communities in the United States. Some important histories of Chinese-American social institutions have appeared since the 1970s,[7] and the task of linking journalism history to social history has only just begun. This chapter looks at the difficulties of doing research on 19th-century Chinese-American newspapers and offers a preliminary look at what they may reveal.

Research Challenges

Doing research on 19th-century Chinese-language newspapers provides a significant challenge because few people apparently saved the newspapers. Karl Lo and H.M. Lai have undertaken the most comprehensive effort to list existing newspapers and their locations. They found that only a few copies of the 19th-century publications survive. "Written information on these papers is skimpy, scattered, and frequently contradictory," and those extant issues of Chinese-language newspapers are difficult for today's readers to understand. They are written in an archaic language that has unique regional characteristics. "Most of the nineteenth-century and some of the pre-1945 papers used a half-classical and half-Cantonese colloquial style of writing," Karl Lo wrote. This dialect is found in neither Cantonese folk literature nor classical literature. "The classical and Cantonese mixture is to be found only in these American newspapers and in private correspondence among Cantonese with two or three years of schooling. When pure classical writing went out of style in the mid-twentieth century, this classical and Cantonese mixture went with it."[8]

And the newspapers' language was unique. Some characters appear to be local creations for names of local places, products, and people. Other Chinese characters appear because they sound like English words. Rather than translating some words from English to Chinese, the editors appear to have used Chinese characters that sound like the English translation. Another difficulty could relate to the fact that the papers are often hand-written for lithographic reproduction, similar to the process used for pictures in the 19th century. With patience, Chinese speakers can figure out the meaning of most words, but some local place names may be difficult to translate. Literate 19th-century readers, however, probably had no difficulty understanding the dialect.

A sampling from the *San Francisco China News* illustrates the simplicity of the original newspapers and the complexity of modern translation. The pages appear to be hand lettered, perhaps all by the same person. The language uses antiquated grammar, and it contains no punctuation.[9] Thus the archaic language, unique dialect, parochial words and expressions, frequent references to local places, and the quality of handwriting contribute to the difficulty of understanding the language. (This author is most grateful to University of Minnesota students Yaijiang [Jane] Zhang and Anchi Chang for translation of articles from the newspapers.)[10]

Missionaries, Chinese, and Newspapers

Early Chinese-language newspapers in the United States served the same groups—missionaries and businessmen—who perpetuated their own imperialistic prejudices and created the U.S. stereotypes in the first place. American missionaries founded newspapers in China and exported them to the United States.

Missionaries and immigrants wrote of a Chinese society in which widespread poverty forced many young men to seek their fortunes outside of China. Reports of gold in California in 1849 attracted Chinese, like immigrants from around the world, to seek riches in the American West. But the Chinese had deep roots in their religion, their homeland and their families. As a result, most Chinese coming to America were male *sojourners* seeking a temporary experience in the United States, hoping to return to China with newfound wealth to help their families. Most of the immigrants and sojourners came from the southeastern provinces which had poor living conditions, political corruption, and exposure to foreign imperialists from churches and businesses.[11]

American missionaries began their work in China as early as 1830 when they settled at the small Anglo-American community at Canton. From this base, historian John K. Fairbank has written, the missionaries planted the seeds that grew into changes later advocated by the Communist government. The missionaries, Fairbank wrote, promoted

the spread of literacy to ordinary people, the publication of journals and pamphlets in the vernacular, education and equality for women, the abolition of arranged child-marriages, the supremacy of public duty over filial obedience and family obligations, increased agricultural productivity through the sinking of wells and improved tools, crops, and breeds, dike and road building for protection against flood and famine, public health clinics to treat common ailments and prevent disease, discussion groups to foster better conduct, student organizations to promote healthy recreation and moral guidance, and the acquisition and Sinification of Western knowledge for use in remaking Chinese life.[12]

For better or worse, the missionaries helped build the confidence of ordinary people to challenge the authority of an imperial government failing to meet their needs.

Missionaries, who often worked as interpreters for the merchants, revealed their attitudes toward China in their contributions to the *Chinese Repository*, a missionary publication in Canton from 1832 to 1851.[13] In their debates in both the religious press and mainstream newspapers, the missionaries expressed their impatience with how slowly China accepted foreign influences. In fact, many missionaries supported blatant British imperialistic attacks, including the so-called Opium and Arrow wars against China.

In the *Chinese Repository,* edited by Elijah Coleman Bridgman and Samuel Wells Williams, American missionaries complained that the "imbecilic" Chinese would insult westerners as long as they met no resistance. In 1834, the editors advocated war after a British lord was humiliated by the Chinese. Force alone would "compel China to a course more consistent with her rights and obligations" to abandon "haughty isolation" which was "in open violation of the law—thou shalt love thy neighbor as thyself." Although advocating force, the editors at first stopped short of demanding an armed invasion of China. But force may be required to change obstinate Chinese attitudes, they said. China was obligated to open its borders to exploitation by British merchants and conversion by Protestant missionaries.[14]

In reaction to an unusual attack from the *New York Herald,* missionaries reacted defensively. Bridgman wrote: "And why not ask: Have the banditti and pirates on the high seas a right to make their own laws? Have they a right to exclude 'foreigners' from what they choose to call their own dominions?"[15] The American missionaries saw China as open as the high seas and its government officials as a gang of pirates. Thus the missionaries felt free to preach in the villages and countryside as seen in the example of two missionaries, who, historian Stuart Creighton Miller wrote, "bragged about physically pushing out of the way Chinese authorities who had attempted to restrain them on one such itinerary, and of disrupting schools and court proceedings to deliver their message of salvation." By 1838 missionaries were blatantly calling for an armed invasion to support their conversion efforts and to help China progress. In 1840, editor/missionary Williams wrote that China needed "a hard knock to rouse her from her fancied goodness and security."[16]

American anti-Chinese sentiment had become so pervasive that Americans seemed to accept shameless exploitation, including drug dealing, by Europeans and Americans on Chinese soil. China's seizure of a British ship loaded with opium for sale in China gave the British a pretext for war and created a crisis of conscience for some missionaries. The Chinese fought the Opium War from 1839 to 1842 to keep the British, with American help, from selling opium in China. But the war opened China's ports to British merchants and gave Hong Kong to Great Britain. An 1844 treaty made it difficult for the weakened dynasty to stop American involvement in the opium trade and provided no incentive for the United States to stop participation by its companies.[17]

Of course, missionaries agreed that opium was evil. But they defended the war as opening China to commerce and civilization—not just drugs. Even negative events such as war and the opium trade, they concluded, could have long-term benefits for humanity. Every Western invasion of China between 1840 and 1900, Miller found, "was almost unanimously conceived of by these American missionaries as an act of Providence." A few missionaries, however, became extremely critical of their colleagues.[18]

Chinese-Language Newspapers

Chinese-language newspapers followed the examples set by early 19th-century American newspapers, which spoke for specific political parties or business interests. Mainstream political leaders expected newspapers to promote their party's ideals, defend the party and its politicians, provide party news, influence public opinion, preach the party line, attack the party's opponents, and provide an electioneering method.[19] Such political control over newspapers remained common, even after the creation of penny newspapers put the press on a commercial basis. By supporting religious and commercial sponsors, early Chinese-language newspapers followed the example of the partisan press.

Contradictory findings of historians seeking the first Chinese-language newspaper illustrate conflicting agendas by the founders and the misunderstandings of historians. "Chinese-American journalism, like that of modern journalism in China, was started by Western missionaries," Karl Lo found. Over the century, the missionaries and later political groups—both those supporting the dynasty and revolutionaries seeking to overthrow it—founded newspapers in the United States to further their interests within both China and the United States. "Throughout the 120 years, the merchant loomed large in the background as the financial supporter, since most of these papers were financial losers."[20]

Historians disagree about when the first Chinese paper appeared in the United States, but most agree it began in San Francisco with a religious mission. In 1851, the Reverend William Speer published a one-sheet religious tract variously referred to as the *Gold Hill News, Golden Hill News,* and *Golden Mountain News.* Speer was corresponding secretary of the Presbyterian Church Board of Education and former missionary in China and in California. At least one directory listed this 1851 effort as the first Chinese newspaper in the United States.

But the first regularly published newspaper, the *Oriental,* a weekly in both English and Chinese, appeared in November 1853 in San Francisco. It was published by a Presbyterian missionary, Lai Sam (or Lee Kan), with Speer's help. Speer defended China as a potential democracy and argued that the Chinese could appreciate American freedoms.[21] In his 1870 autobiography, Speer said the *Oriental* was lithographed in Chinese on one side and printed in English on the other. The Six Companies, a powerful interest group that controlled Chinese immigrants, subsidized the newspaper by paying for the lithography. Other contributions came from people Speer described as "influential gentlemen" of California who "benefited by the presence of the Chinese, and many intelligent and Christian people" who fought repressive legislation against the Chinese.[22]

In his 1858 history of California newspapers, Edward C. Kemble mentioned three newspapers in Chinese, giving different dates from Speer's. The first reference appeared in a list of newspapers founded in 1854: "On the 28th of April the *Golden Hill News,* a weekly lithographed paper, published in Chinese characters and language, was established by Howard & Hudson. It did not live long."[23]

In fact the paper probably failed before the end of its first year, despite religious subsidies. H.M. Lai reports that the paper began on April 22 (not April 28) and promoted Speer's Chinese Mission Chapel. Chapel and press together would combat religious ignorance, explain Chinese laws, and help supply the needs of Chinese residents of the United States. Local news, China news, and shipping and commercial information filled its pages.[24] The *Golden Hills News* promised "to represent the best and enduring interests of the Chinese people...to facilitate their adaptation to American society," and "to bridge the misunderstanding and prejudice between the Chinese and Americans."[25]

Kemble reported that on January 4, 1855,

the *Oriental,* a newspaper printed partly in English and partly in Chinese, was established by the Rev. William Speer, a Presbyterian clergyman, who had been a missionary in China, and understood the tongue. Mr. Lee Kan, a Chinaman, was his associate editor. The paper was religious in its character, and existed two years. It was published thrice a week in Chinese, and one of its issues in each week had one page of English. Its size was twenty-one by twenty-eight inches. It expired in the beginning of '57.[26]

This publication was the first of several 19th-century newspapers to publish a section in English to increase the public's understanding of the Chinese in America. Another was the *Chinese Record* founded in 1876 at the height of the anti-Chinese movement. Other English-language Chinese newspapers founded in 1900 and 1910 sought to increase understanding between the two cultures.[27]

In his 1858 list of Sacramento newspapers, Kemble named the *Chinese News* and added:

It is a little singular that the only paper ever printed in a foreign language in our city should have been a Chinese publication, particularly when we remember the considerable German and French elements in our population. The *News* was a sheet of respectable size and appearance, commenced in December, 1856, by Ze Too Yune, *alias* Hung Tai, a very intelligent native of the Flowery Land residing in our city. It was published not quite two years, first as a daily, next tri-weekly and afterwards irregularly—sometimes once a week and then once a month. It sold at twenty-five cents per week, and had 200 circulation.[29]

The first successful Chinese newspaper took the name of an earlier publication, the *Oriental (Wah-Kee),* in 1875.

In his comprehensive analysis of American newspapers for the U.S. Census Bureau in 1884, S.N.D. North placed the first Chinese newspaper in San Francisco in 1853. He described two such contemporary newspapers and the lithography process necessary to publish them. The *Oriental (Wah Kee)* was published by Yee Jenn, who learned printing in the United States.

He makes use of about 7,000 of the Chinese characters; and, as he has never been able to import Chinese type to this country, all the characters in the paper are formed by hand with a peculiar ink. The sheet, when thus prepared, is impressed upon a smooth stone, over which is constructed a crude machine answering for a press. Upon the stone as thus impressed each separate sheet of the edition is placed, subjected to pressure, and when removed is found to be printed with duplicate characters. The process is one of primitive lithography. When the edition is worked, the stone is chemically cleaned for the next paper.[29]

The *Oriental's* office was at 809 Washington Street and the 21-by-28-inch paper appeared on Fridays. It disappeared for a time but reappeared under the name *Oriental Chinese Newspaper*. The paper disappeared for good in 1903.[30]

North mentioned a second Chinese paper, the *Chinese-English Newspaper (Tong Fan San Bo)*, founded in 1876. The first paper claimed a circulation of 1,000, including many copies sent to China, and the second optimistically claimed a circulation of 750 and growing. Both papers were weeklies; they contained advertisements along with local San Francisco news and excerpts from newspapers in China. Both sold for 10 cents each or $5 per year.[31]

Some Case Studies

A brief tour of newspapers located for this research provides a unique window into American social history as well as the interests of Chinese-American newspapers. They provided an unusual mix of business information and ethnic encouragement. The *San Francisco China News* of 1874 and 1875, for example, was dominated by shipping and marketing information. Typically, tabulations of available products, prices, and shipping schedules dominated the front page and one additional page of the four-page newspaper. Advertisements filled at least one other page, leaving only a small portion of the paper for news and opinion. This remaining space usually listed world news from China and elsewhere. Most news consisted of routine items from afar, but some items reflected concern about the anti-Chinese mood sweeping the country.[32]

The first two issues contained a prospectus for the paper under the heading "Declaration of our company." The newspaper promised to help the Chinese people "to see more, to know more, to let them know the world while living in the room [without traveling]." The editors admitted to some "awkward writing. when translating to Chinese according to sound. When telling the story, we base it on the facts." They asked readers for help. "If there are any awkward places in terms of writing or if we use the wrong word, we need readers to point it out to teach us because to write beautiful lyrics needs ten years. But we are writing an article within one day. How can we satisfy all the expectations?" The first issue announced that the publication would appear every Tuesday.[33]

Nearly all of page 1 was a simple bulletin board, listing commodities and prices. The newspaper contained some local news with a sense of humor. But 30 columns (read vertically) of Chinese characters listed shipping news. For example, a ship arrived from Hong Kong with many letters, guests (probably passengers), silk, linen, mercury, straw mattresses, sacks of pepper and rice, other groceries, 2,559 containers of tea, and 578 containers of tea that stopped in San Francisco and went on to Panama. Another ship left for Hong Kong with wheat, flour and other groceries. A third ship arrived with sardines, white flour, rice, wool, cowhide and eggs. A headline named a company whose steamboat went to Hong Kong and Japan. Departure dates were given in both Chinese and western calendar dates. The boat promised to carry doctors and housekeepers on board—no charge for the doctor if needed. The paper also gave statistics on imports of tea, rice, cigarettes, and on tea going to Peru, Japan, China, and Honolulu.

The newspapers had a straightforward design with many lists and tables, but few illustrations. Like the mainstream press, the Chinese-language newspapers often repeated the same advertisements and illustrations. Standard woodcut illustrations were larger and appeared much less frequently than in most newspapers. The first illustration—a woman sitting at a sewing machine—appeared in an ad on August 4, 1874. A week later, the illustration appeared again along with a second illustration of a sewing machine alone. A few days later, the first illustration appeared again with the face altered to make the woman appear Asian. These three pictures—along with a logo for an insurance company, a beer barrel, and a building facade—were the only illustrations to appear within the year. The building illustration contained a sign stating: "Chenery, Southern & Co. Wholesale Liquor Dealers." On October 17, ads appeared showing the Asian person at sewing machine, building facade, logo, and beer keg. These ads reappear without change for the following six weeks. Between July 1874 and July 1875, the illustration of scales appeared 11 times, a person ironing 8 times, the store front 21 times, the sewing machine alone 7 times, the logo 9 times, beer barrel 5 times, the white woman at sewing machine 6 times and the Asian woman at the sewing machine 26 times. Even though the pictures repeated, the advertisements with them sometimes changed.

Advertisements in *San Francisco China News* promoted the newspaper and its printing business, as well as insurance companies, lawyers, a bakery, shipping schedules, hatters, a businessmen to do taxes and shipping, a circus-like show, a jewelry store, a store selling matches, wooden buckets, ropes, and fish nets, and another vender selling watches, diamonds, guns, and gunpowder. Ads also sold charcoal or coal for cooking, travel to Hong Kong, and medicine to help one quit smoking cigarettes. One store advertised wheat, flour, cooking oil, and ham—prices were printed, but the ad said prices might be negotiable at the store. The most novel repeating advertisement sold fake eyeballs and gold for fake teeth.

Editorials and stories took a moral tone. Page 3 of the first issue contained an editorial associating good and evil with how people were treated, emphasizing an ancient saying: "I don't know what is 'nice' and what is 'evil,' but if they are nice to me, they are nice—if they are bad to me they are evil." The editorial concluded that a shipowner's reputation among Chinese related to how well he treated them. Brief news items came from Shanghai, Canton, the United States, and various shipping companies. Such items were brief digests from other papers. Some articles had been translated into Chinese from other newspapers in the western United States.

In the third issue on page 2, a long editorial reprinted an official statement from the Qing government seeking more authority to maintain order in the San Francisco Chinatown. Other stories often told of appointments of people to business positions, such as the Chinatown Chamber of Commerce. Such stories reported that directors were selected on the basis of their virtue and talent. The Chamber of Commerce, the editorial said, was like a parent, even in small towns.

Like mainstream newspapers, the *San Francisco China News* contained some self-promotion. The newspaper touted new writers to cover the county and its technology, transportation, local culture, and tastes. Crime reporting was promised because it helped readers empathize with victims and therefore strengthen their own resolve. And the newspaper asked readers to promote the paper. The paper promised to print readers' news that was not accusatory or propagandistic. The newspaper also promised advertisers a widespread reach at fair rates. Some news crept into the business statistics. In the fourth issue, for example, the writers warned of the growing influence of Japanese tea in competition with Chinese tea. China profits from tea sales to foreigners, said the article, but sales of new teas from Japan have doubled those from China. Japanese tea flavor described as a little sweeter and more suitable for foreign people because of the Japanese processing method.

The fifth issue contained "Nine Thoughts" in a two-column letter to the editor based on Confucius's admonition to cultivate one's own thinking and to spread virtue. With an endorsement from editors, the writer asked readers to remember the parents, wives, and children back in China as well as ancestors and hometown friends. The article encouraged Confucian virtues of respecting elders, ancestors, and folks left at home while encouraging people to work hard, save, and remain optimistic.

Some editorials and stories contained implicit attacks on white racism. For example, an editorial endorsed China's plan to buy two metal battleships. Japan became aggressive when it bought two such ships, but, the editorial said, Americans thought the Chinese would not be able to operate battleships. Yet, the editorial said, the British and French each had more than 60 such ships while Russia had 32 and the Austria-Hungarian empire 22.

Tabloid-type stories constituted much of the news. In one story, a dying young man sought a wife by searching (like Cinderella's prince) for the owner of a shoe. Another story began with a 60-year-old white religious leader in San Francisco who had disciples, including an intelligent young man he regarded as a son. But the younger man, who had a beautiful wife, became suspicious of his wife's flirtatious demeanor toward the older man, and someone told the younger man that his wife was having an affair with the teacher. Another newspaper in San Francisco then mentioned the affair, while admitting that it might not be true. Still another newspaper said the older man might not be a good person. Toward the end of this article, the writer said the story was possible, whether true or not, because so many older men were going out with younger women.

International news reported that China planned to defend Taiwan in the event of a Japanese invasion. Even though they were barbaric, the newspaper contended, the people of Taiwan should be defended as Chinese. In other news, heavy rains hit Hong Kong, and lightning destroyed a Buddhist temple. A boat near Japan ran into a typhoon. In February, a woman gave birth to a son with three faces. In April, a Chinese police station was struck by lightning, opening the wall to expose three wooden dolls. No one knew why the dolls were there. Too much rain caused crop damage, forcing up the price of rice.

The *San Francisco China News* stood up for the rights of Chinese readers and posted routine legal notices. The paper criticized customs officials for destroying people's clothes while searching their luggage. "This isn't right," the paper contended. "If you know anything about such things, you can report them to an American newspaper so that the officials can know about it so we can stop this." The *News* did not say what newspaper to approach. Another article advised readers that police could not hold them without allowing a call to a friend or relative; if the policeman failed to follow the rule, he could be fined $50 or fired from his job. Another item reported that 60 or 70 stowaways arrived on a boat from Hong Kong and Japan; many business people provided help so the refugees had places to stay and food to eat. "Because we are not in our own country, we all have to help each other," the newspaper said. Another article reported on the suicide of a Hong Kong mother and proposed nurseries for caring for orphaned babies; some businessmen were raising money for that project. Legal notices included a change in the law requiring licenses for laundries and gave the days, hours, and places that fireworks would be permitted during the Chinese New Year.

Slavery among Chinese raised the newspaper's ire and again justified the call for China to intervene. Chinese officials promised to investigate reports that people were being kidnapped into slavery in Cuba. "How sad it is," said the newspaper, "that people have to be separated from their families and to have to suffer as slaves," some even starving to death. The newspaper did not mention the ships transporting the slaves, but it said every house in Cuba had its own prison for housing slaves and preventing rebellion. San Francisco businessmen were trying to figure out a way to set up a legal office for Chinese people, especially with reports of slavery increasing. The newspaper suggested that since all Chinese officials could not come to the United States, San Francisco residents should help the dynasty enforce its laws.

The newspaper said San Francisco Chinese needed government help for business as well as legal support and that Chinese were unfairly discriminated against in the United States while Americans in China were doing very well. One news item under a heading "Metropolitan News" told of a boat arriving with 90 Chinese women. Of these, 22 were very young; they looked like they were prostitutes so the American policeman asked them to go to the police station. The boat's captain took offense, but the women were detained for trial. The newspaper advocated a speedy trial because the women were becoming sick and hysterical.[34]

In August 1876 another newspaper with a remarkably similar name, *San Francisco Chinese Newspaper,* issued its prospectus. In its first issue, the newspaper stressed the importance of news and knowledge. In occasionally classical language, the newspaper promised news from China and anywhere else accessible by train or boat. And, the paper said, people who did not read would become poor in knowledge. Intellectuals knew the importance of knowing what happens in society and whether prices were rising or falling. This newspaper promised to keep track of business and market news, especially about China, day by day, month by month.[35]

The prospectus elaborated in the next issue about how the newspaper helped people help themselves by keeping track of market news. It appealed to traditional views on the importance of storytelling, noting that people without knowledge were not as strong as others. "If we read, we won't be involved in bad things. If we read, we will know what is right. We write articles to survive and to get other people involved," the newspaper said. Short items mixed hard news and helpful tips, such as a warning for sick people to burn contaminated clothing to avoid epidemics.

Local news often involved brothels. A "metro news" item reported a fight in a brothel using "A" and "B" instead of the men's names. Person A threw a knife cutting off part of B's ear. B walked to a Chinese magistrate and asked him to go back to the brothel, but when he got back A was gone. Another item told of two Chinese men fighting over a prospective (white) American customer for their neighboring brothels; one used a knife to stab the leader of the brothel next door. The assailant fled, but police took his landlord captive until the suspect surrendered to police. The landlord called the suspect a gentleman for getting him freed. Another brothel story and editorial told of a madam breaking up a fight when a customer lost his temper; the madam may have saved the young woman's life and prevented the young man from going to jail.[36]

Among other news items, *Chinese Newspaper* in 1877 covered hate groups. The paper objected to political groups that attacked Chinese workers and boycotted businesses hiring Chinese workers. Another story quoted a missionary as saying that host countries should never abuse foreigners within their boundaries. An ongoing story in "metro news" told of a Chinese man murdered near a railroad station. The man had planned to take the train, but anti-Chinese groups waited for him, killed him, and placed his body in a garbage container. In the next issue, the anti-Chinese group denied killing anyone. A spokesman said something went wrong when a factory fired all white American workers and hired all Chinese replacements. Salaries were very low; the Chinese people asked for higher incomes, but the factory owners refused. The newspaper seemed puzzled that the white workers should be angry at the

Chinese willingness to work for less. The paper said white workers had threatened to burn down the homes of the Chinese. Subsequent articles said people who got away with killing the Chinese were allowed to roam around killing others and threatening the employers of Chinese workers.[37]

In 1888, the *American and Chinese Commercial Newspaper* announced its new office in San Francisco, subscriptions for $5 a year, and reasonable rates for job printing. International news on page 2 told of a fictional dragon living in China and a master's negotiations with the dragon to end a drought in the region. One item reported on a creature neither deer, cow, nor horse, living on a mountain in China. Other articles said Russia had invaded Germany and that someone sought information about a missing uncle. Another person sought a missing brother. Local news highlighted a government-sponsored fund-raising effort to build a Chinese hospital in San Francisco. The Chinese ambassador criticized the United States for violating a pledge to protect Chinese in the United States after authorities released a man accused of killing a Chinese man.[38]

A New York newspaper, the *Chinese American* of 1883, contained stories appropriate to a modern supermarket tabloid. A front-page story from China said a falling star, a flock of doves, and the appearance of a dragon supported a theory that the stars might fall from the sky. Another story in the form of a fairy tale told of high officials killed when trying to control a precocious elephant. In retaliation, the emperor became angry and killed the elephant. A more serious story told of a white, wealthy American arrested for getting a Chinese teenager pregnant; he was released from financial responsibility after two of his friends testified that the girl had sex with them. Page 2 of the four-page paper was filled with advertisements, some in English and some in Chinese. Advertisements came from doctors, pharmacists, lawyers, and sellers of professional laundry soaps and equipment. Local news reported a man killed and a woman injured by fumes from a wood-burning stove in their tightly sealed home.[39]

The New York newspaper pointed with pride to Chinese-owned groceries, pharmacies, and liquor stores. The term *Chinatown* was not used, but the newspaper referred to the Chinese business community. Some street performers arrested for their loud contests should have known the police would enforce noise ordinances, the newspaper said. A brief item then informed readers that police keep streets quiet and secure in most areas where (white) Americans live. Another item told of a woman who died from infection after being shot by a Chinese man with whom she had a feud. A Chinese man was beaten by an American while waiting for a bus; both went to court and the American was fined $10. Another notice told of a generous 102-year-old man who allowed poor people to use his garden to grow food; he also helped them pay for food and medicine.[40]

Politically, the newspaper attacked Japanese imperialism and supported the dynasty at a time that other U.S. newspapers and secret societies had begun to work to overthrow the Empress Dowager. Some articles in the newspaper appeared in English. Advertisements heavily favored laundry supplies. One ad for a laundry soap claimed testimony from Chinese laundries. Ads also promoted doctors, medicine, laundry detergent, bleach, other laundry chemicals and supplies, laundry and ironing machinery, sewing supplies, printing, paper, liquor, a service to fix or paint signs and store fronts, restaurants (at least one certified as having a Chinese owner), Japanese goods, and classes to learn English. One advertisement contained the words "American Laundry Machinery Company" in both English and Chinese. Train schedules to Washington and Baltimore were also published.[41]

Printing Challenges

Some mainstream publications noted the challenges of printing Chinese newspapers in their blend of Cantonese and classical Chinese. The turn of the century brought a more modern language and new printing technology. Although the language became simpler, the typical compositor had to become familiar with 11,000 characters in contrast to the 26 letters, 10 figures and other signs and symbols of the English language. "A font of type in the Chinese language," the *Scientific American* reported in 1902,

requires eleven thousand spaces, and in the large and spacious racks here shown each word instead of each letter, as in English, has a place for itself. There is also a peculiar grouping or classification of symbols into groups to further facilitate the mental labors of the typesetters. Thus in the immediate vicinity of the symbol for fish would be found the symbols for scales, net, fins, tail, gills.

The compositor, the magazine said, must be calm and dignified to get through the daily or weekly task of setting a four-page newspaper.[42] Another magazine reported that one newspaper found an efficient production method "by making a contract with an American paper in Oakland to print a daily edition which was first hand-written and then photoengraved and electrotyped."[43]

By the turn of the century, Chinese newspapers had become modernized in other ways as well. "The *World* is probably the most thoroughly Americanized of San Francisco's Oriental papers," wrote one observer in 1910.

It has a staff-photographer, a corps of reporters who can write a news-story in English as well as in Chinese, and who cover the police courts, city hall, incoming and outgoing steamers with remarkable thoroughness. The *World* publishes daily, [has] half-tones of news events, and will soon install an engraving plant—a dignity...which no Oriental paper in American has yet attained.[45]

The *World*, like other Chinese-American newspapers, retained a subsidy. It was supported by reformers seeking to depose the Empress Dowager in China. At the beginning of the 20th century, competing revolutionary leaders found support among Chinese-language newspapers in the United States.

But the Chinese press did not necessarily promote openness. In his study of immigrant newspapers early in the 20th century, sociologist Robert E. Park found it necessary to explain the *tong,* an informal secret society with ties to the home village in China. "Every Chinese is supposed to belong to a *tong,*" Park wrote. Withdrawal from the tong required a public announcement published in the newspaper. He quoted an example from the *Chinese World*:

Mr. Chen: I am a gardener and formerly of *Ho Shin Tong.* Now because I am too much occupied and unable to look after other things, therefore I hand in all the fees and withdraw from the *tong.* Hereafter anything that is connected with the *tong* has nothing to do with me.[45]

One popularized look at Chinese-American life told of an editor's family being kidnapped in China until the editor in the United States published an official statement from the emperor.[46]

Chinese-language newspapers, like their mainstream counterparts, often went after advertising and news for profit-making motives. In 1919, medical advertising dominated the pages, claiming up to 14 percent of the pages in typical foreign-language newspapers. In the largest Chinese daily of the time, nearly 45 percent of advertising was for patent medicines. "Many questionable doctors also advertised. Twenty percent of the medical advertisements in the largest Chinese daily, the *Chung Sai Yat Po,* of San Francisco, are prefaced by the 'flower-willow' symbol, which stands for a venereal disease."[47]

One of five doctors who advertised was an old-fashioned Chinese doctor, Park wrote:

In fact, the whole process of Chinese Americanization can be seen most clearly in the medical advertisements. One doctor in Sonora, Mexico, has his photograph in Chinese dress; another doctor is in white collar and tortoise-shell glasses. These doctors' "ads" consist mostly of testimonials from patients in Hawaii and Canada. There are three kinds of drug store advertising; there is the typical Chinese ginseng and deer's horn, the most expensive Chinese medicines. Then there is the Chinese drug store which advertises twenty to thirty kinds of herb medicines, including brain medicine, and medicine for having children. There is also the American drug store, which advertises some particular remedy—last of all there are the straight patent medicine "ads."[48]

Of course, Chinese newspapers were not alone in their dependence upon patent medicine ads. Like political advocacy, quack medicines had a long tradition in American newspaper advertising.[49]

Conclusions and Suggestions for Further Research

In the 19th century, missionary and business interests founded newspapers in both the United States and China. Ironically, the same interests that competed for access to the Chinese people in China often ran newspapers in the United States with a variety of political agendas. Some supported the dynasty while others organized nationalist movements to overthrow the empire. Nearly all the newspapers gave comfort to sojourners who planned to return home. Such support was in contrast to the ridicule found in much of the maintream press.

Examples for this research affirm the common analysis that the press supported powerful business and missionary interests. In his study of contemporary Chinese-American newspapers in the 1980s, Professor Tsan -Kuo Chang suggested that Chinese-American newspapers retained stronger links to overseas Chinese communities—Hong Kong, the Mainland, and Taiwan—than to the Chinatowns in which they published. As such, the newspapers provided a link between contemporary residents and their roots in the past and their home countries.[50] The Chinese press that developed in the United States provided support for both the dynasty and the revolutionary forces that arose to overthrow it in the early 20th century. Additional research will further illuminate the relationship between these groups and 19th-century Chinese-American newspapers.

Notes

1. Quoted in Lally Weymouth, *America in 1876: The Way We Were* (New York: Vintage, 1976), 161.

2. Mark Twain, *Roughing It* (New York: Signet, 1962), 292, 296-97.

3. *Pajoronian,* 9 November 1871, 16 November, 1871, quoted in Sandy Lydon, *Chinese Gold: The Chinese in the Monterey Bay Region* (Capitola, Calif.: Capitola Book Company, 1985), 133-35.

4. Harold R. Isaacs, *Images of Asia: American Views of China and India* (New York: Harper, 1972), 71.

5. Jack Chen, *The Chinese of America* (San Francisco: Harper & Row, 1981), 6-13.

6. Stuart Creighton Miller, "Ends and Means: Missionary Justification of Force in Nineteenth Century China," in *The Missionary Enterprise in China and America,* ed. John K. Fairbank (Cambridge, Mass: Harvard University Press, 1974), 249-83. Quotation from page 261.

7. See, for example, Lydon, *Chinese Gold*; Stanford Morris Lyman, *Chinatown and Little Tokyo* (Millwood, N.Y.: Associated Faculty Press, 1986); Lyman, *Chinese Americans* (New York: Random House, 1974) and other works by Lyman; Francis L.K. Hsu, *The Challenge of the American Dream: The Chinese in the United States* (Belmont, Calif.: Wadsworth, 1971); Bernard Wong, *Patronage, Brokerage, Entrepreneur-ship and the Chinese Community of New York* (New York: AMS Press, 1988).

8. Karl Lo, preface to *Chinese Newspapers Published in North America, 1854-1975,* by Karl Lo and H.M. Lai (Washington, D.C.: Association of Research Libraries, Center for Chinese Research Materials, 1977), viii, x.

9. For all the above reasons, samples of newspapers located for this research are small and not necessarily representative. Painstaking detective work and extensive travel funds will be required to locate all the existing single copies of 19th-century Chinese-language newspapers. The author is grateful to the University of Minnesota Interlibrary loan office, which searched for two years for 19th-century Chinese-language newspapers available on microfilm.

10. Ms. Zhang, a graduate student from the People's Republic of China, and Ms. Chang, from Taiwan, worked with the author on translation and interpretation from the newspapers in the spring and summer of 1991.

11. Immanuel C.Y. Hsu, *The Rise of Modern China* (New York: Oxford University Press, 1970), 162-79.; John K. Fairbank, Edwin O. Reischauer, Albert M. Craig, *East Asia: The Modern Transformation* (Boston: Houghton Mifflin, 1965), 80-178.

12. John K. Fairbank, "Introduction: The Many Faces of Protestant Missions in China and the United States," *The Missionary Enterprise in China and America,* ed. John K. Fairbank (Cambridge, Mass.: Harvard University Press, 1974), 1-19. Quotation from page 2.

13. Jean Chesneaux, Marianne Bastid, Marie-Claire Bergerc, *China from the Opium Wars to the 1911 Revolution,* trans. Anne Destenay (New York: Pantheon, 1976), 45, 51-52.

14. Miller, "Ends and Means," 249-50. Quotations are from issues of *The Chinese Repository* in 1835.

15. Miller, "Ends and Means," 250-51. Quotations are from issues of *The Chinese Repository* in 1835.

16. Miller, "Ends and Means," 251.

17. John King Fairbank, *Trade and Diplomacy on the China Coast: The Opening of the Treaty Ports, 1842-1854* (Cambridge, Mass.: Harvard University Press, 1953; Stanford, Calif.: Stanford University Press, 1969), 208-09 (page citations are to the reprint edition). The lengths to which the British and Americans would go to sell opium and impose extraterritoriality can be seen in Arthur Waley, *The Opium War Through Chinese Eyes* (London: Allen & Unwin, 1958; Stanford, Calif.: Stanford University Press, 1968) and Hsin-pao Chang, *Commissioner Lin and the Opium War* (Cambridge: Harvard University Press, 1964; New York: Norton, 1970).

18. Miller, "Ends and Means," 249-82.

19. Wm. David Sloan, *The Media in America: A History,* ed. Wm. David Sloan, James G. Stovall, and James D. Startt (Worthington, Ohio: Publishing Horizons, 1989), 68-69.

20. Lo, preface, ix. See also H.M. Lai, "The Chinese-American Press," *The Ethnic Press in the United States: A Historical Analysis and Handbook,* ed. Sally M. Miller (New York: Greenwood Press, 1987), 27-43.

21. Emerson Daggett, supervisor, *History of Foreign Journalism in San Francisco* (San Francisco: Works Progress Administration [WPA Project 10008], 1939), 42-43; Stuart Creighton Miller, *The Unwelcome Immigrant: The American Image of the Chinese, 1785-1882* (Berkeley: University of California Press, 1969) 71, 219.

22. Daggett, *History of Foreign Journalism in San Francisco,* 43-44.

23. Edward C. Kemble and Helen Bretner, *A History of California Newspapers 1846-1858,* printed from a supplement to the Sacramento Union, 25 December 1858 (Los Gatos, Calif.: Talisman Press), 117.

24. H.M. Lai, "A Short History of Chinese Journalism in the U.S. and Canada," *Chinese Newspapers,* 1-15. Quotation from page 2.

25. Quoted in Chin-Chuan Lee, "Preserving Ethnic Pluralism in a Melting Pot: Double Dilemmas of the Chinese-American Press" (paper presented at the annual meeting of the International Communication Association, Chicago, Ill., May 1986).

26. Kemble and Bretnor, *History of California Newspapers,* 119-20.

27. Lai, "The Chinese-American Press," 28.

28. Kemble and Bretnor, *History of California Newspapers,* 117, 119-20, 161.

29. Simon Newton Dexter North, *History and Present Condition of the Newspaper and Periodical Press of the United States* (Washington, D.C.: GPO, 1884), 130.

30. Daggett, *History of Foreign Journalism,* 46-47.

31. North, *History and Present Condition,* 130.

32. Selected issues of *San Francisco China News* from 14 July 1874 to 7 August 1875; on microfilm NMP roll no. 979, University of California. A single issue of *American and Chinese Commercial Newspaper,* no. 266, 13 April 1888, appears on NMP roll no. 4291, University of California, roll 11, item 4.

33. *San Francisco China News,* 14 July 1874; 21 July 1874.

34. News and editorial items from *San Francisco China News,* 21 July 1874; 28 July 1874.

35. *San Francisco Chinese Newspaper* 1:1 (26 August 1876); reel 11, no. 34.

36. *San Francisco Chinese Newspaper,* 1:2 (2 September 1876).

37. *Chinese Newspaper* 1:29 (17 March 1877), 4; 1:30 (24 March 1877); 1:31 (31 March 1877), 1; 1:32 (2 June 1877), 1, 3.

38. Single issue of *American and Chinese Commercial Newpaper,* 13 April 1888.

39. *Chinese American* (New York) 1:1 (3 February 1883); 1: 2 (10 February 1883). One issue of this newspaper is on microfilm at the University of Minnesota Library.

40. *Chinese American* (New York), 3 February 1883; 10 February 1883.

41. *Chinese American* (New York), 3 February 1883.

42. Charles P. Holder, "The Chinese Press in America," *Scientific American* 87 (October 1902), 241.

43. Louis J. Stellmann, "Yellow Journals: San Francisco's Oriental Newspapers," *Sunset* 14:2 (February 1910), 197-201. Quotation from p. 200.

44. Stellman, "Yellow Journals," 199.

45. Robert E. Park, *The Immigrant Press and Its Control* (New York: Harper & Brothers, 1922; Westport, Conn.: Greenwood Press, 1970), 127-29 (page citations are to the reprint edition).

46. Alexander McLeod, *Pigtails and Gold Dust* (Caldwell, Idaho: Caxton Printers, 1947), 146-47.

47. Park, *The Immigrant Press,* 121-22.

48. Park, *The Immigrant Press,* 370-71.

49. Frank Presbrey, *The History and Development of Advertising* (Garden City: Doubleday, Doran & Company, 1929), 289-301.

50. Tsan-Kuo Chang, "The Chinese Press in U.S.: A Linkage to the Past" (paper presented at the annual meeting of the Association for Education in Journalism and Mass Communication, Corvallis, Oregon, August 1983).

5

Newspaper Representation
of China and Chinese Americans

William E. Huntzicker

The Union Pacific Railroad opened the first coal mine at Rock Springs, Wyoming Territory, in 1868, hiring the Wyoming Coal and Mining Company, in which railroad officials owned nine-tenths of the stock, to operate it. Unlike neighboring Montana and Colorado in the 1850s, Wyoming Territory offered little hope to gold miners who became disillusioned with California and headed for inland mining frontiers. So Wyoming leaders expected their wealth to come from coal rather than gold.

But labor troubles soon erupted. In 1871, the Wyoming Coal and Mining Company fired all of its employees who walked out on strike, replacing them with Scandinavians who worked for $2 a day. Federal troops had to protect the replacement workers. In 1874 the Union Pacific Railroad created a coal department to replace the company, and in 1875, the railroad cut the piecework pay to miners but promised to cut its charge to miners for clothing and provisions. Workers struck again when the company broke the agreement.

This time, the railroad replaced striking workers with Chinese miners recruited from farther west. Emerging labor unions and grass roots politicians reacted angrily. The local newspaper, the *Rock Springs Independent,* said the company planned to turn Rock Springs into a Chinatown. "Let the demand go up from one end of the Union Pacific to the other, 'The Chinese must go,'" the newspaper said. The *Independent* condemned the "powerful corporation" for "the employment of leprous aliens."[1]

In 1876, Wyoming Territory's Republican Party resolved that "the introduction of Chinese labor into this country is fraught with serious and dangerous consequences." But the railroad found that Chinese workers were unusually productive and continued to import them. Two weeks after the 1875 strike, 150 Chinese and 50 whites worked the Rock

93

Springs coal mines; ten years later, 331 Chinese and 150 whites worked the Rock Springs mines.[2]

Stable wages and plentiful coal reduced tension between white and Chinese miners for a time. But economic hard times and the depletion of quality coal veins soon led the railroad again to cut wages and reduce many miners to piecework pay. Whites were assigned the best mines to work, while the more challenging ones went to Chinese miners. Resentment grew in both camps. Some white miners accused the railroad of letting the Chinese work the richest veins. Supported by their emerging labor unions, white miners hated both the Chinese workers and the Union Pacific as local symbols of monopoly and capital.[3]

On September 3, 1885, a fistfight between Chinese and white miners did not stop with whites' beating up some Chinese miners. Labor leaders called a mass meeting at the local Knights of Labor hall. The mob ordered the two most unpopular foremen to leave town, which they did hastily on the next train. Then the mob took pistols and rifles and marched into the local Chinatown to set fire to buildings and shoot people who did not get out of town fast enough. Refugees scattered into the hills. "The next day when the bodies were picked out of the ashes and dragged in from the surrounding sagebrush," historian Alexander Saxton wrote, "the official count came to twenty-eight Chinese killed, fifteen wounded. In addition, property amounting to $150,000 had been destroyed." Craig Storti's more recent study placed the death toll at 51, the highest of any race riot in American history.[4]

The riot captured national attention, including strong, indignant play in the two major national weekly magazines, *Harper's Weekly* and *Frank Leslie's Illustrated Newspaper*. Public reaction illustrates the stereotypes and other difficulties Chinese Americans faced in the 19th century. This chapter looks at 19th-century coverage of Chinese issues in mainstream newspapers, examines reaction to the massacre of Chinese workers at Rock Springs in 1885, and analyzes the anti-Chinese movement. The last section looks at *Frank Leslie's Illustrated Newspaper* to provide case studies in stereotypes of China and Chinese Americans.

Rock Springs: A Case Study

On its cover, *Frank Leslie's Illustrated Newspaper* for October 3, 1885, pictured a meeting of rough-looking miners and cowboys above the caption "THE CHINESE TROUBLES IN WYOMING—SUNDAY MORNING SERVICE IN A MINING CAMP."[5] A large picture and short article summarized the event. The magazine blamed the union and a Wild West mentality, but *Leslie's* coverage seems more antiunion than pro-Chinese. *Harper's Weekly*, however, expressed sympathy for the union.

"Our illustration of Sunday morning service in the Wyoming mining region," *Leslie's* said, "gives a vivid idea of the characteristics of the men who participated in the recent butchery of Chinamen." In less than 4.5 column inches, *Leslie's* described the white miners as "men of wild and lawless character, capable of any desperate deed which a savage impulse may suggest. With them the pistol is the arbitrator of all disputes, and the restraints of law and morality are always secondary to the gratification of personal rancor." The magazine said the threat of organized labor could cost the railroad dearly in profits and possible dynamite explosions, adding that the Knights of Labor had the power to stop every wheel on the Union Pacific if it declared a strike. Miners who would prefer orderly methods to settle disputes were powerless, except for the support from troops sent by President Grover Cleveland.[6]

Leslie's major competitor covered the event with more substance. A full-page illustration in *Harper's Weekly* depicted Chinese workers shot down as they ran away from angry miners.[7] The story began with historical background on the company's use of Chinese labor in the coal mines. *Harper's* said the riot followed a quarrel in which four Chinese were wounded, one fatally; white miners then armed themselves, met in the streets, and vowed that "John Chinaman" must go.[8]

To present both the facts and the tone of local racism, *Harper's* lifted part of its story from the *Rock Springs Independent,* which spoke for white miners. Between 60 and 70 armed miners gave the Chinese ("John Chinaman") an hour to leave town. "But the men grew impatient," the *Independent* reported.

They thought John was too slow in getting out, and might be preparing to defend his position. In about half an hour an advance was made on the enemy's works, with much shooting and shouting. The hint was sufficient. Without offering any resistance, the Chinamen snatched up whatever they could lay their hands on and started east on a run. Some were bareheaded and barefooted, others carried a small bundle in a handkerchief, while a number had rolls of bedding. They fled like a flock of sheep, scrambling and tumbling down the steep banks of Bitter Creek, then through the sage-brush and over the railroad, and up into the hills east of Burning Mountain. Some of the men were engaged in searching the houses and driving out the stray Chinamen who were in hiding, while others followed up the retreating Chinamen, encouraging their flight with showers of bullets fired over their heads.[9]

This Rock Springs account, *Harper's* declared, showed that the Chinese offered no resistance, that the whites were not drunk, and that Chinatown was not empty when miners set it afire.

Half choked with fire and smoke, numbers of Chinamen came rushing from the burning buildings, and with blankets and bed-quilts over their heads to protect them from stray rifle-shots, they followed their retreating brothers into the hills at the top of their speed.

Some burned to death while digging holes in which to protect themselves from the flames; the smell of burning flesh was in the air. "The utter fiendishness of the mob was almost inconceivable," *Harper's* wrote. A coroner's jury reported that eleven people burned to death and that four were shot by parties unknown. Hogs found one body and began mutilating it.[10]

The territorial governor immediately asked for the return of federal troops to protect the Chinese miners and to escort refugees back to Rock Springs. Within a week, *Harper's* reported, 200 soldiers escorted the 650 miners—probably an exaggerated number—back to work.

Some of them began to dig in the ruins of their houses, and it is said that as much as $12,000 was unearthed, which the "hated Chinese" had managed to save on the same wages as were received by the "superior" race, though on smaller daily earnings."

The company fired some of the miners who persecuted the Chinese.[11]

The governor called the riot "the most damnable and brutal outrage that ever occurred in any country." And he called the perpetrators "tramps and outlaws," some of whom were fugitives, and "the dregs of the lowest order of immigrants, ignorant and brutal by nature, never having had an opportunity to learn any better than to be led into such performances." The Chinese government listed property losses to Chinese subjects in Rock Springs at $147,748.74, which Congress agreed to pay. Federal troops remained at Camp Pilot Butte near Rock Springs until the Spanish-American War began 13 years later.[12]

While condemning the massacre, *Harper's Weekly* praised the union, but warned that its secrecy encouraged suspicion.

Nothing, however, would be more unjust than to question the right and often the practical wisdom of such organizations, which in this free country, if nowhere else, are inevitable. All that we have heard of one of them, called the Knights of Labor, is so honorable that we were greatly surprised to see them denounced as the allies of the foreign miners in the recent appalling massacre of the Chinese laborers at Rock Springs, Wyoming. That crime was so wanton and inhuman that any organization of American citizens which was privy to it would be justly odious to every true American.

The editorial then reported that the Knights of Labor offered to settle a dispute with the Union Pacific without a strike. The newspaper said a strike would undermine organized labor and endorse the massacre of Chinese workers.[13]

Wyoming newspapers generally disapproved of the massacre as well, but the Chinese in Wyoming soon learned that outrage against murder did not translate into defense of civil rights. Although 16 men, including a legislator-elect, were arrested for the killings, a grand jury refused to return any indictments. The governor gained a national reputation, the support of capitalists who liked Chinese laborers, and an extended term for his support of the Rock Springs victims. By January, however, he had joined the anti-Chinese movement. "The Chinese do not assimilate with our people," he said, "and therefore are not to be regarded as a desirable element in our civilization." Throughout the controversy, the *Rock Springs Independent* repeated the slogan "The Chinese must go." Many Chinese people left Wyoming.

The visible success of the anti-Chinese movement in Rock Springs inspired a wave of mob violence against Chinese people throughout the West, forcing thousands to seek refuge in urban San Francisco.[14] In November, *Harper's Weekly* expressed outrage at the triumphs of "hoodlum persecutors" of Chinese along the Pacific coast. For one example, a jury acquitted the killers of two Chinese men after a 30-minute deliberation in Washington Territory. Rumors indicated that acquitting the remaining defendants would be an easy task. "No doubt! And the task of covering the name of American justice with disgrace and contempt in every civilized land will be an easy one if this sort of thing is to go on." Tacoma residents forced Chinese from their homes onto the prairie in winter.

Of course it is a League of alleged "workingmen" that has driven these quiet toilers out, in the very same spirit as that which, thirty years ago, assailed the Germans and Irish landing at New York, because they sent a part of their earnings home, and were willing to work for less than the wages paid to those who had been here longer. It is a stinging reproach to us all that such an outrage can occur on American soil.

The magazine concluded by calling on law-abiding citizens to protect Chinese people from abuse.[15]

Even before the Rock Springs massacre, newspapers spread hatred of the Chinese throughout the West faster than immigrants arrived. The Silver City, Idaho, newspaper summed up a common attitude in 1866: "They are in many respects a disgusting element of the population but not wholly unprofitable." Even those who hated the Chinese admitted their dependence upon them. "We don't mind hearing of a Chinaman being killed now and then," a Montana journalist declared in 1873, "but it has been coming too thick of late." He warned that violence would leave the West with a shortage of cheap labor. An Arizona editor declared in 1882 that the Chinese were the least desirable immigrants:

The most we can do is insist that he is a heathen, a devourer of soup made from the fragrant juice of the rat, filthy, disagreeable, and undesirable generally, an incumbrance that we do not know how to get rid of, but whose tribe we have determined shall not increase in this part of the world.[16]

The Rock Springs example also illustrates dilemmas created by U.S. policy toward Chinese residents. International treaties and local laws provided ways for racial discrimination to bypass post-Civil War civil rights laws. Unlike African-American slaves who were at least given legal freedom with Constitutional amendments after the Civil War, Chinese workers were denied citizenship. They could not vote, own property, or testify in court against whites. Like slave and free blacks, they became scapegoats for labor leaders among immigrant groups threatened by the introduction of additional cheap labor.

Although Rock Springs was perhaps the largest inland incident against the Chinese, it was only one among many. "Murdering Chinese," historian B.L. Sung writes,

became such a commonplace occurrence that the newspapers seldom bothered to print the stories. Police officials winked at the attacks, and politicians all but incited more of the same. There were thousands of cases of murder, robbery, and assault, but in only two or three instances were the guilty brought to justice.[17]

The miners' real target was the railroad and coal companies, but their anger was directed toward Chinese, who were perceived as the tools of the big corporations. In fact, the Chinese were the most exploited of the western workers. Ironically, the Chinese were among the smallest ethnic groups in the West and, by 1885, their numbers were declining rapidly. Systematic legal discrimination discouraged their permanent settlement and the Chinese Exclusion Act of 1882 prohibited Chinese immigration. In 1885, only 22 Chinese entered the United States, down from a peak of 39,579 in 1882, the year the gates closed.[18]

Two basic illusions underlay the Rock Springs violence: first, the miners said the Chinese received favored treatment and, second, they thought masses of Chinese would threaten their economic stability. Illusions of favored treatment of Chinese workers against the reality of Chinatown poverty and exploitation were kept alive through the newspapers, which emphasized differences between the Chinese and white society. Some of the stereotypes were perpetuated by the same media that expressed outrage at ethnic violence.

Neglecting, Stereotyping, and Blaming the Victims

A California newspaper said Chinese immigrants threatened American progress in 1876:

We have won this glorious land inch by inch from the red man in vain; we have beaten back the legions of George the Third for nothing; we have suppressed rebellion and maintained the integrity of our country for no good purpose whatsoever, if we are now to surrender it to a horde of Chinese, simply because they are so degraded that they can live on almost nothing, and underbid our own flesh and blood in the labor market. The people of California cannot endure it.

In the first major academic study of the anti-Chinese movements, E.C. Sandmeyer found the agitation against racial and ethnic groups a recurring theme in American history.[19]

The image of invading hordes of Chinese threatening to take over the country became so pervasive that Jack Chen opens his history of the Chinese in America with statistics to refute the myth. The California Gold Rush, the first event to bring Chinese in any great numbers, attracted 325 Chinese among the 100,000 men who converged on the territory in 1849. Even in 1882, when Congress passed the Exclusion Act, Chinese constituted less than 0.2 percent of the U.S. population, only 107,488 of the nation's 63 million people. When exclusion was repealed in 1943, the share had dropped to 0.05 percent and by 1970 it had again reached 0.2 percent.[20] Even among those who came, most were sojourners seeking a temporary experience in the United States, hoping to return to China with newfound wealth to help families who remained in poverty at home.[21]

The image of Chinese as slaves comes from the coolie trade of the 1840s. With prohibitions against the slave trade, plantation owners in Latin America and the West Indies looked to cheap Chinese labor to replace slaves. Pirates, Chinese brokers and shippers misled, forced, and kidnapped people for the coolie trade. Local fears were reflected in the word *shanghaied*, which became part of the English language. "News of the possibilities in the coolie traffic soon spread throughout the New World," writes Shih-shan Henry Tsai; "from 1847 to 1859 the number of

Chinese coolies transported by American shippers to Cuba alone averaged over 6,000 per year." Conditions on board ship and in the plantations rivaled those of slavery. Despite winking at American shippers' involvement in the coolie trade, the U.S. Congress refused to allow coolies to be brought into the United States.

Chinese entering the United States came as contract laborers or indentured servants under agreements requiring them to work to pay the costs of their transportation. Historian Gunther Barth says a system of control by foreign importers and Chinese middlemen kept these workers just "one step removed from the despotism of the coolie trade." But the laborers entered the trade by their own volition, and many paid their debts and returned home much better off than countrymen who remained to work in China. The slave analogy was aided by an unsuccessful effort by Mississippi and Arkansas plantation owners to replace their slaves with Chinese workers after the Civil War.[22]

Emphasis on the differences between Chinese and whites permeated the mass media, even in the most sympathetic publications. The *Overland Monthly,* a national magazine in San Francisco—which housed the largest Chinese population in the United States—published many widely reprinted articles about the Chinese. These were among the most reliable descriptions of Chinatown in the 19th century.

Yet even this magazine perpetuated common stereotypes. "The most persistent, general, and, of course superficial impression conveyed by the *Overland* writers of the Chinese was that they all looked alike," wrote Li-min Chu in a comprehensive study of Chinese images in the magazine,

and since for many years almost every Chinese immigrant was an illiterate laborer, most writers had in mind the image of a coolie when a Chinese was described. The usual facets of his characteristic image included a pigtail, almond-shaped or slanted eyes, a tawny skin, a tireless body, loose garments, a shuffling gait, and a proneness for living in a hole as cramped as a dog-kennel. Likened to the Negro, who was another stereotype in the popular imagination, the "Chinaman" could be hired cheaply and remained the least respected of men. In all such casual descriptions, he remained virtually faceless because to these writers all the Chinese faces looked the same.[23]

The stereotyped Chinese worked in the mines or at other menial jobs, belonged to secret societies, worshiped idols, smoked opium, gambled, and visited prostitutes. All Chinese women entering the United States were assumed to be prostitutes. In fact, most Chinese who came were skilled, male workers who remained devoutly loyal to their families in China. Like thousands who rushed into California, their hope was to strike it rich on the "mountain of gold" and return to China where their families remained in relative poverty. The Chinese spent little money on themselves, sending it home or saving it for their return. These Chinese immigrants and sojourners posed little threat to American workers.

Perceptions, of course, diverged from reality. E.C. Sandmeyer found the motives for the anti-Chinese movement in three broad categories: economic, moral and religious, and social and political. Cheap contract labor threatened other new immigrants already in the job market. Religious reformers constantly attacked Chinatowns for their alleged opium dens, gambling casinos, and brothels. And because political parties in post-Civil War California found themselves evenly matched, politicians could easily gain votes by attacking the Chinese workers for their perceived immorality and threats to white workers.[24]

Disseminated through books, magazines, and newspapers, these stereotypes reflected the special interests of the first Americans to visit China: traders, diplomats, and Protestant missionaries with inflated expectations about the number of potential markets and converts. Instead, they encountered corrupt petty bureaucrats of a crumbling dynasty who rejected their trade and religion. These disillusioned envoys wrote about Chinese peculiarities, dishonesty, xenophobia, vices, and backwardness as well as commenting more favorably about crafts, agriculture, and Confucian virtues. The records of these insiders who visited China prepared the United States for the Chinese who would emigrate. These records show, as Stuart Creighton Miller writes,

that the majority of Americans who journeyed to China before 1840 regarded the Chinese as ridiculously clad, superstition-ridden, dishonest, crafty, cruel, and marginal members of the human race who lacked the courage, intelligence, skill, and will to do anything about the oppressive despotism under which they lived or the stagnating social conditions that surrounded them.

In addition to spreading their biases, these traders, diplomats, and missionaries often accepted and repeated one another's misinformation and rumors.[25]

News of the Opium War, in which China went to war to prevent Great Britain and American merchants from dealing drugs within China, reached New York at a time when circulation-based penny newspapers placed a premium on weird and sensational information. James Gordon Bennett, editor of the *New York Herald,* sent messengers to ships arriving from China to get the latest developments, which he could rush into extras for quick sale on the street. "Not only was the Celestial Empire being vanquished," historian Miller writes, "but that 'lazy, rotten, corrupt, unprincipled, ignorant, barbarian, selfish, bankrupt, dying Wall Street press' was suffering a similar fate in the process." Reflecting a decade of magazine coverage, a Boston newspaper described Chinese people as absurdly ugly and intellectually deficient and China as "the land of many letters, many lanterns, and few ideas." Many events kept China and these stereotypes in the public eye at the same time as the mass media grew more competitive and sensational.[26]

Ironically, opium came to symbolize Chinese vice and corruption in stories that ignored U.S. involvement in the Chinese drug trade. "The opium pipe," Miller writes, "became as much a symbol of Chinese culture as the queue or the tea cup, and the mass media gave the impression that Chinese adults of all classes were universally addicted to this pernicious drug."[27] Seemingly factual stories dwelled on the details of opium smoking. But the stereotype outran reality. Ironically, American employers of Chinese workers never complained of substance abuse. Quite the contrary, Chinese railroad workers never caused the problems from drinking and fighting as did most white work crews.[28]

Stereotypes overwhelmed any reality of a Chinese threat to white workers. Stuart Creighton Miller provides the best explanation for the phenomenon by drawing on both E.C. Sandmeyer and Walter Lippmann, who discuss the human tendency to observe those stimuli that reinforce previously held generalizations and stereotypes. For Lippmann, isolated facts merely support the preconceived "pictures in our heads"—stereotypes of unexperienced places and people. Thus Miller contends that Americans had ready-made stereotypes of Chinese immigrants before they met any.[29] For example, voters in West Virginia, a state without a single known Chinese resident in the 19th century, supported the Exclusion Law in 1882.[30]

Completion of the transcontinental railroad in 1869 brought hard times to Chinese workers. Thousands lost their jobs when the work was completed, and the trains now brought more unemployed workers from the East to compete for jobs. Politicians quickly took up the resentment of Chinese laborers and their big-business employers. Railroad magnate Leland Stanford had praised the diligence and efficiency of the Chinese worker, but later Stanford, as politician, found Chinese-baiting expedient. California's state constitution denied voting rights to insane persons and natives of China. Some, including President Cleveland, advocated excluding Chinese people because U.S. law enforcement was unable to defend them from its citizens. Historian Patricia Nelson Limerick sees this reasoning as "the old 'humanitarian' argument for

Indian removal—the solution to crime was to banish the victim."[31] In some respects, science seemed to support this view, especially in light of contemporary theories about the spread of germs. Thus, rumors of disease or sickness in Chinatown became the basis for community defense. The solution again: banish the victim.[32]

"Jostling Pairs" of Stereotypes

Stereotypes of Chinese have not all been negative. At the height of Cold War hostility toward China in the 1950s, researcher Harold R. Isaacs found a deep American ambivalence toward China, showing pleasant and hostile perceptions at the same time. Isaacs interviewed 181 American opinion leaders, including reporters and editors, to determine their attitudes toward China and the Chinese people. His interviewees applied such qualities as cruel, barbaric, inhuman, faceless, devious, and heathen to Chinese people. But they also applied opposite qualities, including high intelligence, persistent industry, peaceableness, filial piety, and stoicism. One stereotype stressed ancient greatness and wisdom; the other swarming hordes of faceless heathens.[33]

These perceptions which Isaacs described as "jostling pairs" of opposite stereotypes have been persistent themes in American popular culture. "The Chinese are seen as a superior people and an inferior people; devilishly exasperating heathens and wonderfully attractive humanists; wise sages and sadistic executioners; thrifty and honorable men and sly and devious villains; comic opera soldiers and dangerous fighters."[34]

Miller found the long-standing ambivalence toward China reflected in 19th-century press coverage. "The cycle of sublime hope, frustration, and bitter disappointment which is so clearly patterned in the reports of missionaries is also discernible, although less pronounced, in most of the press that commented on China." But, he said, editorial positions were not always predictable. "It is exceedingly dangerous to generalize about a newspaper's position regarding the Chinese without following the editorial twists, turns, and reversals over many months."[35]

Examples from "Leslie's"

On December 15, 1855, *Frank Leslie's Illustrated Newspaper*'s first issue carried two seemingly unrelated items. One was a small notice among other news from California:

The Chinese are leaving California. The discriminating tax upon foreign miners, under which the Chinese are now compelled to pay $72 per annum into State Treasury, and which is to be increased $24 each succeeding year, will necessarily induce their speedy departure from the mines. The *Challenger* sailed on November 1, for Hong Kong, taking four hundred Chinese as passengers.

The other item contained the history of plans to build a Pacific railroad, which *Leslie's* supported.[36]

More than 13 years later, *Leslie's* covered the ceremony celebrating the driving of a golden spike at Promontory Point in Utah with an Associated Press report dated May 10, 1869. Telegraph offices in Chicago, New York, New Orleans, Boston, and Omaha were connected, ready to receive simultaneously the message when the final spike completed the coast-to-coast railroad.

[A]t about 2:27 p.m., many of the offices in different parts of the country began to make all sorts of inquiries of the office at Omaha, from which point the circuit was to be started. That office replied: "To everybody: Keep quiet. When the last spike is driven Promontory Point, we will say 'Done.' Don't break the circuit, but watch for the signals of the blows of the hammer."

After a request to remove hats for a moment of prayer, three taps over the wire at 2:47 P.M. indicated that the spike had been driven. *Leslie's* called its cover pictures "strict copies of the photographs taken expressly for *Frank Leslie's Illustrated Newspaper*…we can imagine no pictures more interesting to the civilized world."[37]

Although the contribution of Chinese workers on the transcontinental railroad had been mentioned occasionally, the Chinese were only casually mentioned in coverage of the ceremony:

[A]t a quarter to eleven the Chinese workmen commenced leveling the bed of the road with picks and shovels, preparatory to placing the ties. These Chinese are of lighter color and more regular features than the Chinese seen in the streets of New York. At quarter past eleven the Governor's train arrived. The engine was gaily decorated with little flags and ribbons, the red, white and blue.

Chinese workers, who were so prominent in the railroad's construction, are not obvious in any of the illustrations of the completion ceremony.[38]

Coverage of both routine and unusual events in the illustrated magazines displayed the national ambivalence toward China. Like penny newspapers, the illustrated press eagerly printed quaint or strange ideas and images, especially as they supported prevailing political views or stereotypes. Chinese images made exotic copy.

Even a brief story and illustration of a fast-moving wagon contained cultural and racial bias. Thus *Frank Leslie's Illustrated Newspaper* in 1868 described the picture of a horse-drawn cart and trumpeted U.S. superiority:

While the American nation, with untiring assiduity, is striving to span the continent of North America with the iron girdle of the railroad, Asia is still content to rely upon the service of horse, camel, or mule, as did their fathers before them. It is true that the introduction of foreigners has had some effect in facilitating communication by giving the lazy Orientals an idea of speed and regularity.[39]

Like dozens of others, this reporter assumed that Chinese people were content with ancient ways and that contemporary China reflected centuries of static culture. A casual reference further illustrated this attitude. In an editorial against wooden ships in the U.S. Navy, *Leslie's* evoked another familiar image of China, calling wooden ships "as completely warlike impostures as the wooden fortifications and the sham guns of a Chinese commander." In other words, the ships were considered worthless.[40]

Yet in the same year, *Leslie's* dwelt romantically on the cultural and technological contributions of the Chinese to Western civilization. The occasion was the Chinese mission to the United States headed by Anson Burlingame, an American diplomat hired by the Chinese to protect their interests in the United States. Burlingame's appointment, said *Leslie's,* bestowed honor on both him and his new employers. And the mission deserved considerable space in *Leslie's* magazine: "[I]t is naturally gratifying to our national pride that a citizen of our young and vigorous Republic has been selected to represent the vast and ancient Eastern Empire." The embassy should communicate better "under the direction of an American gentleman of intelligence, experience, and liberal and progressive spirit." Besides Burlingame, the embassy included two other Caucasians, two Mandarin ministers, and Chinese staff members.

Stories and pictures provide details, including descriptions of preparing and eating food:

The two mandarins occupied seats at the head and foot of the table, and, with the exception of the interpreters, were the only ones who indulged in conversation during the repast. As will be seen, the process of catering to the wants of the inner man is quite similar to the ordinary or European method; the only marked difference being in the use of ivory chop-sticks.... The dexterity and precision evinced in handling these instruments is...wonderful, and the appearance of a man plunging a couple of white sticks into a bowl of soup or a dish of peas, taking soundings about the receptacle for a moment, and then withdrawing them with a little green ball or a dripping piece of potato skillfully poised at one end, and with a hasty movement depositing them in the mouth, was a sight highly amusing to our Yankee minds. With the Chinese, dinner-eating seems as much a matter of business, requiring close application, as the facetious harangues of a Bowery auctioneer, or the dash and excitement of a Wall street broker, and they take but little notice of persons and things from the time they sit down until they wipe their chop-sticks and fold their napkins at the conclusion of the exercise.[41]

In the following week, *Leslie's* published pictorial and word portraits of Burlingame, a former Free Soil Republican and President Lincoln's ambassador to China. Articles and pictures of a diplomatic reception and a ceremony raising the Chinese flag over a Washington hotel also appear in the issue.[42]

In a cover story, *Leslie's* praised Secretary of State William Seward for ignoring traditional protocol that would have prevented recognition of an American as a diplomat from another country. The magazine praised Burlingame's indication that China would join the "laws of nations," abandoning its traditional isolation as the Middle Kingdom. *Leslie's* proclaimed that the announcement brought one-fourth of the human race into modern civilization. "It is the clasping of hands between the Occident and the Orient, effected through the intermediation of the United States, which henceforth is to be the next friend and advisor of numerically the greatest nation on the planet."[43]

The U.S. agenda stressed an open policy for China, allowing equal access to China by all European powers. Under such a process, the United States could receive its share of the action. And the article again evoked China's antiquity and flowering civilization while sustaining U.S. superiority:

When we consider the antiquity of China, the stability as well as the extent of her government and the powerful character of her civilization, which differs more in form than in essences from our own, we are sometimes led to think that she alone possesses the true elements of national prosperity and permanence—which, joined with our strength of intellect and the moral elements of our social life, shall produce a new and world-wide organization of society and government, under which the wise and the virtuous shall alone be rulers, and mankind reach its highest point of perfection.[44]

Yet China must show a deeper interest in the "civilized world." The writer gave China credit for the centuries-old inventions of the compass, gunpowder, and printing and for towns that rival "the greatest capitals in our part of the world." Besides material advantages, the study of Chinese history and institutions would "throw an important light on the growth and arrangement of the social system and receive the attention of the statesman, philosopher, student, and Christian philanthropist." Official functions offered additional opportunities for *Leslie's* illustrations. Chinese cooks prepared the state dinner at the Metropolitan Hotel and the embassy staff attended a play at the National Theater. In September, Burlingame's departure for Europe provided an occasion for another cover illustration.[45]

By August, *Leslie's* view of China seemed to have undergone a transformation. In an editorial on international trade, the Great Wall became a metaphor and Chinese political trends a model for the United States as the Middle Kingdom moved away from the isolation the wall represented. In "Sale of the Great Chinese Wall," *Leslie's* made a case for listing the Great Wall among the world's seven wonders, switched to politics, and then typically mixed metaphors and subjects:

Metaphorically speaking, then, China has, in taking away the barriers between herself and the "outside barbarians," sold her Wall, and we think it will not be difficult to show, of course only in a metaphorical sense, that it is we—the great American nation—who have bought it.

We cannot pretend that there was a word about this in the treaty recently signed. On the contrary, the treaty seems to stipulate that we shall pull down part of our wall, if the Celestials will pull down part of theirs.... [W]e shall find on examination plenty of proof elsewhere that we are now owners of the Wall. Thus we read in a recent debate in the French Chambers it was stated that the United States had laid heavy duties, that is, built a wall against French wines and brandies, and it was proposed, in retaliation, to build a wall against American produce. But as it was shown, on argument, that we only injured ourselves, the French wall-builders abandoned their project.

The rambling article says China had been opening as America closed, and it criticized those who wished to make the Pacific Ocean an American lake. This effort could lead only to the isolation and stagnation that China had tried for thousands of years. A Great American Wall could promote certain internal interests and stabilize employment, but it would also result in higher taxes, decreased competition, and reduced commerce.[46]

Within nine months of 1868, readers of *Frank Leslie's Illustrated Newspaper* saw China transform from barbarous, backward nation in January to ancient, honorable civilization in June. By August, the Celestial Empire had learned an ancient lesson and should be the model for the United States in opening to international trade. Surprisingly, *Leslie's* said little about immigration in its coverage of the Burlingame Treaty, the document that provided the legal basis for Chinese immigration until passage of the Exclusion Act in 1882. Burlingame loosened rules for Chinese immigration, but subsequent legislation gradually tightened them.

Without acknowledging swings in its own attitudes toward China and the Chinese, *Leslie's* wrote in 1869, there was no comprehensive, English-language view of China. Most American information on China came from missionaries while most British information came from traders, *Leslie's* said.

Reflecting men are rapidly coming to understand that China is a country of far deeper interest than the narrow-minded religious enthusiast or the selfish trader have [*sic*] represented it. An empire which up to this century contained half the people in the world, the authentic history of which as a single power dates back five thousand years, and which, beginning its life as a paternal despotism, has undergone political and social changes without revolution, until it now presents itself to us in the form of the most democratic monarchy upon earth—that is a picture of some interest.

Confucian society and politics remained vital by providing opportunities for individuals on the basis of merit. This and other topics about China, *Leslie's* said, needed additional study by American scholars and officials.[47]

In 1870, *Leslie's* praised the self-sufficiency of the American Chinese community. Sacramento residents lost many of their possessions in a flood, but the Six Companies from San Francisco cared for its Chinese flood victims. Nevertheless, the magazine could not resist an opportunity to expound upon Chinese vices and virtues. It even presumed to tell the Chinese ("John Chinaman") how to do laundry. "One arm of the river at Sacramento is so frequented by the Oriental washermen, that it has received the name of Chinese Slough. On any pleasant day the work of cleansing linen may be seen in progress, and in some features it differs from the American mode." Exposure to the United States improves the Chinese ability to do laundry:

John has a way of pounding linen, that is not always conducive to its integrity; and it is sometimes necessary to teach him that he should be a preserver rather than a destroyer. To his credit be it said, that he improves, as a washerman, by coming to America; in China he will ruin any linen article in half a dozen washings, and when he wishes to get through his work rapidly, he will put fine gravel into the garments before pounding them. There he has no rival and can do as he pleases; but, in California, he comes in competition with Bridget, and Katrina, and governs himself accordingly.

Stereotypes abound. "A Chinese in San Francisco takes as naturally to washing clothes as an Irishman does to hod-carrying or dray-driving."[48] Two sketches of Chinese in the Sacramento Valley accompany the story, one of men in a tent along the railroad and the other of men doing laundry.

The nation's centennial ushered in a period of hard economic times and anti-Chinese agitation, especially in California. Raising the old specter of Chinese hordes, the *New York World,* which had stimulated antidraft riots among Irish immigrants worried about free black workers, preached against the Chinese. "Asiatics," the newspaper said, "are cunning, treacherous and vicious, possessing no conception of American civilization." Western states, the *World* warned, were degenerating into Chinese colonies that threatened the American way of life. Both national political parties included anti-Chinese statements in their platforms in 1876.[49]

In 1876, *Leslie's* covered China and the Chinese in America several times. In January, an article lifted from a Denver newspaper reported that You, a Chinese in Montana's territorial prison, was innocent of a crime for which he had been convicted. The man, a model prisoner working in the kitchen, "revels in dishwater like a Naiad among coral groves. There is nothing very singular about this. But it now turns out that You is innocent and with fixed contented purpose has become the scapegoat of the guilty parties, whom he knew for a consideration." You received $3 per day of his prison term and had earned $2,100 so far toward his three-year goal of $3,285.

It would hardly strike an American as a good speculation, but a Chinaman may look at it singularly, and take a different view of the project. Anyhow, You seems to be content, and the real thieves are probably more punished by the constant drain upon their exchequer and the apprehension of future revelations and punishment than they would be if in his place.

The magazine reported this event under the heading: "Another Chinese Enterprise."[50]

A week later, *Leslie's* reported on extreme poverty and suffering in China. Mechanics and laborers were receiving 10 to 20 cents per day, which involved 12 to 14 hours. Skilled mechanics could earn 25 to 75 cents per day. Observers reported widespread begging, despite the presence of "many rich Chinamen...not inclined to works of charity; they hold and hoard. There is no properly organized system of charity; relatives and friends are supposed to take care of the sick and the unfortunate." Government, said the magazine, helps in only the most extreme cases; its most conspicuous charity was a hospital.[52]

A week later, Chinese New Year provided a more festive occasion for a story. Chinese residents of Belleville, N.J.,

have experienced much annoyance at the circulation of reports derogatory to their character, a feeling quite generally shared by the citizens, who have found the deportment of the Chinamen to be most quiet, unassuming and gentlemanly. They have been quite regular attendants at the churches and Sunday-schools, and evince great earnestness in the pursuit of a knowledge of the English language and of American customs.

Several boys organized a New Year's celebration combining elements of both American and Chinese ceremonies. Small invitation cards were sent to 200 people. Displays of native handiwork, a painting, and colorful flowers adorned the Joss House temple. Flags and other ornaments decorated the exterior. Fireworks displays, musical performances, and parades highlighted the activities.[52]

In April *Leslie's* reported on progress and stated the importance of educating and Christianizing the Chinese residents of San Francisco. These tasks are mandated by the increasing number of Chinese residents and the prospect that they may vote some day. The mission schools, operated by Presbyterian, Baptist, and Methodist churches, were founded by the Women's Missionary Society of the Pacific Coast to rescue young Chinese women from prostitution. *Leslie's* described the society's rooms in the Methodist Chinese Mission House as "an asylum for any Chinese women who wished to escape from their life of slavery and shame, and secure Christian protection." Two hundred women had participated; 20 of whom married "respectable men." Women usually received sponsorship of $5, the men paying their own tuition of $1. The mission also founded a Chinese YMCA with 57 members and branches in Sacramento, Stockton, San Jose, and Oakland. The Chinese were said to be eager students.[53]

Yet after an April anti-Chinese riot in San Francisco, *Leslie's* strongly reflects the racist tone of the Workingman's Party:

The anti-Chinese meeting held at Union Hall, San Francisco on the evening of April 5th, was the first protest by the people *en masse* against the Asiatic plague that threatens the ruin of California.... Resolutions were adopted setting forth the evils flowing from the Chinese immigration, and urging that, as local measures of relief had been exhausted, the only resource remaining was an appeal to the treaty-making power of the Government.... Fears have been entertained for several months past that the animosity felt towards the Chinese might culminate in a riot or war of extermination. This impression has been gravely considered by the organizations known as the "Six Companies," and the managers claim that they have telegraphed to China to have the immigration stopped at once.[54]

Leslie's attitude toward the Chinese had certainly changed from the days of the Burlingame mission eight years earlier. Critics charged that the Six Companies

practically buy and sell young girls and women for the purpose of prostitution; that their regulations are so strict...no Chinaman dare testify either against the Companies or a fellow-countryman; that they punish violations of their laws by great cruelty, and frequently death; and that the startling increase in the arrivals of Chinese threatens to take from all other people the means of obtaining a livelihood.

Leslie's also charged that the Six Companies "have been quietly arming and drilling their subjects for two or three years past." Thus *Leslie's* expected Chinatown to become more violent.[55]

From violence to celebration again, the 1876 Chinese image returned to the quaint when *Leslie's* visited China's entry into the U.S. Centennial Exposition. Among the 35 countries in the main building, China exhibited an indoor pagoda which was built in Canton and moved in sections to the exhibition.[56]

In *Frank Leslie's Illustrated Newspaper,* a reader can easily see over time wild swings in images of China from near worship of the Celestial Empire to racist vilification of its subjects. The jostling pairs of stereotypes Harold Isaacs found had been prevalent in the American newspapers since the Opium War of the 1830s.

Notes

1. Clayton D. Laurie, "Civil Disorder and the Military in Rock Springs, Wyoming," *Montana: The Magazine of Western History* 40, no. 3 (summer 1990): 44-59; the newspaper stories are from pages 54 and 56. See also Craig Storti, *Incident at Bitter Creek: The Story of the Rock Springs Massacre* (Ames: Iowa State University Press, 1991).

2. T.A. Larson, *History of Wyoming*, 2nd ed., rev. (Lincoln: University of Nebraska Press, 1978), 112-15, 141.

3. Alexander Saxton, *The Indispensable Enemy: Labor and the Anti-Chinese Movement in California* (Berkeley: University of California Press, 1971), 201-05; Rodman Paul, *The Far West and the Great Plains in Transition 1859-1900* (New York: Harper & Row, 1988), 166-67.

4. Saxton, *Indispensable Enemy*, 202; Storti, *Incident at Bitter Creek*, 142. See also Paul Crane and T.A. Larson, "The Chinese Massacre," *Annals of Wyoming* 12, nos. 1, 2 (January 1940, April 1940), 47-55, 153-161.

5. *Frank Leslie's Illustrated Newspaper*, 3 October 1885, cover, 97.

6. *Frank Leslie's Illustrated Newspaper*, 3 October 1885, 103.

7. *Harper's Weekly*, 26 September 1885, 637.

8. "The Chase of the Chinese," *Harper's Weekly*, 26 September, 1885, 638.

9. *Rock Springs Independent* quoted in "The Chase of the Chinese," 638.

10. "The Chase of the Chinese," 638.

11. "The Chase of the Chinese," 638.

12. "The Chase of the Chinese," 638; Larson, *History of Wyoming*, 143, 144.

13. "The Knights of Labor," *Harper's Weekly*, 10 October 1885, 659.

14. Larson, *History of Wyoming*, 141-44; Saxton, *Indispensable Enemy*, 205-13.

15. *Harper's Weekly*, 14 November 1885, 194.

16. *Owyhee Avalanche* (Silver City, Idaho), 23 June 1866; *Montanian*, 27 March 1873; *Tombstone Epitaph*, 13 February 1882. All are quoted in Stanford M. Lyman, *The Asian in the West* (Reno: University of Nevada Desert Research Institute, 1970), 14-15, 134.

17. B.L. Sung, *Mountain of Gold: The Story of the Chinese in America* (New York: Macmillan, 1967), 44.

18. Sung, *Mountain of Gold*, 52.

19. *Marin Journal*, 13 April 1876; E.C. Sandmeyer, *The Anti-Chinese Movement in California* (1939; reprint,Urbana: University of Illinois Press, 1973), 38 (page citation is to the reprint edition).

20. Jack Chen, *The Chinese of America* (San Francisco: Harper & Row, 1981), 3. Some evidence indicates that Chinese landed on the North American

continent before Europeans (about 499 A.D.) and that a few Chinese were among Spanish conquistadors who settled early California. The British East India Company built a settlement in 1788 with Chinese residents on Vancouver Island. Nothing is known of the descendants of these Chinese. Chen, 4, 5; Stan Steiner, *Fusang: The Chinese Who Built America* (New York: Harper, 1979), 3-5, 79-106.

21. Immanuel C.Y. Hsu, *The Rise of Modern China* (New York: Oxford University Press, 1970), 162-179; John K. Fairbank, Edwin O. Reischauer, Albert M. Craig, *East Asia: The Modern Transformation* (Boston: Houghton Mifflin, 1965), 80-178; Chen, *Chinese*, 6-13.

22. Shih-shan Henry Tsai, *The Chinese Experience in America* (Bloomington: Indiana University Press, 1986), 3-10; Chen, *Chinese,* 20-46; Gunther Barth, *Bitter Strength: A History of the Chinese in the United States 1850-1870* (Cambridge Mass.: Harvard University Press, 1964), 50-76.

23. Li-min Chu, *The Images of China and the Chinese in the "Overland Monthly"* (Saratoga, Calif.: R and E Research Associates, 1974), 63. This is a reprint of a 1965 doctoral dissertation from Duke University.

24. Sandmeyer, *Anti-Chinese Movement in California,* 25-39.

25. Stuart Creighton Miller, *The Unwelcome Immigrant: The American Image of the Chinese, 1785-1882* (Berkeley: University of California Press, 1969), 36, 78-80.

26. Miller, *Unwelcome Immigrant,* 84, quoting from the *New York Herald,* 23 March and 24 November 1840, and the *Boston Evening Transcript,* 11 June 1840.

27. Miller, *Unwelcome Immigrant,* 148.

28. John Debo Galloway, *The First Transcontinental Railroad* (New York: Dorset Press, 1989), 144-45, 162.

29. Miller, *Unwelcome Immigrant,* 148; Walter Lippmann, *Public Opinion* (New York: Macmillan, 1922; New York: Free Press, 1965), 3-7, 53-62.

30. Jack L. Hammersmith, "West Virginia, the 'Heathen Chinese,' and the 'California Conspiracy,'" *West Virginia History* 34, no. 3 (April 1973), 291-96.

31. Patricia Nelson Limerick, *The Legacy of Conquest* (New York: Norton, 1987), 260-69; Tsai, *Chinese Experience in America,* 17.

32. Miller, *Unwelcome Immigrant,* 160-66, 197-98.

33. Harold R. Isaacs, *Images of Asia: American Views of China and India* (New York: Harper Torchbooks, 1972), 13-14, 62-63. This book was originally published as *Scratches on our Minds* in 1958.

34. Isaacs, *Images of Asia,* 70-71.

35. Miller, *Unwelcome Immigrant,* 204.

36. *Frank Leslie's Illustrated Newspaper,* 15 December 1855, 2, 14.

37. *Frank Leslie's Illustrated Newspaper,* 5 June 1869, cover, 183.

38. *Frank Leslie's Illustrated Newspaper,* 5 June 1869, cover, 183.

39. "Chinese Carrying Dispatches," *Frank Leslie's Illustrated Newspaper*, 11 January 1868, 268.

40. *Frank Leslie's Illustrated Newspaper*, 2 May 1868, 99.

41. "The Chinese Embassy," *Frank Leslie's Illustrated Newspaper*, 13 June 1868, 195. Illustrations appear on several other pages of the same issue.

42. *Frank Leslie's Illustrated Newspaper*, 20 June 1868, 211.

43. *Frank Leslie's Illustrated Newspaper*, 27 June 1868, cover.

44. *Frank Leslie's Illustrated Newspaper*, June 27, 1868, cover.

45. *Frank Leslie's Illustrated Newspaper*, June 27, 1868, 225-26, 231; 26 September 1868, cover.

46. *Frank Leslie's Illustrated Newspaper*, 15 August 1868, 338.

47. *Frank Leslie's Illustrated Newspaper*, 31 July 1869, 306.

48. *Frank Leslie's Illustrated Newspaper*, 11 June 1970, 265.

49. Lally Weymouth, *America in 1876: The Way We Were* (New York: Vintage Books, 1976), 158; Saxton, *Indispensable Enemy*, 105.

50. *Frank Leslie's Illustrated Newspaper*, 29 January 1876, 342.

51. "Chinese Pauperism," *Frank Leslie's Illustrated Newspaper*, 5 February 1876, 355.

52. "Chinese New Year's Reception at Belleville, N.J.," *Frank Leslie's Illustrated Newspaper*, 12 February 1876, 372.

53. "Christianizing the Chinese in San Francisco," *Frank Leslie's Illustrated Newspaper*, 15 April 1876, 99. Illustration from a photograph is on page 97.

54. "The Chinese on the Pacific Slope: Hostility to the Celestials in San Francisco," *Frank Leslie's Illustrated Newspaper*, 6 May 1876, 141.

55. "The Chinese on the Pacific Slope," 141.

56. *Frank Leslie's Illustrated Newspaper*, 3 June 1876, cover, 210-11.

6

Elias Boudinot and "Indian Removal"

Barbara F. Luebke

All I want in this creation,
Is a pretty little wife and a big plantation
Away up yonder in the Cherokee nation[1]

Westward moving white America was land hungry in the early 19th century, and what some Americans wanted most was the land that the Cherokees had called their own since as far back as their grandparents' grandparents could remember. As the whites pressed their claims, what came to be called "the removal story" developed—a full-fledged battle between southern Native American tribes and the governments of the United States and Georgia.

The *Cherokee Phoenix*, the first newspaper published by a Native American tribe (and thus the first newspaper to give voice to the American "insiders" who were forced to become "outsiders"), was an important player in the removal drama. The newspaper's first editor, Elias Boudinot—an outsider first as an outspoken removal opponent and later as a removal proponent—was an important player, too. His newspaper was the only Georgia paper to protest the natives' removal.[2] As the "principal voice for one of the parties of the conflict," the *Phoenix* excelled in covering the removal story.[3] The paper "was a potent ized by the scores of newspapers that quoted it, by ; who sought to control it, and by federal officials who t."[4] Elias Boudinot's leadership was essential; a man of "keen discernment, eloquent and fearless," he proved to be a "publicist to be dreaded."[5] The father of Native American journalism also proved to be just one of countless 19th-century editors who demonstrated that the press is an essential tool for outsiders, too.

History generally has neglected the Native American press, and until recently, in fact, journalism history barely acknowledged the existence of native publications. While the total number of 19th-century native publications depends on how one defines them, four other tribal newspapers were published—all by the Cherokees and the Choctaws.[6] More common were nontribal papers, "those that were not tribal organs in any sense but were Indian owned, operated or edited."[7] Most of these were published in Indian Territory or by members of Indian Territory tribes. At least 20, of varying duration, appealed primarily to native readers.[8]

When the *Cherokee Phoenix* was established in February 1828 as the official newspaper of the Cherokee Nation, the possibility of the tribe's removal to west of the Mississippi River was a growing rumble of thunder. Lightning was to strike soon. The *Phoenix* could not have escaped the storm, although with a less articulate editor the paper's defense of the natives would not have been so eloquent. An examination of how Elias Boudinot handled the removal story demonstrates that even though the tribal leaders' arguments did not prevail (indeed, Boudinot ultimately came to see their futility and himself reversed position), the Cherokees' own press magnified the outsiders' voice in important ways. Further, by reading the story as reported and editorialized by Boudinot, one hears that voice unfiltered. Finally, the story reveals Elias Boudinot as an editor who, to the end, fought for what he believed in. He saw a need and met the challenge,[9] and in doing so set a noble standard for all Native editors.

The Optimistic Editor

The Cherokees resisted removal from their homeland longest and most strongly—not only for themselves but for all the southern tribes;[10] Their newspaper's name change of February 11, 1829—from the *Cherokee Phoenix* to the *Cherokee Phoenix, and Indians' Advocate*—reflected this. As editor Boudinot wrote in that issue, when the first volume was on the eve of closing:

The paper is sacred to the cause of Indians, and the editor will feel himself especially bound as far as his time, talents and information will permit, to render it as instructive and entertaining as possible to his brethren, and endeavor to enlist the friendly feelings and sympathies of his subscribers abroad, in favor of the aborigines.

As the present policy of the General Government, the removal of all the Indians beyond the limits of organized States or territories, is assuming an important aspect, the editor will feel himself bound to lay before his readers all that may be said on this subject, particularly the objections against this measure of the Government.

In November 1828, Andrew Jackson, an avowed Indian-hater, had been elected President of the United States. A month later, the Georgia

Legislature had passed an act to annex that part of the Cherokee Nation within its limits and to extend state jurisdiction over the natives. The resolution affirmed that the state "had the power and the right to possess herself, by any means she might choose, of the lands in dispute, and to extend over them her authority and laws."[11] The idea of this edict, to go into effect June 1, 1830, was to put the Cherokee Nation under the thumb of Georgia law—eventually forcing the Cherokees out. More than just land was at stake. Gold had been discovered in the Cherokee Nation, and "intruders" soon were flocking to dig it.

The escalating troubles confronting the Cherokees were reflected in Boudinot's *Phoenix* columns from the beginning. So was the general sentiment that, in the end, the natives would not be forced west. The second issue of the newspaper carried part of a report on the native lands prepared by a committee in the Georgia legislature. True to his promise to publish a newspaper whose aim was to inform and benefit the Cherokees, the editor explained:

We think it proper that those of our readers in this Nation, who have not seen this extraordinary document, should be informed of the proceedings of some of those we are accustomed to call, elder brothers. This report is drest [*sic*] with very strong language, and had we never before realized a similar specimen of "*moderation*" from that quarter, we should consider ourselves in a serious dilemma.

The Cherokees were fortunate, Boudinot continued, that their future did not depend on the committee. But he was unwilling to blame the citizens of Georgia, "for we are unwilling to suppose, that the principles contained in the report can ever meet with the approbation of the people of a Christian state." Boudinot wondered if "perhaps it is the lot of Indians, never to find a resting place, never to enjoy a spot of ground which they can call their own, and which their white brethren will ever condescend to them the kindness if not justice, to acknowledge as such." He admitted that in the past the Cherokees had asked for government aid and had received it. Trustingly, he concluded, "We have full reason to believe that it will not now forsake us, and deliver us up to those who seek our hurt."[12]

A week later, Boudinot, tossing in something of a history lesson, commented further on the efforts of the committee.

The situation of Indians is peculiar in the history of man; and the disadvantages in the way of their becoming an enlightened people, which they are obliged to encounter, are numerous and formidable. Such has been the case from the discovery of America to the present moment, and for aught we can say, will still continue to be so. Enemies to Indian improvement, would do well to consider these disadvantages. When they are properly and candidly considered, we cannot but believe, instead of creating astonishment why the Indians have not been civilized before, they will at least suggest the enquiry why they have not degenerated more. What but pernicious effect must such a document as the report of the joint Committee in the legislature of Georgia, have on the interest and improvement of the Indians? Who will expect from the Cherokees, a rapid progress in education, religion, agriculture, and the various arts of civilized life, when resolutions are passed in a civilized and Christian Legislature, (whose daily sessions, we are told, commenced with a prayer to Almighty God) to wrest their country from them, and strange to tell, with the point of a bayonet, if nothing else will do? Is it in the nature of things, that the Cherokees will build them good and comfortable houses and make them great farms, when they know not but that their possessions will fall into the hands of strangers & invaders? How is it possible that they will establish for themselves good laws, when an attempt is made to crush their first feeble effort towards it? These are sad facts, & we beg our readers to bear with us, when we express ourselves so freely & frequently on a subject which we consider to be of vital importance to the Indian race. But amidst troubles, difficulties and evil wishes, we can look around us with much satisfaction and see those who are truly our friends, not only in profession but in deed.[13]

Another time, he minced no words in evaluating removal: "It is calculated upon probable suppositions, in order to remove the whole Cherokee Nation, it will require about Three Millions of Dollars. We should think with this sum every Indian tribe in the U. States might be civilized and rendered happy."[14]

The series of acts passed by Georgia made it unlawful for the Cherokee council to assemble within the state except to relinquish lands. Whites who attempted to live in the Cherokee Nation after March 1, 1831, were to be imprisoned. And Cherokees were not allowed to bring suit in Georgia courts or to testify against whites in those courts.[15] The Cherokees' independence was in jeopardy; their fate had been sealed back in 1822, when in a message to the United States Senate "they declared, once for all, officially as a nation, that they would not sell another foot of land."[16] Georgia would not be satisfied until it got what it wanted. That determination, coupled with Andrew Jackson's policies, left little doubt in Boudinot's mind about the struggle ahead.

President Jackson has, as a neighboring editor remarks, "recognized the doctrine contended for by Georgia in its full extent." It is to be regretted that we were not undeceived long ago, while we were hunters and in our savage state. It appears now, from the communication of the Secretary of War to the Cherokee Delegation, that the illustrious Washington, Jefferson, Madison and Monroe were only tantalizing us, when they encouraged us in the pursuit of agriculture and Government, and when they afforded us the protection of the United States, by which we have been preserved to this present time as a nation.

Why, Boudinot wondered, had not the Cherokees been told earlier that they could not establish their own government. "Then we could have borne disappointment much easier than now." Boudinot pointed out:

The pretext for Georgia to extend her jurisdiction over the Cherokees has always existed. The Cherokees have always had a government of their own. Nothing, however, was said when we were governed by savage laws, when the abominable law of retaliation carried death in our midst, when it was a lawful act to shed the blood of a person charged with witchcraft, when a brother could kill a brother with impunity, or an innocent man suffer for an offending relative. At that time it might have been a matter of charity to have extended over us the mantle of Christian laws and regulations.

Why, asked the editor, had the Georgians now, suddenly, seen the need for jurisdiction over the natives?

But how happens it now, after being fostered by the U. States, & advised by great and good men to establish a government of regular law; when the aid and protection of the General Government have been pledged to us; when we, as dutiful "children" of the President, have followed his instructions and advice, and have established for ourselves a government of regular law; when every thing looks so promising around us, that a storm is raised by the extension of tyrannical and unchristian laws, which threatens to blast all our rising hopes and expectations?

Boudinot suggested, however, that the "great rejoicing in Georgia" was premature. "It is even reported that the Cherokees have come to the conclusion to sell, and move off to the west of the Mississippi—not so fast. We are yet at our homes, at our peaceful firesides...attending to our farms and useful occupations." Then, as if he had overstepped his editorial bounds, Boudinot ended his commentary with this paragraph:

We had concluded to give our readers fully our thoughts on the subject, which we, in the above remarks, have merely introduced, but upon reflection & remembering our promise, that we will be moderate, we have suppressed ourselves, and have withheld, what we had intended should occupy our editorial columns. We do not wish by any means, unnecessarily to excite the minds of the Cherokees. To our home readers we submit the subject without any special comment. They will judge for themselves. To our distant readers, who may wish to know how we feel under present circumstances, we recommend the memorial, the leading article in our present number. We believe it justly contains the views of the nation.[17]

In spite of mounting evidence to the contrary, Boudinot continued to be charitable toward his white brothers. But that was not always easy. The editor was growing more puzzled, more angry.

When we reflect upon the prospects of the Cherokees and their kindred tribes, and the methods and devices of interested white people to obtain the lands, we feel what is not in our power to express. We feel indignant at such arbitrary measures.—We often ask ourselves are we in the United States, the refuge of the oppressed—the land of christian light and liberty?—Where is the superior excellence of republicanism? While we feel indignant at the persecuting civil power which would bear us down to the ground, we mourn for the apathy & indifference of the christian community on the subject. How few are there who will venture to speak a word in our favor? For our part we think, if the public opinion is not for the Indians, we must fall in spite of laws and treaties, for the signs of the times convince us that laws and treaties will form no barrier to the cupidity of our white brothers. But will not justice be outraged? It will be an easy thing for the state of Georgia, whenever she shall think it necessary, to possess the country by force of arms—even if she should be resisted, the poor Indians can easily be crushed to the dust; but a day will come when impartial justice must have its course.[18]

The discovery of gold in the Cherokee Nation turned out to be another nail in what ultimately would be the natives' coffin. Cherokee law stated that metals found within native borders belonged to the Cherokee Nation. Cherokee law did not mean much. When the whites began to "intrude" into the Cherokee lands in order to prospect, the natives asked the United States agent to get rid of them. He brought in federal troops, but there were too few of them to be helpful. Besides, the Georgians complained about the troops and asked President Jackson to order them removed, which he did. The state created the Georgia Guard and gave it jurisdiction over the entire Cherokee Nation.[19] Neither government was fully successful in keeping order, as Boudinot's columns reflected.

In the *Phoenix* of December 16, 1829, he reported on "three eruptions" of white Georgians, "which we will denominate *savage hostilities.*" He described the situation "without comment."

A party of whitemen eight in number, well armed with guns, in the dead of the night, a few days since, came into Hightower and forcibly entering a house, kidnapped three negroes, two of whom were free, and made their escape into Georgia. Another party, also well armed, came over to arrest "thirteen Cherokee Indians," for punishing a notorious thief.... At the same time another party from Habershain County, fifteen in number, we believe, entered another part of the nation, with hostile intentions. After killing a hog, and robbing the Indians, and doing other insufferable acts, some of the Cherokees showed signs of resistance, & demanded of the savage invaders, that they should make remuneration for the hog they had killed, and for other mischief they had done. They not being very disposed to accede to this very reasonable demand, the Cherokees forcibly took one of their guns—after which they escaped into Georgia. This band of robbers will in all probability...have warrants issued against those Cherokees who have had the hardihood to stop their proceedings.

Two weeks later, the confused nature of the situation was evident. The editor reported that the secretary of war had countermanded his order to remove the intruders. "What," asked Boudinot rhetorically, "does the executive intend to do with us? To wear us out by degrees undoubtedly." In his column, he was able to ask publicly what many others undoubtedly must have been thinking:

Where is the faith and justice of the nation, if treaties are thus to be disregarded merely because the state of Ga. has alledged [*sic*] an unfounded claim to a portion of our country. We repeat what we have heretofore said, if the state has any claim, let her first establish that claim upon equitable principles, not by such disgraceful proceedings which [have] characterized her conduct, in the mean time let intruders in kept at a distance.

Boudinot further expressed "serious apprehensions" that justice would be done, especially considering that the order was the fourth by the War Department concerning the intruders—"two for their removal, and both have been countermanded. Such a course of conduct would justly subject any individual to the charge of instability."[20]

"Overrun with Indian Matter"

The Georgia Acts went into effect on June 1, 1830. The Cherokees officially were made outsiders in their own nation. Their laws and customs were declared null; no person of native blood or descent living within "Indian country" could be a witness in a suit with a white defendant; the territory was mapped into counties and surveyed into "land lots" and "gold lots," which were lotteried to whites. Another law required white men living in the Cherokee Nation to take an oath of allegiance to Georgia. The Cherokees were forbidden to hold councils, to assemble for public purposes or to dig for gold. On May 29, 1830, editor Boudinot wrote in his *Phoenix* column:

The day is now at hand—the Cherokees have looked to it deliberately—they have anticipated its approach, but they are still here, on the land of their fathers. So conscious are they of their rights as a people that they have thought it not best to avoid the threatened operation of *civilized* and *republican* not to say *religious* laws, by a precipate flight to the western wilds. They are still here, but not to agree or consent to come under these laws. This they never will do—they have protested against the measure, and will always protest against it.

When the time comes that state laws are to be executed by rigor, as they no doubt will be, backed by the executive of the United States, and the late decision of the Senate, upon the reprobate Cherokees, we are unable to say what the effects will be. To us, the future is but darkness. One thing we Know, *there will be suffering*. The Cherokees will be a prey to the cupidity of white men— every indignity and every oppression will be heaped upon them. They have already undergone much, when the time is merely in anticipation,—how will it be when full licence [*sic*] is given to their oppressors?

Boudinot reminded his readers that there was good reason to be pessimistic, judging from incidents previously reported in the *Phoenix*. And if these were not enough, he told of yet another "indignity" by "civilized men toward savages."

In the neighborhood of Tarrapin Creek, there lives a Creek man by the name of Hog, who, by his industrious habits, has been enabled to accumulate some property, consisting, chiefly, of large stocks of horses and cattle. Living as he does near his white brothers, who are clamorous for the removal of the Indians, that they may not be harassed by savage neighbors, his best horses became the objects of much desire to some of them. By the precaution of the Hog and the constant watch he kept about his stables and lots, he was able to preserve these horses. Finding they could not steal them, we understand another expedient was resorted to lately by these members of the "Poney Club." Four whitemen came to this Indian's house, two of whom were armed with rifles. Finding the Hog alone with his wife, one of the men who was armed, proposed to buy his horse, and offered his gun for compensation. The Creek Indian refused to sell for such a trifle. The white man then proposed to exchange with the Indian. The offer was again rejected, the Indian's horse being greatly superior in value to the other. At this the white man observed he would have the horse, and proceeded towards the lot with a bridle. Hog's wife, discovering the intention of these men, followed, and in attempting to prevent them from catching the horse, was knocked down by the other armed man with a gun. She fell senseless to the ground. Hog ran into the horse lot, & by driving off the horses, & giving the alarm, prevented these robbers from accomplishing their design. The woman lay for some time apparently dead, but finally came to herself. We understand she is better, and is likely to recover.

Then, although characteristically saying comment was unnecessary, Boudinot concluded his column this way:

We intreat you, respected reader,—we implore you, to pause after perusing the above facts, and reflect upon the effects of *civilized* legislation over poor *savages*. The laws which are the result of this legislation, are framed expressly against us, and not a clause in our favor. We cannot be a party or a witness in any of the courts where a white man is a party. Here is the secret. *Full licence* [sic] *to our oppressors, and every avenue of justice* closed against us. Yes, this is the bitter cup prepared for us by a *republican* and *religious* Government—we shall drink it to the very dregs.

Already, Cherokees had died at the hands of the Georgians. In a rare headlined *Phoenix* article, Boudinot had announced the story this way: "FIRST BLOOD SHED BY THE GEORGIANS!!" He wrote that he was not surprised such a circumstance, long dreaded, finally had occurred. But, he judged, it was better that a Cherokee had been murdered by a white man than had a Cherokee murdered a white. "It has been the desire of our enemies that the Cherokees may be urged to some desperate act— thus far this desire has never been realized, and we hope, notwithstanding the great injury now sustained, their wonted forbearance will be continued." Boudinot advised, "If our word will have any weight with our countrymen in this very trying time, we would say, forbear, forbear—revenge not, but leave the vengeance to him "to whom vengeance belongeth."[21]

The *Phoenix* was changing, and the 1830 issue in which the Cherokee murder was reported was typical. Native-related news filled more and more of the space in the newspaper. In his own column that week, Boudinot even noted, "We are so overrun with Indian matter, that we are not only obliged to withhold our own remarks, but of necessity omit many interesting and important pieces."[22] Not all the issues published in 1830 were so filled with native material, but Boudinot had altered the tone of the paper considerably. One of the recurring topics was the debate of the "Indian Removal Bill" that had been introduced into the U.S. House and Senate early in 1830. The proposal was to move all the southeastern natives to the Great Plains west of the Mississippi River. The *Phoenix* reported the speeches at length, often filling as many as one-third of its columns with legislative orations. For example, the speech of freshman New Jersey Senator Theodore Frelinghuysen, which took six hours over three days, was published in the June 12 and June 19 issues. Frelinghuysen's position was not unlike that of other humanitarians, in and out of Congress, who spoke against the removal legislation.

Mr. President, it is really a subject of wonder, that after these repeated and solemn recognitions of right of soil, territory and jurisdiction, in these aboriginal nations, it should be gravely asserted that they are mere occupants at our will; and, what is absolutely marvelous, that they are a part of the Georgia population—a district of her territory, and amenable to her laws, whenever she chooses to extend them.[23]

The humanitarians—and the natives—lost. The bill passed May 28, 1830, making it possible for President Jackson to initiate removal of any tribe anywhere.[24] Shortly thereafter, Indian agents were told to begin distributing annuities to individual natives instead of tribes. The point was made especially not to pay the Cherokee treasurer, ostensibly to break down tribal authority and deprive leaders of money for the *Phoenix*. Boudinot's antiremoval position had angered the United States government. For example, in a column written after the Senate had passed the removal bill and rejected amendments proposed by Frelinghuysen, Boudinot had strong words for the Congress.

It has been a matter of doubt with us for some time, whether there were sufficient virtue and independence in the two houses of Congress, to sustain the plighted faith of the Republic, which has been most palpably sacrificed by the convenience of the Executive. Our doubts are now at an end—the *August Senate* of the United States of America...has followed the heels of the President, and deliberately laid aside their treaties.... When it comes to this, we have indeed fallen upon evil times.

Anticipating House approval of the bill, Boudinot voiced what would become a familiar theme: faith that the Cherokees would find justice in the courts. He wrote that we confidently think justice will be done, even if the Cherokees are not in the land of the living to receive it—posterity will give a correct verdict. But we are not now making such an appeal—we hope we are not yet at the end of our row—we hope there is yet a *tribunal* where our injured rights may be defended and protected, and where self interest, party and sectional feelings have nothing to do.

As he would do countless times, he admonished,

Let the Cherokees be *firm* and *united.*—Fellow citizens, we have asserted our rights, we have defended them thus far, and we will defend them yet by all lawful and peaceable means.—We will no more beg, pray and implore, but we will *demand* justice, and before we give up and allow ourselves to despondency we will, if we can, have the solemn adjudication of a tribunal, whose province is to interpret the treaties, *the supreme law of the land.* Let us then be *firm* and *united.*[25]

Boudinot's very public position left him vulnerable to criticism, some of it as scurrilous as any leveled against white frontier editors. His Cherokee ancestry often was questioned by those who continued to assert that a native could not edit a newspaper, let alone ably. He answered one such attack this way:

The Augusta *Chronicle* tells its readers, (which, by the way, is not so,) that the editor of the *Cherokee Phoenix* is a halfbreed. If this were true we know not what good purpose it would answer the *Chronicle* to tell it. Upon reflection, however, our readers will find it to be an ingenious turn to get out of a difficulty. Some of the Georgia papers have confidently asserted that only whites and half breeds in this nation were opposed to emigration. It is ascertained by the editor of the *Chronicle,* that the editor of the *Phoenix* is opposed to emigration, therefore he must be a half breed.[26]

Another time, Boudinot reprinted a letter from the head of the Georgia Guard to Governor George R. Gilmer that ended,

It is with feelings of indignation therefore that I have viewed the foul aspersions cast upon the guard and upon those conducting its operations, emanating as they do from that most polluted of all receptacles, the *Cherokee Phoenix*—they would have passed me as does the idle wind, but for their introduction into other columns and their dissemination abroad.—They are as false sir, as the canting and hypocritical fanatic who indites [*sic*] them.[27]

The editor responded this way:

We are sorry Col. Sanford does not hold our print in a little better estimation than he seems to do. If the *Cherokee Phoenix* is, in his view, of all others the most polluted, we are happy to know that a great majority of its readers think differently. They believe truths have been published in it, which a mere fiat denial cannot invalidate.[28]

The Cherokees Fight Back

In January 1831, the Cherokee Nation challenged the State of Georgia in the Supreme Court of the United States. Great confidence had been placed in the court by the Cherokees, as evidenced in a column Boudinot had written six months earlier.

Every man must know, who has watched the progress of the Indian question during the last six months, & who has been familiar with the doings of the Congress of the United States respecting the Cherokees and other tribes, and the proceedings of the state of Georgia, that, by the refusal of the former to protect, and the extension of the jurisdiction of the latter over them, they are placed under new and very trying circumstances, and that their views, feelings, and the course they have determined to pursue should be speedily made known to the world. This is fully expressed in the address [of the National Committee and Council published on page 1], which, after a most attentive observation, we can freely testify, contains the sentiments of the nation at large. Indeed we have never known the people so firm and united as at the present time.—Their eyes are turned, not to the western country, but to that period when, by the judicial decision of the Courts of the United States, they must be either satisfied that they have rights, or that they have none. They intend to wait for that time. It is therefore considered by them perfectly idle to talk about exchanging countries, or entering into treaties, while the great question remains unsettled. If we are removed, say they, by the United States, from our land and possessions, we wish to leave in the records of her judicial tribunals, for future generations to read, when we are gone, ample testimony that she acted *justly* or *unjustly*. The reasonableness of this determination must appear evident to every mind.

The Cherokees think they have rights, secured to them under their various treaties and the laws of the United States.—This opinion has never been shaken by all that the general Government has done, and the proceedings and oppressive laws of the state of Georgia. Their views in regard to their rights, for which they have so strenuously contended, are supported by some of the ablest lawyers of the United States. Of this we have the most ample evidence. And now that protection is withheld, and licence [*sic*] given for the abrogation of those laws and treaties by State legislation, what must be done? Surely the Supreme Court of the United States is the proper tribunal where the great question at issue must be settled. To this tribunal the Cherokees will freely refer their case.[29]

But the Cherokees lost. They had argued that Georgia laws were null because of the Constitution and the Indians Trade and Intercourse Acts of 1802. They also had contended that various treaties made with the United States recognized the right of the Cherokee Nation to exist and that treaties, according to the Constitution, were part of the supreme law of the land. Further, they had argued that the Supreme Court had jurisdiction over treaty cases involving the federal government and "foreign" nations. The court ruled, however, that the Cherokee Nation was not a "foreign" nation; Native tribes were "domestic dependent nations." Thus, the court had no jurisdiction over Cherokee lands. Boudinot provided *Phoenix* readers with both the text of the decision and his analysis of it.[30] In dissecting Chief Justice John Marshall's opinion, Boudinot decided that it placed his people

in a peculiar situation.—While most of the rights which we have contended are most explicitly acknowledged and conceded by the Court, we are at the same time considered to be in a state of "pupilage," unable to sue for those rights in the judicial tribunals. This is certainly no enviable position. Having rights, important rights, but no redress, except it be in the Executive and Congress of the United States, and those have already proved but a broken reed which has been piercing us to our very vitals.

Boudinot noted that there remained the question about whether individual Cherokees could find redress in the federal courts; the only question before the Supreme Court had been whether the Cherokee Nation could be considered a foreign state. As for the impact of the court's decision, the Cherokee editor stated he so far had seen only one Georgia newspaper, from which he copied a paragraph:

"It will be seen, by the following letter from a respected correspondent at Washington that the Supreme Court has decided entirely in favor of the State of Georgia, in the case of the injunction prayed by the Cherokees, to prevent the operation of the State laws over them—declining to take jurisdiction. Thus, the views of the State, with regard to her entire jurisdiction over the Indians within her limits, are fully sustained, in the last resort, and the Cherokees, therefore, must either submit altogether to our laws or emigrate to the West of the Mississippi."

Continuing his own analysis, Boudinot contended optimistically that the court had not fully sustained the claims of Georgia against the Cherokees:

Does the Court say that the Cherokees have no property in the soil, but are merely tenants at will? that they have no right of self-government, but are subjects of the states? that the treaties are not binding, and the intercourse law unconstitutional? These are the views of Georgia. Now does the opinion of the Court sustain them? Far from it. No language can be plainer than the following: "So much of the argument," says the Court, "as was intended to prove the character of the Cherokees as a state, as a distinct political society, separate from others, capable of managing its own affairs and government itself, has in the opinion of the majority of the judges, been completely successful." If this sustains the views of Georgia and General Jackson (for we are told he also considered his views sustained by the Court) then we have all along been utterly ignorant as to what these views were.[31]

In the next *Phoenix,* Boudinot included the first of many remarks on the Supreme Court decision from several publications, including the *New York Journal of Commerce,* the *New York Spectator* and the *National Intelligencer.*[32] Boudinot, "the outsider," wrote a second commentary on the decision, expanding on his previous analysis. He said he feared that the public was being misled.

It is said by some that the case is "settled," forever put to rest, and a hope is entertained that nothing more will be said on the subject. Now we apprehend this is doing injustice to the Supreme Court. The case is not settled for the great question at issue between the State of Georgia and the Cherokees was not before that tribunal. The only question before it was, whether it had original jurisdiction—whether the Cherokee nation was a foreign state in the sense of the constitution, & the decision went no further than to say, as we understand it, that the Court had *not* original jurisdiction, and that the Cherokee nation was *not* a foreign state in the sense of the constitution. How such a decision can be understood and construed as sustaining the pretensions of Georgia and the views of the President of the United States, we are not able to say.

In comparing the judgment of the court with the "pretensions of Georgia and the views" of Gen. Jackson, Boudinot concluded:

It is true the Court says that it cannot protect the Cherokees as a nation, but does it say that they are not entitled to protection of the Gen. Government? The opinion plainly intimates that it is the duty of the Executive and Congress of the

United States to redress the wrongs, and to guard the rights of the Cherokees if they are oppressed. The whole responsibility is thus thrown, by a judicial decision, upon those branches of the Government. The rights of the Cherokees are as plain, as sacred, as they have been, and the duty of the Government to secure those rights is as binding as ever.

He suggested that the Cherokees had no option but to "remain peaceably where they are, and continue to call upon the people of the U. States to fulfill their engagements, their solemn promises which have been repeatedly made." Nothing could be foreseen, wrote the editor, that would change the minds of the determined Cherokees.

The land is theirs—their right to it is "unquestionable," and it cannot be taken away from them without great injustice to them and everlasting infamy to the United States. They stand upon a perfectly safe ground as regards themselves— if they suffer, they will suffer unrighteously—if their rights and their property are forceably [*sic*] taken away from them the responsibility will not be upon them, but upon their treacherous "guardians."

Boudinot reminded his readers that "the Cherokees are for peace—they have been in amity with the United States for the last forty years." And he reassured those who feared the worst.

Why should they now fly to rash and unavailable measures to vindicate their injured rights? They will not, at least we think they will not; and such is our advice. It is more blessed to suffer than to be the oppressors—It is more blessed to lose, than to gain by unrighteous means. If the white man *must* oppress—if he must have the land, and throw us penniless upon the wild world, and if our cries and expostulations will avail nothing at the door of those who have promised to be our guardians and protectors, *let it be so.* We are in the path of duty, and the Judge of all the earth will vindicate our cause in his own way and in his own good time.[33]

Gloom settled over the Cherokee Nation when the Supreme Court decision first was delivered, but influential tribal leaders used the part of the decision that acknowledged the tribe as a political entity with rights under the law to buoy spirits, to encourage the people to believe that the battle with Georgia had not yet been lost.[34] Boudinot continued to publish commentaries on the decision and citizens' "memorials" favoring the tribe. When the editor believed a writer was misinformed or had misrepresented the Cherokees, he did not hesitate to add his own editorial comment. For example, he once wrote:

"The Cherokees and Georgia—It will be seen by reference to another column that the attempt of the Cherokees to obtain an injunction from the Supreme Court to stay the action of the laws of the State of Georgia over their territory has failed & the court has decided it that [sic] has no jurisdiction in the case. The National Gov. have also declared that the Cherokees are within the chartered limits of Georgia & consequently subject to her laws & will not interfere in the rights of that State in extending her laws and authority over them."

We find the above in the North Carolina *Spectator* published in Rutherfordton. The editor seems to have fallen into a mistake in common with many others, in regard to the decision of the Supreme Court. To say that the Court decided that it has no jurisdiction in the case is to say what is in fact true, yet the expression may be used by some, and understood by indifferent readers to mean widely different from the sense intended to be conveyed by the Court. What was the case upon which the Judges of the Supreme Court were called upon to decide? It was this: Is the Cherokee nation a *foreign* state in the sense of the constitution and has the Supreme Court *original* jurisdiction? This was the question, and they may with propriety say, as they have said, that the Cherokee nation is not a foreign state, and of course they *cannot* exercise *original* jurisdiction, yet at the same time they may entertain a case wherein is involved the question at issue between the State of Georgia and the Cherokees. It is in this light that we understand the decision of the Supreme Court. Whether our understanding is correct or not every reader will judge for himself, as the opinion is now before the public.[35]

Moving Toward Denouement

In March 1831, the law requiring loyalty oaths of whites in the Cherokee Nation went into effect and, as Boudinot had predicted, the Georgia Guard moved to arrest violators. Among those detained were John Wheeler, the *Phoenix* printer who had married one of Boudinot's sisters, and Boudinot's best friend, the Reverend Samuel Worcester. The editor provided an unusually long and detailed account of the arrests in the Phoenix of March 19; it was Boudinot the reporter at his best. He set out "simply to give facts as they have occurred before our eyes, and not to indulge ourselves in remarks." He observed that the court might acquit the arrested men, and so "it does not become us...to...comment upon those proceedings at this time." Boudinot acknowledged that the arresting Guard officers only were doing their duty, but he was critical of how they had made the arrests and when—a Sunday. And he was outraged that he once again was forced to counter charges that it was Worcester, the white missionary, and not he, who edited the *Phoenix*.[36]

The loyalty oath law specified a sentence of four years imprisonment for those who refused to sign, but Boudinot was optimistic that the detainees would be acquitted. Shortly, a judge ruled that the missionaries could not be held under Georgia law because they were agents of the federal government. In Worcester's case, in addition, was the fact that he was a postmaster. Soon, the prisoners were freed.[37] But it was not long before Worcester received a letter notifying him that he had been relieved of his postmaster's job. And it was not long before the secretary of war ruled that the missionaries were not agents of his government.

On July 7, the missionaries were arrested again. In September, they were tried and convicted of violating the loyalty oath law. They were sentenced to prison. Boudinot reported those facts and added only: "It is unnecessary to add a word of comment on this closing scene."[38] About a month later, however, he published the remarks made by the judge in sentencing the men. Boudinot found it "a curious document—entirely foreign to the question brought before his honor for decision." What, asked the editor, did the matter of Indian removal have to do with "his duties as a Judge called upon to interpret a plain law making it a crime for any white man to reside within the Georgia charter without taking an oath of allegiance?" There should have been no relationship, the editor wrote.

Nor can we conceive what connexion [sic] there should be between the trial of these men & the behavior of the Cherokees towards Georgia and its officers and towards the President and his officers, if indeed their resentment has been wrought to the highest pitch against these sacred personages. His Honor even alludes to this press as being engaged in insulting and calumniating "officers of every grade"—If this were true we cannot see what propriety, to say the least, there was in introducing this topic in his address.[39]

The experiences of the missionaries were widely reported, with the *Phoenix* serving as the "principal and only on-the-scene source of news and comment favorable" to the arrested men. "No campaign that Boudinot could have devised would have created so much support for the Cherokee cause as Georgia's harassment of the missionaries."[40] On October 1, the newspaper was able to report that nine of the men, having agreed to leave Georgia, had been released. Two missionaries, including Worcester, stood firm on their refusal to sign the loyalty oath, and they were sent to the penitentiary.[41]

Boudinot was devastated. He also was growing weary of doing battle with the authorities—in print and in person. In his commentaries,

Boudinot was blunt; there was nothing subtle about the antigovernment sentiments he expressed in his editorials. A year earlier, for example, in writing about Georgia, he ended a column thus:

In making these remarks, we do by no means hold in contempt the power of the state—she is powerful, and we are weak. She can soon destroy us if she takes us in hand. We are bound, however, to tell the truth—our readers will not, therefore, consider us out of the way of propriety when we merely tell them that if *Georgia intends to use force, when peaceable means fail, she will have to do it.* We do not say what the Cherokees will do—they have born [*sic*] a great deal, and they may bear a great deal more.[42]

That straightforward approach may not have been the best approach, as one official of the American Board of Commissioners for Foreign Missions remarked to Worcester: "It is hardly worth while to tell an enemy how he may vex & injure you most effectually."[43] But it was Boudinot's approach, and so not surprisingly, when the Georgians had stepped up their harassment of Cherokee Nation residents, Boudinot was a target. Not long after the missionaries had been arrested for the second time, the *Phoenix* editor was "lectured" by the commander of the Georgia Guard, Colonel C.H. Nelson. Boudinot explained the events to his readers in three long and eloquent columns he titled "Liberty of the Press."

The first column, published August 12, 1831, explained why the editor had been summoned by Nelson, who was visiting the Cherokee capital of New Echota:

The Col. observed to us that there has been a great deal of lies, & abusive & libelous articles published in the *Phoenix.*—These slanders have been directed against the State of Georgia and the Georgia Guard. Heretofore they (the Guard) had exercised forbearance towards us on account (as we understand him to say) of Mr. Worcester's connections with the *Phoenix.* Now they had got rid of Mr. Worcester, and we must now look out.—He also observed that as they could not prosecute us for libel, the only way that we could be punished would be to deal with us in their individual and private capacity, to tie us to a tree and give us a sound whipping. And this assuredly will be done if any more slanders are published.

In defending himself, Boudinot repeated a common theme, that "truth *has* been our object, and truth *shall* be our object." The only reason he could see for Nelson's actions was "an attempt to frown us down."

Apparently convinced that the editor had not responded "properly" to his first lecture, Nelson asked to see Boudinot again before the colonel left New Echota. Boudinot refused. As the editor reported in the August 19 *Phoenix,* he told the unarmed Guardsmen sent to fetch him that he did not feel bound to comply "inasmuch as I was ignorant of his object. He had before sent a similar message, and it was only for the purpose of lecturing and threatening me." Boudinot did say that if Nelson had "friendly business" in mind, he would gladly meet with him, or Nelson could visit Boudinot's home.

The Guardsmen soon returned "with four others, as I anticipated, all armed. They came into my yard. One of them observed that it was the wish of the Col. that I should walk up. I said, 'You then take me as a prisoner, Sir?' 'Yes Sir,' was his reply." When Boudinot reached the colonel, he was released. As the men talked, Nelson wondered aloud why Boudinot had not come when summoned and explained that he had wished only to tell Boudinot of a "misstatement" about their last meeting. The problem, it seemed, was that Nelson still believed Boudinot was publishing statements of the missionaries in his editorial columns and presenting them as his own.

They (the Guard) considered me as a peaceable, passive, inoffensive and ignorant kind of man, and as not possessing sufficient talents to write (as I understood him to say) the editorial articles which had appeared in the *Phoenix.* He intimated that the missionaries were the authors of those articles, and he blamed me for claiming them as mine. He requested me to make this correction, which I have done now according to my understanding of his language.

To make certain he would "not be guilty of misstating things," Boudinot asked Nelson about the grounds for his arrest. Nelson said it was for firing a gun at Guardsmen, a charge Boudinot had denied.

He took the opportunity, also, of repeating his former threat of flagellation. I observed to him that as to his threat I did not care anything about it, he could execute it if he pleased. He replied to his effect, "Don't be short here—if you do I will mount you d—— quick." & again, "If you do," meaning I suppose that if I make any more misstatements, "I will send to you," or something like it. I inquired if he had now done with me. He said yes, and I returned. It is proper that I should here observe, that when I said I did not care about his threat, I meant his threat would have no influence on my course as Editor of the *Phoenix.*

In a third column, published August 27, Boudinot impressed upon his readers that Nelson's actions were so much in conflict with "one great liberty guarantied" by the U.S. Constitution that he thought it important to discuss the matter again. The editor explained that prior to his first meeting with Nelson, he had heard rumors that Guardsmen had threatened him: "I had understood that one of the officers had said, if it were not for pity's sake, 'he would whip me within an inch of my life.' Another had declared, he would castigate & flagellate me." And when he first talked with Nelson, he was forced to deal with the colonel's preconceived conclusions about the *Phoenix*.

I found there was a determination to consider me a libeller without making a single specification, and that the rod was to bring me to my senses without allowing me the privilege of making reparation, if indeed I had been (as a nominal editor) guilty of slandering and abusing the Guard.

And regarding the charges made at the second meeting, that the missionaries ran the *Phoenix*, Boudinot wrote they were "too foolish to demand my attention." What he did want to talk about again was his statement that he did not care about Nelson's threats.

I did not mean to dare his threat, or to intimate that the punishment, if inflicted, would be nothing to me. I believe I should feel as keenly as any other man the indignity offered to my person, if my back were indeed subjected to the lash; but yet that would be but a trifling consideration in my mind when compared with the dictates of my conscience, and what I consider to be the line of honesty. I could not abandon these on account of threats. That was my meaning. And why should I care about a threat if I really thought I was doing my duty, and felt on the workings of a guilty conscience? I should be unworthy of the confidence of my countrymen and friends, if, for fear of a personal chastisement, I should be guilty of a dereliction of duty.

In conclusion, Boudinot wondered if a white editor would have been treated as he had been, and if so,

what would be the feelings of the people? In this free country, where the liberty of the press is solemnly guarantied is this the way to obtain satisfaction for an alleged injury committed in a newspaper. I claim nothing but what I have a right to claim as a man—I complain of nothing of which a privileged white editor would not complain.

A Break from Editing

A few months after his run-in with Nelson, Elias Boudinot was forced to interrupt his *Phoenix* duties. The Cherokee Nation was in serious need of financial assistance; the U.S. government had cut off its annuity, which had drained the Cherokee treasury. Tribal leaders called on the eloquent Boudinot to travel north to raise money to replenish it. His expenses were to be defrayed out of the money he collected, and he was to receive 10 percent of the funds as compensation for his efforts.[44] His traveling companions would be members of a delegation appointed to present Congress with a "memorial" detailing the Cherokees' grievances. The December 3, 1831, issue of the *Phoenix* included a note from Boudinot explaining why he was about to leave the Nation for several months. He informed readers that his brother, Stand Watie, would serve as acting editor.[45]

Boudinot corresponded regularly with his brother, who now and then published excerpts of those letters under the absent editor's familiar editorial heading. The first came from Augusta, Georgia. Boudinot noted that just two days out of New Echota, his group had passed a spot where, they were told, an officer of the Georgia Guard planned to settle. The editor wondered why and by what authority. He also reported hearing little talk about the imprisoned missionaries and the "Indian question." He found this strangely encouraging.

The people appear to be more indifferent than I expected to find them; it is not at all improbable that, if it were not for the leading men, another demagogue [apparently soon-to-be Governor Wilson Lumpkin] who cannot obtain the votes of the people but by promising the *Indian land*, the Cherokees would be permitted to remain peaceable on the soil of their fathers.

Boudinot also noted that he had seen a report that the Georgia House had passed a bill authorizing the immediate surveying and occupancy of Cherokee lands. Senate approval was expected. He predicted that the action "cannot effect the determination of the Cherokees. They have taken their stand, are contending for vital principles."[46]

By the middle of December, the Cherokees had reached Richmond, Virginia. The *Phoenix* carried another optimistic excerpt from Boudinot to his brother. He wrote that while traveling through Georgia, he had talked with several persons whom he labeled friends of the Cherokees. "These worthy people feel a great interest in the condition of the Cherokees—they believe they have justice on their side and that the state is committing an act of the most oppressive kind." But, Boudinot wrote, it was unpopular and unwise to speak out in favor of the natives; "hence those who do not wish to displease the sovereign people will remain in silence, and if they are compelled by circumstances to speak out, it is generally to extenuate the acts of their Government." That, he said, was the case with most Georgians.[47]

The turn of the year found Boudinot in Philadelphia, where he and the others dined with the editor's nemesis, Thomas L. McKenney of the Office of Indian Affairs. McKenney had "swallowed his pride" and agreed to meet with the Cherokees at their hotel.[48] The Cherokees were able to report to him, and to tribal officials back in the Cherokee Nation, that the trip had so far been successful. They explained to McKenney that they were raising money, speaking about the Cherokee situation and assessing public opinion about the removal question. And they told him how gratified they were to learn "how much light our Little *Phoenix* has had in this city."[49]

At the end of January, the *Phoenix* carried another excerpt from a Boudinot letter in which he commented on the "land bill," which by then had been passed by both houses of the Georgia legislature. Ever the optimist, Boudinot suggested that one obstacle remained in the way of the Georgians' taking Cherokee lands—the "when" was left to the discretion of the governor. "His *discretion* may tell him to wait, until the Indian title is properly extinguished, from a fear of coming in conflict with the General Government, or from motives of policy." If that did not happen, Boudinot wondered if Congress could remain silent. Once again he confidently predicted that, regardless of the actions of the governments, "it cannot, in the least, affect the determination of the Cherokees. They have taken their stand, and there they will stand! Let the crisis arrive, and it is better that it should come soon. We will test the government to the last, so that we may know what to depend on hereafter."[50]

Then, on March 3, 1832, as a result of the imprisoned missionaries' efforts to free themselves, the break the Cherokees had been hoping for occurred. Chief Justice John Marshall of the United States Supreme Court handed down the decision that declared Georgia's jurisdiction over the Cherokee Nation unconstitutional. Boudinot, in Boston when the historic ruling was announced, described the scene at the offices of the American Board of Commissioners for Foreign Missions when the men there heard the news.

Expectation has for the last few days been upon tip-toe—fears and hopes alternately took possession of our minds until two or three hours ago Mr. John Tappan came in to see us.... He then told us the true story of the case, and produced a paper which contained an account, and tried to read to us, but he was so agitated with joy that he could hardly proceed.[51]

The Cherokees were equally ecstatic. Boudinot wrote to his brother: "It is a glorious news.... It is a great triumph on the part of the Cherokees so far as the question of their rights were concerned."[52]

The *Phoenix* carried news of the decision in the March 24, 1832, issue. A short time later, Principal Chief John Ross noted: "Our adversaries are generally down in the mouth—there are rejoicings throughout the Nation.... Traitors and internal enemies are seeking places where to hide their heads."[53] The Cherokees interpreted the decision to mean their difficulties were over; their position had been vindicated by the high court that had so disappointed them with its earlier decision on the "foreign nation" status of the Cherokee Nation. Wrote Boudinot, "The question is forever settled as to who is right & who is wrong & this controversy is exactly where it ought to be.... It is not now before the great state of Georgia & the poor Cherokees, but between the friend of the judiciary, and the *enemies* of the judiciary."[54]

A Change of Heart

The jubilation and optimism that followed the Supreme Court decision proved to be premature. Georgia ignored the order to release the missionaries. President Jackson boasted that "John Marshall has made his decision; now let him enforce it."[55] The decision became the justice's "most famous scrap of paper."[56] And the U.S. government's failure to uphold what its highest court had mandated seems to have been the fatal blow to Elias Boudinot's steadfast belief that the Cherokees eventually would find justice. He returned to the Cherokee Nation in the summer of 1832, "disillusioned by the obvious impotency of the Supreme Court decision...and discouraged by powerful friends in Washington and the East, [expressing] doubt about continuing the struggle against unequal odds."[57] On August 11, 1832, Boudinot resigned as editor of the *Cherokee Phoenix, and Indians' Advocate.*

What it was that finally destroyed the optimism and hard-line antiremoval policy espoused by Boudinot from the time he assumed the mantle of editorial leadership is unclear. The fund-raising trip north had sapped his strength; late in the trip he wrote his brother that he had been "very feeble" and housebound for four days, so ill he had canceled appointments.[58] The separation from his family could only have reinforced for Boudinot how occupied his life was with Cherokee matters and how little time he had to spend with the children and wife he loved dearly. Too, his detention by the Georgia Guard must have impressed upon the editor that he was in a most vulnerable position. The very job that week after week called upon him to plead the cause of the natives also meant that he was one of the most visible antiremoval spokesmen. To date, the Georgia Guard had only detained him, only lectured him. He was well aware that, if they chose to, Georgia authorities could find some reason to imprison him, even as they had the missionaries.

There were additional reasons for the editor's dramatic change of heart, too. One was the apathy of the American people as the governments of Georgia and the United States balked at releasing the missionaries and recognizing the Cherokee Nation's independence. In a poignant column shortly after his return to New Echota, Boudinot's pain was obvious.

What do the good people of the United States think of the distressed condition of the Cherokees? Is their private attention so completely engrossed in their own private affairs that they cannot even find time to shed a tear at the recollection of such accumulated oppressions heaped upon their fellow creatures? Has the cause of the Indians been swallowed up in other questions...? For how can we account for the silence which pervades the public in regard to the conduct of the General government and the state of Georgia towards the Cherokees?

Boudinot could not understand how measures that had been declared unconstitutional "are still pushed forward with a degree of impudence truly remarkable and alarming." The conduct of the President also amazed him:

He will not move his little finger to support the constitution and laws of the country, and save his once Indian allies from utter destruction, & yet he sends, at the suggestion of the Governor of a neighboring state, a company of his troops, to drive off a half dozen gold diggers!

As for Georgia,

While a few half starved gold diggers are to be expelled at the point of the bayonet, she has been permitted and encouraged to send in five hundred surveyors to violate the laws and treaties of the United States, by running lines, marking trees &c. To this great company, agents or instruments of robbers, cultivated fields were no obstacles. Corn fields, wheat fields, and what not, were as waste lands, and those who owned them were like the wild beasts of the forest, so insignificant & contemptible were they in the eyes of this Christian people!

Further, Boudinot wrote,

They *glory* in their shame—triumph over their own laws, and smile at the cries of the subjects of their cruelty! What signifie [*sic*] to tell it, when the complaints of the oppressed are *unheeded* by those in high places, and *regarded* by the people only in *silence!*[59]

In certain respects, Boudinot's blind faith in "good Christian people" also contributed to his disillusionment. He was "incapable of measuring the malice in the forces that he opposed."[60] His missionary-teachers had done their jobs well; the Christian Boudinot turned the other cheek, and then once again. Even as the evidence mounted that the Cherokees did not stand a chance of remaining on their homeland, he continued to proclaim their determination to do just that. But something snapped. When the principal chief called for a day of fasting and prayer, Boudinot's despair was evident. "What can be more proper!" he wrote in the *Phoenix*. "We have need to go to the Ruler of the universe in this day of deep affliction. We have been too long trusting to an arm of flesh, which has proved to be but a broken reed."[61]

Elias Boudinot had had his first exposure to tribal factionalism when, as a youngster, he watched his father leave home to fight with a Cherokee regiment formed to help put down an uprising of a faction of Creeks.[62] Now, as he became less sure of his antiremoval position, he was on the cutting edge of an embryonic Cherokee faction, even though he denied it.

We would respectfully caution our Cherokee friends against the many reports which are circulating about *certain things* and *certain persons*. This is no time to be impugning each other's motives, and doubting each other's patriotism. We hope there will be no attempt made to create the idea that there is a faction formed or forming.... We know of no such faction—we say to all, be *national*—look to the interest of the people—*nothing but the interest of the* PEOPLE.[63]

Boudinot realized that harmony was a strong guiding principle in Cherokee politics; a good man did not cause discord. If and when conflict could not be avoided, "he was expected to withdraw both emotionally and, if possible, physically."[64] To the *Phoenix* editor, it now was clear that "the act of Georgia and the United States compelled the natives to consider the question of removal. The columns of the *Phoenix* seemed to him a proper place to carry on a public discussion."[65] It was also clear that this change of heart was making him unpopular with many Cherokees, not just tribal leaders, even as his original stand had made him unpopular with government officials. He was, in a sense, a victim of his own persuasive antiremoval commentary. One too many letters like the one admonishing "Hang the Traitor" above a crude sketch surrounded by the legends "Shoot him," "Cut his throat," "Death to the Rebbell" finally convinced Boudinot that it was time to step down as *Phoenix* editor.

Boudinot Explains Himself

In his final editorial column, Boudinot included a copy of his resignation letter to Principal Chief John Ross. In that letter, he attempted to explain why he was stepping down. For one thing, he wrote, the newspaper had "succeeded *all the purpose* that it can be expected to achieve hereafter." He elaborated:

Two of the great objects which the nation had in view in supporting the paper were, the defense of our *rights* and the proper representation of our *grievances* to the people of the United States.—In regard to the *former,* we can add nothing to the full & thor'o investigation that has taken place, especially after the decision of the Supreme Court, which has forever closed the question of our conventional rights. In regard to the *latter,* we can say nothing which will have more effect than what we have already said. The public is as fully apprised, as we can ever expect it to be, of our grievances. It knows our troubles, and yet never was it more silent than at present.

Further, Boudinot wrote, since these "great and important objects of the paper" no longer existed, the Nation's precious financial resources could be better used elsewhere. Thirdly, he explained,

Were I to continue as Editor, I should feel myself in a most peculiar and delicate situation. I do not know whether I could satisfy my own views and the views of the authorities of the nation at the same time. My situation would then be as embarrassing as it would be peculiar and delicate. I do conscientiously believe to be the duty of every citizen to reflect upon the dangers with which we are surrounded—to view the darkness which seems to lie before our beloved people—our prospects, and the evils with which we are threatened—to talk over all these matters, and, if possible, come to some definite and satisfactory conclusion, while there is time, as to what ought to be done in the last alternative.

Boudinot added that it would not be possible for him to edit the *Phoenix* "without having the right and privilege of discussing these important matters." But if he did that, it had become apparent already that he would be considered "an enemy to the interest of my beloved country and people." For the last time in print, Boudinot pledged his devotion to truth:

I love my country and I love my people, as my own heart bears me witness, and for that very reason I should think it my duty to tell them the whole truth, or what I believe to be the truth. I cannot tell them that we will be reinstated in our rights when I have no such hope.[66]

In accepting Boudinot's resignation, Principal Chief John Ross said the *Cherokee Phoenix, and Indians' Advocate* would be continued.

The views of the public authorities should continue and ever be in accordance with the will of the people; and the views of the Editor of the National paper be the same. The toleration of diversified views to the columns of such a paper would not fail to create fermentation and confusion among our citizens and, in the end prove injurious to the welfare of the Nation. The love of our country and people demands unity of sentiment and action for the good of all.[67]

Ross's position—that the tribally funded newspaper must reflect the views of the tribal government—and Boudinot's adherence to a basic premise of a democratic press—the freedom to and necessity of expressing contrary points of view—had come to an inevitable conclusion.

The history of Native American journalism includes the stories of countless other editors, their native loyalty often questioned, who sooner or later found themselves confronted with the same dilemma. Elias Boudinot defined his own patriotism simply, and in so doing set a standard for all the editors who have followed him. His patriotism, Boudinot wrote in a letter the *Phoenix* refused to publish after his resignation, "consist[ed] in the love of the country, and the love of the People."[68]

Notes

1. Quoted in Joel Chandler Harris, *Georgia* (New York: Appleton, 1896), 216.

2. Louis Turner Griffith and John E. Talmadge, *Georgia Journalism 1763-1950* (Athens: University of Georgia Press, 1951), 33.

3. Cullen Joe Holland, "The Cherokee Indian Newspapers, 1828-1906: The Tribal Voice of a People in Transition," (Ph.D. diss., University of Minnesota, 1956), 140.

4. Holland, "Cherokee," 142. See also Henry Thompson Malone, *Cherokees of the Old South* (Athens: University of Georgia Press, 1956), especially 166.

5. Jack Gregory and Rennard Strickland, eds., *Starr's History of the Cherokee Indians* (Fayetteville, Ark.: Indian Heritage Association, 1967), 113.

6. Daniel F. Littlefield, Jr., and James W. Parins, *American Indian and Alaska Native Newspapers and Periodicals, 1826-1924* (Westport: Greenwood Press, 1984), xii.

7. Littlefield, Parins, *American Indian and Alaska Native Newspapers,* xiii.

8. Littlefield, Parins, *American Indian and Alaska Native Newspapers,* xiv-xvi.

9. "A Memorial to the Cherokees Before 1907" reads, "These few represent some of the early leaders who saw a need and met the challenge." The memorial is located at TSA-LA-GI, the Cherokee Heritage Center, in Tahlequah, Oklahoma.

10. The Choctaw removal treaty was signed September 27, 1830; the Creek treaty March 24, 1832; the Seminole treaty May 9, 1832; the Chickasaw treaty October 20, 1832; and the Cherokee treaty December 29, 1835. Sam G. Riley, "The Cherokee Phoenix: The Short, Unhappy Life of the First American Indian Newspaper," *Journalism Quarterly* 53 (winter 1976), 668.

11. James Mooney, *Historical Sketch of the Cherokee* (Chicago: Aldine Publishing, 1975), 110; Donald Grinde, "Cherokee Removal and American Politics," *The Indian Historian* 8 (summer 1975): 39; Malone, *Cherokees of the Old South: A People in Transition,* 172-76.

12. *Cherokee Phoenix,* 28 February 1828.

13. *Cherokee Phoenix,* 6 March 1828.

14. *Cherokee Phoenix,* 18 March 1829.

15. Grinde, "Cherokee Removal and American Politics," 38.

16. Helen Hunt Jackson, *A Century of Dishonor* (New York: Harper Brothers, 1881; Harper Torchbooks, 1965), 272 (page citation is to the reprint edition).

17. *Cherokee Phoenix,* 17 June 1829.

18. *Cherokee Phoenix,* 1 July 1829.

19. Malone, *Cherokees of the Old South,* 172.

20. *Cherokee Phoenix,* 30 December 1829.

21. *Cherokee Phoenix,* 10 February 1830.

22. *Cherokee Phoenix,* 10 February 1830.

23. *Cherokee Phoenix,* 19 June 1830.

24. Grant Foreman, *The Last Trek of the Indians* (Chicago: University of Chicago Press, 1946), 59.

25. Herman J. Viola, *Thomas L. McKenney, Architect of America's Early Indian Policy: 1816-1830* (Chicago: Swallow Press, 1974), 234; *Cherokee Phoenix,* 15 May 1830.

26. *Cherokee Phoenix,* 19 August 1829.

27. *Cherokee Phoenix,* 17 September 1831.

28. *Cherokee Phoenix,* 17 September 1831.

29. *Cherokee Phoenix,* 24 July 1830.

30. Grinde, "Cherokee Removal and American Politics," 40; Holland, "Cherokee Indian Newspapers," 154 n, states that the *Phoenix* "probably was the first newspaper to obtain the text of Marshall's opinion."

31. *Cherokee Phoenix,* 9 April 1831.

32. *Cherokee Phoenix,* 16 April 1831.

33. *Cherokee Phoenix,* 16 April 1831.

34. Grant Foreman, *Indian Removal: The Emigration of the Five Civilized Tribes of Indians* (Norman: University of Oklahoma Press, 1932), 234.

35. *Cherokee Phoenix,* 30 April 1831.

36. This charge had plagued Boudinot from the earliest days of his editorship, as he explained in his report on the arrests: "The first public statement to this effect was made soon after the commencement of the paper, by a certain religious Editor in Knoxville. This statement was followed by a disclaimer from Mr. Worcester." *Cherokee Phoenix,* 19 March 1831.

37. Holland, "Cherokee Indian Newspapers," 182.

38. *Cherokee Phoenix,* 24 September 1831.

39. *Cherokee Phoenix,* 15 October 1831.

40. Holland, "Cherokee Indian Newspapers," 178, 175-90.

41. The missionaries spent 16 months doing hard labor. More than 160 years later—on November 25, 1992—acknowledging it made a mistake, the state of Georgia formally pardoned the two men! *New York Times,* 23 November 1992.

42. *Cherokee Phoenix,* 16 October 1830.

43. David Greene to Samuel Worcester, quoted in Althea Bass, *Cherokee Messenger* (Norman: University of Oklahoma Press, 1936), 164-65.

44. John Ross Papers, 31-14, Thomas Gilcrease Institute of American History and Art, Tulsa, Oklahoma. In the February 18, 1832, *Cherokee Phoenix,* Stand Watie corrected the "misimpression" that Boudinot was part of the Cherokee delegation to Washington, D.C., saying that he was collecting funds for the Cherokee treasury.

45. Later, there would be long-distance instructions. On March 7, 1832, Boudinot wrote to Watie: "Publish nothing in regard to the Presidential election—about Clay or Jackson, and copy little of what is said about the S.C. [Supreme Court]. A great deal will be said but let us only look on and see." *Niles National Register* 56 (17 August 1839), 7. On April 6, 1832, cousin John Ridge wrote to Watie: "Allow me to suggest the propriety of presenting all you can of what is in the minds of the whites and encouraging our people to communicate the facts to you from various quarters by letters which you can publish." *Niles National Register* 56 (17 August 1839), 9-10.

46. *Cherokee Phoenix,* 24 December 1831.

47. *Cherokee Phoenix,* 31 December 1831.

48. Viola, *Thomas L. McKenney,* 263.

49. John Ridge to John Ross, 12 January 1832, John Ross Papers, 32-1, Thomas Gilcrease Institute of American History and Art, Tulsa, Oklahoma. See also, John Ridge to John Ross, 3 April 1832, John Ross Papers, 32-33.

50. *Cherokee Phoenix,* 28 January 1832.

51. Elias Boudinot to Stand Watie, 7 March 1832, Cherokee Nation Papers, Western History Collections, University of Oklahoma, Norman, Oklahoma.

52. Elias Boudinot to Stand Watie, 7 March 1832, Cherokee Nation Papers.

53. *Cherokee Phoenix,* May 12, 1832.

54. Elias Boudinot to Stand Watie, 7 March 1832, Cherokee Nation Papers.

55. Quoted in Jack F. Kilpatrick and Anna G. Kilpatrick, eds., *New Echota Letters* (Dallas: Southern Methodist University Press, 1968), 116.

56. Ralph Henry Gabriel, *Elias Boudinot, Cherokee & His America* (Norman: University of Oklahoma Press, 1941), 133. The missionaries finally were released January 14, 1833. See Bass, *Cherokee Messenger,* 156-59.

57. Holland, "Cherokee Indian Newspapers," 89.

58. Elias Boudinot to Stand Watie, 7 March 1832, Cherokee Nation Papers.

59. *Cherokee Phoenix,* 7 July 1832.

60. J.F. Kilpatrick and A.G. Kilpatrick, *New Echota Letters,* 4.

61. *Cherokee Phoenix,* 14 July 1832.

62. Kenny A. Franks, *Stand Watie and the Agony of the Cherokee Nation* (Memphis: Memphis State University Press, 1979), 3.

63. *Cherokee Phoenix,* 21 July 1832.

64. V. Richard Persico, Jr., "Early Nineteenth-Century Cherokee Political Organization," in *The Cherokee Indian Nation,* ed. Duane H. King (Knoxville: University of Tennessee Press, 1979), 94.

65. Gabriel, *Elias Boudinot,* 134.

66. *Cherokee Phoenix,* 11 August 1832.

67. *Cherokee Phoenix,* 11 August 1832.

68. Elias Boudinot, *Letters and Other Papers Relating to Cherokee Affairs* (Athens, Ga.: Office of the *Southern Banner,* 1837), 15-16.

7

Explaining the Little Bighorn

John M. Coward

As battles go, the most famous Indian fight of the 19th century was a minor affair, its death and suffering dwarfed by Civil War horrors at places like Shiloh, Antietam, and Gettysburg. But the violence near the banks of the Little Bighorn River on June 25, 1876, soon became a powerful symbol of America's manifest destiny. With the help of the newspapers, the illustrated press, and dime novels, the Battle of the Little Bighorn was soon transformed into Custer's Last Stand, a name which not only recognized the fate of Custer and his command but also marked the closing days of the Indian frontier.

Custer's colorful life and dramatic demise have been the subject of several shelves of articles and books, many of which document the press contribution to the Custer legend.[1] Western historian Robert M. Utley, for example, opens his 1988 Custer biography with sensational headlines from the Bismarck *Tribune* and goes on to describe the "avalanche of emotional prose" which followed Custer's defeat.[2] Journalism historians have also analyzed the newspaper role in shaping the Custer legend. Oliver Knight found that the reporters who covered the Sioux campaign of 1876 made significant—and often erroneous—contributions to the Custer legend.[3] Given Custer's love of the spotlight, it is little wonder that his defeat became a rallying cry for a final campaign against the Indians of the northern plains.[4]

The scholarly emphasis on the press and Custer myth has focused almost entirely on mainstream publications. But several native newspapers, all published in Indian Territory (now Oklahoma) in 1876, had a more culturally complex task. Indian newspapers, after all, were founded to promote and defend Indian rights and their pages contained many stories documenting the education and advancement of particular tribes.[5] The Sioux and Cheyenne victory over Custer threatened such ideas and put native editors in a precarious position. If they cheered too loudly for the Indian victors, they would risk the goodwill of many whites. If they condemned the Indian victory, they would risk the

145

support of their Indian readers. This study describes the social and political role of the two most active Indian Territory newspapers around the time of the Little Bighorn, when Indian-white relations were especially strained. The study examines the ideology of race and progress which appeared in these papers as well as the public relations strategies they used to explain the Indian victory over Custer to their native and non-native readers. As a case study, the research shows how minority newspapers used language and ideas to mediate and defuse a threatening political position.

Race and Progress in the Native Press

Indian Territory had five newspapers in 1876: the *Indian Herald* at Pawhuska, the *Vindicator* at Atoka, the *Oklahoma Star* at Caddo, the *Cherokee Advocate* at Tahlequah, and the *Indian Journal* at Muskogee.[6] In widely differing ways, all five papers saw themselves as instruments of Indian "progress." The *Oklahoma Star*, for example, carried the motto "Progress and a Higher Civilization." The *Herald* was "devoted to the cause of Indian civilization."[7] The *Indian Journal* said it was "devoted to the interests of the Indian race and the dissemination of knowledge among them at home."[8] The *Vindicator* asserted that it would be an exponent of the Indians' "upward struggle for progressive civilization."[9] In his first editorial, William Penn Boudinot, editor of the *Advocate,* noted the progress of the Cherokee Nation, "where a small tribe of North American Indians are struggling from a state of complete savagism to reach a state of high civilization."[10]

The similarity of this language suggests that, despite many differences, these papers all subscribed to the idea of "civilized progress" for American Indians. According to this ideology, humankind advanced from the lesser to the greater good, from the simple to the complex, from "savagism" to civilization.[11] Such ideas explain why Indian Territory editors did not condemn white society; it was, after all, a society they usually sought to emulate. Indeed, Indian Territory papers were filled with stories of native success in education, agriculture, self-government, and the like. Although some papers did criticize white politicians and institutions concerning Indian issues, as will be seen, such criticism was developed on a case-by-case basis and was tempered by notions of "civilized progress."

This commitment to progress, however, masked a host of political differences. The *Herald*, the *Vindicator*, and the *Star* were published by whites, ostensibly on behalf of local tribes. In the case of the *Herald*, W. McKay Dougan, the Osage agency physician, served as editor. Dougan used the paper to publicize Osage achievements and defend the tribe against detractors.[12] The *Vindicator*, founded in 1872 and edited by another physician, J.H. Moore, claimed to be "devoted to the interest of the Choctaws and Chickasaws." Despite this claim, Moore advocated the allotment of tribal land to individual Indians, an idea opposed by many tribal leaders.[13] The *Star* also advocated allotment. Edited by a white man who had married a Choctaw, the *Star* pushed hard for a new territorial government and attacked the Choctaw council as "illiberal and oppressive."[14]

The two largest and most progressive native papers were the *Cherokee Advocate* and the *Indian Journal*. The *Advocate*, founded in 1844, was a descendant of the *Cherokee Phoenix*, the first Native American newspaper.[15] Elias Boudinot, founding editor of the *Phoenix*, published many stories celebrating tribal advances. Like the *Phoenix*, the *Advocate* was designed to improve Cherokee society and to project a positive image of the tribe. When the *Advocate* was revived in early 1876, its new editor, William Penn Boudinot, son of Elias, expressed his faith in the public relations role of native journalism: "If the people of the United States had access to reliable sources of information of the affairs of this territory—had they both sides of the case before them— there would be less danger to us of the result."[16]

The *Indian Journal*, edited by William Potter Ross, was an intertribal paper established in May 1876.[17] Like his famous uncle, Chief John Ross, W.P. Ross spent his life defending and promoting Cherokee interests. An 1842 graduate of the College of New Jersey (now Princeton), Ross was a former Cherokee chief, the founding editor of the *Advocate*, a former correspondent for Chicago's *Inter-Ocean*, and a lawyer. He was, one historian said, the best qualified person to head the Territory's first intertribal newspaper.[18]

The Indian Territory press served two audiences: local readers, both native and white, and white readers outside the Territory. To serve their native readers, the *Vindicator* and the *Advocate* regularly published material in native languages and the *Journal* kept its subscription price intentionally low.[19] The papers published many reports from Washington on the status of Indian legislation, news of considerable importance in Indian Territory. The papers also published reports from Indian agents and missionaries, many of which provided evidence of Indian progress for both native and non-native readers.

By most accounts, the circulation of the Indian Territory press was limited. The *Advocate* claimed a circulation of 1,300 in 1877, though another source listed the circulation at 500 the next year.[20] In 1876, after only four issues, the *Indian Journal* boasted of subscribers in 17 states, as far away as New York, Pennsylvania, Michigan, Ohio, Indiana,

Illinois, Wisconsin, Minnesota, and Iowa. This was evidence, the paper said, of the general interest in Indian issues by the larger public.[21] Despite such claims, it seems likely that the primary influence of the Indian Territory press was in the Territory itself.

In mid-1876, then, Indian Territory had a variety of editorial voices, all committed to some form of Indian advancement. The most influential papers—and the two most committed to the native point of view—were the *Cherokee Advocate* and the *Indian Journal*, papers edited by progressive native leaders who were highly attuned to the political realities of 1876.

The most important reality was the continuing pressure to open tribal lands to white settlement, an action vehemently opposed by the *Advocate* and the *Journal*.[22] To defend tribal land rights, Boudinot and Ross often published evidence of progress in Indian Territory. On June 1, 1876, for example, the *Journal* referred to a government report that praised the Seminoles as "a sober, industrious people," a fact the paper thought should dishearten "advocates of the 'Open up the Territory' policy."[23] When the New York *World* ran an article critical of Indians, the *Journal* reprinted the response of a friendly newspaper: "The five great nations which inhabit the Indian Territory have ... jumped into the traces of civilization with wonderful alacrity, and their works of progress stand to-day [*sic*] a proud monument to their industry and skill."[24] This recognition of native progress by non-Indians bolstered the ongoing argument that Indian rights should be respected.

Similarly, the *Advocate* responded to an article critical of Indians by citing Territorial developments: "If there is ever to be a distinction between civilized and uncivilized red men to the credit of the former, it would be in consequence of our own good conduct and enterprising policy as a Nation in conjunction with other tribes of this territory."[25]

This appeal to native advancement included an important and related assertion: that all Indians were not alike. On this point, the *Advocate* and the *Journal* were of two minds. Boudinot and Ross sometimes claimed special status for the Indian Territory tribes—tribes known as the Five Civilized Tribes. At other times, they argued for Indian as well as racial solidarity. Responding to an exchange copy of the *Indian Herald*, for example, Ross wrote in expansive terms: "The noble stand it [the *Herald*] takes in behalf of the Indian race, will make it always welcome in the homes of our people."[26] On another occasion, Ross drew connections between the problems of Indians and other minorities. In mid-June, 1876, he wrote a commentary on "anti-coolie" and anti-African-American activities in the news and asked a rhetorical question: "Can any one inform us of the cause of so much 'class hatred'—of ill will toward the people of the negro, Chinee [*sic*], or Indian race, by the citizens of the United States, as witnessed in the past few months?"[27] When the progress of Indian Territory was not at issue, Ross more readily used the *Journal* to promote racial tolerance and fight against racial injustice. When native rights in Indian Territory were at risk—as in the case of the Little Bighorn—both the *Journal* and the *Advocate* had compelling reasons to drop all notions of racial solidarity.

Before the Battle

Calls for racial brotherhood can be found in the *Advocate* and the *Journal* in the months leading up to the Little Bighorn. The first issue of the revived *Advocate* in 1876 mentioned Custer as a threat to racial solidarity. In a page-one article, abolitionist and Indian activist Wendell Phillips wrote, "The good men who wrote the words 'all men are created free and equal' really made two exceptions—Indians and negroes." To prove his point, Phillips cited Custer's 1868 attack on Black Kettle's village:

The inhabitants were peacefully and harmlessly asleep, dreaming of anything but dangers. Silently in the still, peaceful night [Brevet] General Custer drew his troops about the defenceless village, and, everything disposed, a loud shout was raised and drums were beaten. The Indians came rushing out in alarm, and as they appeared the troops poured in volley and volley and shot them all down. Sheridan then telegraphed, "A glorious victory."[28]

Thus the *Advocate* portrayed the attack on Black Kettle, the basis of Custer's reputation as an Indian fighter, as a massacre of innocents. It is instructive, however, that this criticism came not from Boudinot himself, but from Phillips, an outspoken Boston reformer. Boudinot was fully capable of defending Indian interests but he often published the words of white sympathizers, a public relations strategy that let readers see that all Indians had allies in the dominant society.

The *Indian Journal* was less circumspect in the weeks leading up to the battle. On June 1, 1876, for example, Ross questioned the "subject and purpose" of the army's Sioux campaign: "Are not the Sioux trying, by negotiation, to conclude the sale of lands already stolen from them, in advance by whites?" Ross then put the Sioux campaign in terms that native readers in Indian Territory would understand: "Is not the whole thing a scheme of the Territorial-politician, and the landgrabber? It looks like it."[29] In short, Ross cast the Sioux campaign as an assault on Indian land rights, the same rights he and others in Indian Territory were seeking to strengthen.

In another column, Ross posed the Sioux dilemma in "us" versus "them" terms: "The troops are not coming to protect us as promised, but to make war, not to remove intruders, but to punish us, and for what: because we do not wish to sell our land at the price offered?"[30] Such language indicates, perhaps, the depth of Ross's sympathy with the Sioux before the Little Bighorn, a position he quickly abandoned after the battle.

Continuing reports from the Sioux campaign in June 1876 provided other opportunities to criticize the government and defend Indian interests. The *Journal* reprinted a Texas newspaper story, for example, about Sioux attacks on miners in the Black Hills, attacks that could have been prevented if the government had stopped miners from entering Indian lands. "We regard the government responsible for every murder committed, every outrage perpetuated," the story concluded.[31]

Yet there were limits to Ross's sympathy with the Sioux. In a report on the Battle of the Rosebud, the *Journal* emphasized the role of Gen. Crook's Indian scouts: "GEN. CROOK'S ARMY SURPRISED—SAVED FROM DESTRUCTION BY THEIR INDIAN ALLIES," the headline read.[32] Crook's official report on the battle was headed by a sarcastic editorial note asking for the same report from "Gen. Sittingbull ... so that our readers may have two sides of the case, as two opposing generals rarely ever see the results of a great battle in the same light." The *Journal* also ran a report from one Reverend Cook on the sad state of the reservations of the northern plains. The Sioux, Cook wrote, "are almost wholly dependent upon the government for the food to keep body and soul together."[33] To the readers of the *Journal*, it would have been clear that the Sioux were much less civilized than Indians in the Territory.

Explaining the Indian Victory

The Battle of the Little Bighorn was fought June 25, but the news broke in Indian Territory on July 13. At first, the *Journal* responded to the Little Bighorn with sadness: "But few persons...can more profoundly regret than the Indian Journal, the state of warfare existing in the Black Hills."[34] But Ross soon dropped any pretense of solidarity with the Sioux, now a political liability in Indian Territory and in the larger society as well: "It is exceedingly ungenerous to attempt to excite a sentiment of hostility towards the people of this Territory, because of the bloody outrages that have grown out of the discovery of gold in the Black Hills."[35]

The *Journal* used Gen. Alfred Terry's official report for its news account of the battle. Both the story and its headlines took the army's point of view: "BLACK HILLS/CUSTER'S DEFEAT/250 SOLDIERS KILLED" and

"NOT A SOUL OF THE COMMAND LEFT TO TELL THE TALE."[36] The report included no mention of the Sioux or any of their leaders—people Ross had vigorously defended only weeks before.

Ross, it seems clear, was determined not to the let the victory at the Little Bighorn undermine tribal land rights in Indian Territory. That may also explain why Boudinot did not mention the Little Bighorn until another week had passed. Even then Boudinot offered no page-one commentary of his own. Instead, he published a front-page story paraphrasing Ross and criticizing "the manifest purpose of certain persons to take advantage of it to 'cry havoc, and let slip the dogs of war' against the whole Indian race."[37] Thus the *Advocate's* first response to the battle was secondhand and conservative. By republishing the comments of Ross, Boudinot deferred to a respected Cherokee leader and former *Advocate* editor who was ten years his senior. By republishing Ross's *Journal* comments on page one, Boudinot avoided a major editorial risk at a precarious time in Indian-white relations. Ross and Boudinot, it seems, agreed that the best editorial response was to emphasize that the tribes of Indian Territory were not to blame for Custer's defeat.

The conservative nature of this response is underscored by the very fact that Boudinot and Ross were on the same side of this issue despite a long-standing and bloody feud between their families. As the nephew of Chief John Ross, W.P. Ross was a leader of the antitreaty faction, those Cherokees who had resisted the removal from their southeastern homelands in the 1830s. The Boudinots were leaders of the treaty faction, Cherokees who eventually agreed to move west, a position which would lead to Elias Boudinot's assassination in 1839. Despite this bitter history, William Penn Boudinot, Elias's son, embraced the words of William Potter Ross in response to the Battle of the Little Bighorn.

Boudinot's agreement with Ross is also evident in his reprinting of another Ross commentary in the *Advocate*. Ross, the *Advocate* said,

recognizes the fact which must be obvious to every one, that there are good, bad and indifferent among them all. The good will command, the indifferent pity, and the bad condemn—whether red, white or black, when occasion requires. Further, [Ross] believes that a majority of all classes of people in this country are governed in their general deportment by proper motives, and that these who are really perverse and inclined to do evil, form the exceptions among them and not the rule.[38]

Ross's words, published in the two leading Indian Territory newspapers, separated the Sioux and Cheyenne from Indian Territory tribes and reminded white readers that these five tribes, the Cherokee, Chickasaw, Choctaw, Creek, and Seminole, considered themselves civilized. Ross and Boudinot were taking politically safe positions, the better to defend themselves and their tribes from the howls of racism which followed the Custer defeat.

On July 22, the *Advocate* also reprinted an editorial on the Little Bighorn from the Denver *Mirror*. The editorial attacked the government's conduct of Indian policy, a point Boudinot emphasized in his editor's note: "We have not seen a single paper commenting on the battle between Custar [*sic*] and Sitting Bull...that does not criticize the United States authorities severely for their attempt to take forcible possession of the Black Hills country." Though the editorial warned that the battle had stirred up talk of extermination in the West, it noted that Custer and his men "succumbed to the fate of war in the enemy's country. They were not shot down unresisting or defenseless, but with gun, rifle, pistol and sword in thier [sic] hands, trying to kill as many as possible of their assailants." The *Mirror* editorial ended with a reminder that must have pleased the *Advocate*'s native readers:

Dreadful as the result is, painful to the relatives and friends of the fallen, disgraceful to the Government, the fact should not be lost sight of, that the Indians were fighting on their own ground, vindicating, as they deemed it their own guaranteed rights, and in defense of their lodges (homes), wives and children.[39]

Such comments from others helped Boudinot explain and defend the Indian point of view in an especially powerful way. These views insulated the *Advocate* from directly criticizing Custer or the government and showed readers that the Indian cause had some support even in the western press, a forum often unsympathetic to Indians.

Yet Boudinot was not content to let others do all the thinking about the Custer affair. In his July 22 editorial, Boudinot criticized the federal government, though in rather restrained language. He opened by casting doubt on the War Department's statement that the conflict had "nothing do to with the invasion of the Black Hills by miners in search of gold or with the breaking of the Sioux treaty." Boudinot responded that "the country will be slow to believe it. The Sioux expected to be protected in possession of their reservation and were not."[40] Boudinot concluded that Custer typified more general attitudes of whites toward Indians:

Undoubtedly the plan of General Custer was a good one if the Indians he was to fight had been of the same class as the Indians he had been accustomed to fight before.... But unfortunately for him they were not of that class. He made the mistake so often made of confounding all Indians alike. The mistake cost him his life if not his reputation.[41]

Boudinot's editorial response to the Little Bighorn, then, was carefully measured. Although he criticized the War Department generally, he did not name names or point the finger at the army or the Grant administration. And although he expressed some admiration for the "class" of the Sioux and Cheyenne warriors, he stopped far short of an endorsement of their victory. Boudinot knew that the *Advocate* could neither condemn all whites nor celebrate the death of Custer. To do so would have invited white reprisals against the Cherokees and threatened their own rights.

Boudinot used the white press to offer a mild defense of the Sioux, though in a highly selective way. When white newspapers defended the Indian cause or criticized federal policy, Boudinot was apt to quote them. But he did not reprint any stories or editorials from the white press that called for retribution or Indian extermination. The *Advocate* mentioned such comments only in order to defend Indians against these hostile attacks.

Such was the case with an editorial from the New York *Sun* printed on the front page of the August 5 issue. The *Sun* had asked, "WHO IS RESPONSIBLE?" and answered, not surprisingly, the administration. According to the *Sun,* the Sioux were only defending themselves:

If Custer had wiped out Sitting Bull and his whole band, he would have been applauded to the skies. Do those editors who rail like fishwomen at the Indians, think that the Sioux ought to have stood still and permitted themselves to be killed without resistance when our troops overtook and attacked them?[42]

The *Sun* editorialist thought that the Sioux warriors were savages, but acknowledged that "our own methods of war are not always such as ought to characterize Christian civilized countries." The Democratic *Sun* concluded its review of the Custer disaster with a partisan attack:

It is the Republican Administration that is really responsible for the lamentable death of Custer and his associates...[and] all the difficulties with the Sioux originated in schemes of plunder for the benefit of the notorious Indian Ring, which has had its headquarters in the Interior Department from almost the beginning of Grant's administration.[43]

This was an especially useful piece for Boudinot and the *Advocate.* It defended the Sioux by placing most of the blame on Washington corruption.

The *Journal* employed a similar strategy. More than a year after the battle, the paper published an account of the 1782 massacre at Gnadenhatten, the Moravian Missionary Settlement in Ohio. Author Rev. W.P. Nobles compared the Ohio massacre to the Little Bighorn:

Let us place side by side the Custer massacre, so called (was it not a fair fight. The gage of battle thrown down by the gallant Custer, and as gallantly accepted by the distinguished warrior of the Sioux) and the massacre of Indians at Gnadenhatten.[44]

According to Nobles, the Ohio incident was a true massacre. It involved 97 worshipping Indians, including many women and 34 children, who were "massacred, scalped, and then hacked to pieces by white men who claimed that the Indians were foreordained to be destroyed from off the face of the earth." Here again, the native press effectively used outside commentary. By reprinting the words of Rev. Nobles, the *Journal* could defend Indians and criticize Custer supporters without having to do so directly. Moreover, such commentaries reminded native readers of the *Journal* that they still had friends in the white community.

Conclusions

If native newspapers were pleased about the Indian victory over Custer, they were reluctant to say so directly. In fact, they seemed to be aware that the Sioux and Cheyenne victory was hollow, and that the glory days of the plains Indian were quickly passing. A small, unsigned piece, which appeared in the *Journal* in March 1877 under the headline "MUSKOGEE ITEMS," lamented the end of the buffalo:

The last link is broken that binds poor lo [the Indian] to the past. The buffalo no longer roams free as the winds of heaven upon the plains. He has been caught, tamed and harnessed, and driven through our streets on Sunday last, tied behind an emigrant wagon, ignominiously hitched to a rickety cart, with head bowed low—clothed in sack-cloth and dust he sadly passed on his way, ruminating on the departed glory of his race and species. We drop a tear.[45]

If the end of the buffalo meant the end of the old Indian life on the plains, it did not mean the end of the progressive native journalism. The *Cherokee Advocate* and the *Indian Journal* remained dedicated to the social, moral, political, and economic improvement of their people.

The Battle of the Little Bighorn threatened to undermine such efforts. With white passions inflamed by the Indian victory, the native press sought ways to continue supporting the Indian cause without agitating white critics. Thus the papers consistently emphasized the civilized nature of the tribes in Indian Territory, separating themselves from the Indians of northern plains. But they stopped short of condemning the Sioux and Cheyenne warriors. In fact, the *Advocate* and the *Journal* took pains to explain that the Sioux and Cheyenne were only defending their territory from invading whites and that these whites were not innocent civilians but fully armed soldiers. By reprinting attacks from white newspapers papers, the native press could appear restrained in its response to the Little Bighorn yet still criticize government policy.

The immediate cause of the native press's restrained response to the Little Bighorn was the controversy over land rights in Indian Territory. Even before the battle, Boudinot and Ross knew that both national and regional forces were seeking control of tribal land; Custer's defeat was merely an excuse to carry out such plans. As assimilated Indian leaders, Boudinot and Ross knew that celebrations over Custer's death or fierce attacks on government policy would be counterproductive. They also knew that the tribes of Indian Territory—still dependent on the Interior Department for annuities and deeply suspicious that their land would be taken once again—would not be helped by a militant editorial response.

More significantly, the response of the *Advocate* and *Journal* reflects the continuing progressive ideology embodied in these papers. Because they saw themselves as instruments of civilization and enlightenment, the *Advocate* and the *Journal* emphasized assimilation rather than criticism or protest. Driven by this editorial philosophy, the *Advocate* and the *Journal* muted their criticisms of whites and of government policy after the Little Bighorn.

Notes

1. See, for example, Brian W. Dippie, *Custer's Last Stand: The Anatomy of an American Myth* (Missoula: University of Montana, 1976); Bruce A. Rosenberg, *Custer and the Epic of Defeat* (University Park: Pennsylvania State University Press, 1974); Kent Ladd Steckmesser, *The Western Hero in History and Legend* (Norman: University of Oklahoma Press, 1965); Robert M. Utley, *Cavalier in Buckskin* (Norman: University of Oklahoma Press, 1988). Also see Paul Andrew Hutton, ed. *The Custer Reader* (Lincoln: University of Nebraska Press, 1992) and Roger L. Nichols, "Printer's Ink and Red Skins: Western Newspapermen and the Indians," *Kansas Quarterly* 3 (fall 1971): 82-88.

2. Utley, *Cavalier in Buckskin*, 4.

3. Oliver Knight, *Following the Indian Wars* (Norman: University of Oklahoma Press, 1960). Other studies of the press and Custer include Warren E. (Sandy) Barnard, "New York Herald: Origins of the Custer Legend," (Paper delivered at American Journalism Historians Association, Atlanta, Ga., 1989), and William E. Huntzicker, "Custer's Pictorial Images: Heroism and Racism in the Illustrated Press," in *Speaking About Custer*, ed. Sandy Barnard (Terre Haute, Ind.: AST Press, 1991).

4. William Huntzicker, "The Frontier Press, 1800-1900" in *The Media in America*, ed. Wm. David Sloan and James G. Stovall (Worthington, Ohio: Publishing Horizons, 1989), 179-80.

5. James E. Murphy and Sharon M. Murphy, *Let My People Know: American Indian Journalism, 1828-1978* (Norman: University of Oklahoma Press, 1981), 16-17.

6. These papers are discussed in Daniel F. Littlefield and James W. Parins, *American Indian and Alaska Native Newspapers and Periodicals, 1826-1924* (Westport, Conn.: Greenwood Press, 1984).

7. *Indian Herald*, February 1875, 2.

8. *Indian Journal*, 15 June 1876, 4. Also see Sam G. Riley, "*Indian Journal*, Voice of the Creek Tribe, Now Oklahoma's Oldest Newspaper," *Journalism Quarterly* 59 (spring 1982): 46-51, 183.

9. Littlefield and Parins, *American Indian and Alaska Native Newspapers*, 322.

10. *Cherokee Advocate*, 1 March 1876, 2.

11. An excellent discussion of these ideas in American history can be found in Roy Harvey Pearce, *Savagism and Civilization* (Berkeley: University of California Press, 1988).

12. *Indian Herald*, 20 June 1876, 2. Unfortunately, few copies of the *Herald* have survived. See Littlefield and Parins, *American Indian and Alaska Native Newspapers*, 184.

13. Littlefield and Parins, *American Indian and Alaska Native Newspapers*, 371-372. Also see Carolyn Thomas Foreman, *Oklahoma Imprints, 1835-1907* (Norman: University of Oklahoma Press, 1936), 143-44.

14. Littlefield and Parins, *American Indian and Alaska Native Newspapers*, 349-50.

15. Littlefield and Parins, *American Indian and Alaska Native Newspapers*, 20-21. Also see Cullen Joe Holland, *The Cherokee Indian Newspapers, 1828-1906: The Tribal Voice of a People in Transition* (Ph.D. diss., University of Minnesota, 1956).

16. *Cherokee Advocate*, 1 March 1876, 2.

17. Littlefield and Parins, *American Indian and Alaska Native Newspapers*, 189.

18. Foreman, *Oklahoma Imprints*, 77.

19. A house ad in the *Journal* explained that the cost of the paper was low "[so] that all the Indian people who read English might be able to spare that amount from their scanty income." *Indian Journal*, 15 June 1876, 4.

20. Figures from 1876 show the *Star* with 459 subscribers and the *Vindicator* with 300. These figures are from Foreman, *Oklahoma Imprints*. She cites two sources: George P. Rowell, *Centennial Newspaper Exhibition, 1876* (New York, 1876) and S.M. Pettengill, *Newspaper Directory and Advertisers' Handbook* (New York, 1877).

21. *Indian Journal*, 1 June 1876, 3.

22. Angie Debo, *The Road to Disappearance* (Norman: University of Oklahoma Press, 1941), 233. Also see Holland, *The Cherokee Indian Newspapers,* 399 and 420-23, who notes that Boudinot was responding to fears of white control of Indian land in the *Advocate* as early as 1870-71.

23. *Indian Journal*, 1 June 1876, 2.

24. *Indian Journal*, 15 June 1876, 1. The five nations, also known as the "Five Civilized Tribes" were the Cherokee, Chickasaw, Choctaw, Creek, and Seminole tribes.

25. *Cherokee Advocate*, 22 April 1876, 2.

26. *Cherokee Advocate,* 1 June 1876, 3.

27. *Indian Journal*, 15 June 1876, 1.

28. *Cherokee Advocate,* 1 March 1876, 1. Custer was reduced in rank to lieutenant colonel following the Civil War, though he was often referred to as "General."

29. *Indian Journal*, 1 June 1876, 2.

30. *Indian Journal*, 1 June 1876, 2.

31. *Indian Journal*, 29 June 1876, 1.

32. *Indian Journal*, 29 June 1876, 2.

33. *Indian Journal*, 6 July 1876, 2.

34. *Indian Journal*, 13 July 1876, 2.

35. *Indian Journal*, 13 July 1876, 2.

36. *Indian Journal*, 13 July 1876, 2.

37. *Cherokee Advocate*, 22 July 1876, 1.

38. *Cherokee Advocate*, 22 July 1876, 1.

39. *Cherokee Advocate*, 22 July 1876, 1.

40. *Cherokee Advocate*, 22 July 1876, 2.

41. *Cherokee Advocate*, 22 July 1876, 2.

42. *Cherokee Advocate*, 22 July 1876, 2.

43. *Cherokee Advocate*, 22 July 1876, 2.

44. *Indian Journal*, 18 August 1877, 2.

45. *Indian Journal*, 22 March 1877, 3.

8

Historiography on the Woman's Rights Press

Catherine C. Mitchell

Traditional American history explains that one of the immediate outcomes of the American Civil War was the passage of the Fifteenth Amendment to the United States Constitution saying that no one could be denied the right to vote based on "race, color, or previous condition of servitude."[1] Not generally discussed is the fact that the Fourteenth Amendment also passed just after the Civil War defined eligible voters as "male." Because these two amendments effectively preserved the disenfranchisement of women, Elizabeth Cady Stanton and Susan B. Anthony used their newspaper, the *Revolution,* to oppose passage of these amendments and the enfranchisement of African-American men.

This chapter proposes the women's studies concept of privilege as a way of understanding the *Revolution*'s position on the right to vote for African-Americans. Drawing heavily on current thinking in women's studies, the chapter discusses privilege in terms of scholarship of the woman's rights press and issues for African-American women, but the concept of privilege could well aid scholars examining other journalism history also. The chapter urges media historians to use the idea of privilege as a unit of analysis for examining both media content and the personal backgrounds of great figures in media history.

As used here the term privilege refers to issues both of race and of income level. In women's studies terms, privilege means working from the assumption that an upper-income white woman has certain advantages in American society that are lacking to both an upper-income woman from a racial or ethnic minority and a lower-income white or minority woman. The women's studies theorist Peggy McIntosh observes that if racism causes disadvantages for African-Americans, then a corollary must be that white privilege brings with it advantages. She defines privilege as "an invisible package of unearned assets."[2]

With this concept in mind, the chapter argues that a historian looking at the woman's rights press should ask whether or to what extent these newspapers crusaded for the rights of all women. Did the editors concentrate primarily on issues of concern to women like themselves, or did they display concern for issues of concern to women much different from themselves? Until scholars complete this work, the chapter argues, historians need to avoid assuming the woman's rights press crusaded for the common good.

Revision in Women's History

In the 1980s, scholars began incorporating into women's studies the idea of feminists as elitists unaware of multicultural issues. The push for revision originated among African-American writers who found they had little in common with the experience and issues raised by a feminism dominated by middle-class white women. In 1981, Angela Davis pointed out racism in the 19th-century woman's rights movement. In 1983 the novelist and poet Alice Walker coined the term "womanist" to signify these differences. She defined a womanist as "a black feminist or feminist of color." In 1984 theorist bell hooks pointed out the comfortable status of many white feminists: "Privileged feminists have largely been unable to speak to, with, and for diverse groups of women because they either do not understand fully the inter-relatedness of sex, race, and income oppression or refuse to take this inter-relatedness seriously." In a 1991 article, Elsa Barkley Brown argued that any good work of women's history must acknowledge the context of race, class, time, and place in which the events occurred.[3]

Observations like those of Davis, Walker, hooks, and Brown helped create a heightened interest in multiculturalism. Contributions to cultural diversity in the study of mass communication include two books about African-Americans and the mass media, one written by Clint Wilson and Félix Gutiérrez and one edited by Jannette L. Dates and William Barlow.[4]

This new awareness has spurred a very fertile re-examination in women's history. An outstanding example of the new approach, Christine Stansell's *City of Women,* discusses efforts of middle-income reformers in the Children's Aid Society in New York City in the 1850s. These sincerely caring reformers tried to help the poor by encouraging them to emulate middle-class behavior. For instance, reformers, thinking women could find happiness only if they literally stayed in their homes, drove impoverished women and children off city streets. In the process, Stansell found, reformers destroyed an important part of the urban day care system of the working poor.[5]

Famous Women's Stories

The idea of privilege needs incorporation into the history of the woman's rights press. Intense study of women working in journalism began with the publication in 1977 of Marion Marzolf's *Up from the Footnote*. Since then most writers of the history of women in journalism have concentrated on telling the stories of women who worked in journalism and the newspapers for which they worked. Histories of the woman's rights press have generally used this approach. They have written biographies of the woman's rights editors and described the content of their newspapers.[6] Any new branch of history must start with this baseline work, but historiographers have called for the history of women in journalism to move on to an examination of more complex research questions about women journalists.[7]

Woman's rights scholars should consider moving toward cultural history. James Carey, an influential proponent of this approach, argues that journalism history, by concentrating too narrowly on telling the stories of newspapers, lacks a "sense of historical time" and connections to other historical research. Others have agreed. For instance, John Stevens and Hazel Dicken Garcia say most journalism histories have ignored cultural forces and treated "individuals as shapers of American media." David Paul Nord has pioneered in writing social histories of newspapers. He says he tries to describe how "the institutions of mass media have been involved with the changing nature of community life in urban America."[8] Historians of the woman's rights press would do well to take up this theme.

One recent book, *A Voice of Their Own* edited by Martha Solomon in 1991, goes beyond just narrating the stories of famous women. Many of the chapters concentrate on telling the basic stories of different woman's rights newspapers, but they also discuss the influence of the rhetoric in those newspapers. Linda Steiner's chapter concentrates on the rhetorical positions taken by the woman's rights press and explains how this rhetoric played an important part in the formation of the suffrage community. Martha Solomon looks at interrelationships between the various newspapers and their editors. Other scholarship like *The Revolution in Words*, a 1990 collection of excerpts from the *Revolution*, edited by Lana F. Rakow and Cheris Kramarae, has more limited value. These reprints give a good picture of the newspapers' views on such women's issues as dress reform, child rearing, and divorce, but the new availability of the entire *Revolution* on microfilm dates the volume.[9]

Looking at privilege would give woman's rights press scholars a way to fit these newspapers into the broader American culture of the

19th century. A few scholars of the woman's rights press do briefly discuss factors involved in privilege. For example, *The Radical Women's Press of the 1850s,* by Ann Russo and Cheris Kramarae, incorporates some information on income and race differences. This collection of articles from the antebellum woman's rights press does include one article that discusses whether white northern woman's rights advocates should concern themselves with abolition. Lynne Masel-Walters gives two pages of a 1980 article to an income-and-race analysis of the readers of woman's rights newspapers.[10] In the main, however, the 19th-century woman's rights press still awaits detailed analysis that places these newspapers within the cultural context of their times.

Backgrounds of Woman's Rights Editors

A look at the backgrounds of the woman's rights editors shows how such an analysis might prove useful. The editors' biographies indicate they were a homogeneous group, the small-town daughters and wives of white, professional men. For instance, Amelia Bloomer, editor of the *Lily,* was the daughter of a small business owner. She worked as a schoolteacher until she married an attorney who served as town clerk and co-editor of a newspaper. Elizabeth Cady Stanton, editor of the *Revolution,* was the daughter of a state legislator and judge, and married Henry Stanton, a journalist, lawyer, and member of the state legislature. *Woman's Journal* editor Lucy Stone, one of the first American women to earn a college degree, was married to a hardware merchant. Paulina Wright Davis, editor of *Una,* was the daughter of a military officer. Her second husband, a jewelry manufacturer, later became a United States congressman from Rhode Island. Mari Boor Tonn calls her "a wealthy young Rhode Island socialite." Susan B. Anthony, publisher of the *Revolution,* was the daughter of the owner of a small textile mill, and she studied with a private tutor. Never married, she worked as a schoolteacher until she took up the cause of woman's rights full-time.[11]

Born in the United States, these editors grew up in Protestant homes. Many were Quakers. None of the editors were factory workers, immigrants, Roman Catholics, Jews, or African-Americans.[12] The editors of the woman's rights press, then, were privileged, white, and financially comfortable.

To Change Middle-Class Ideas

The woman's rights press clearly contradicted the dominant cultural ideology of the Cult of True Womanhood espoused by mainstream publications in the 19th century. This ideology rested on several assumptions: Men and women have very different natures. Men should operate in the greater world of commerce and politics while women should stay in the home. The ideology cast women as morally superior with a primary duty to raise children, but these standards of True Womanhood applied only to middle-class women with enough income to stay at home. Many women worked long hours in textile mills while American culture preached the virtues of a womanly life in the home. Linda Steiner says the woman's rights press as a whole wanted to replace the dominant idea of the "true woman" with the idea of the "new woman," a woman active in public affairs including the electoral process, but leaders "carefully chose both dress and hairstyle to demonstrate how the new woman could be different without appearing abrasive or 'unwomanly.' "[13]

Advocates of a woman's right to make public speeches, to vote, to hold property even if married, and to serve on juries definitely represented a radical viewpoint in the 19th century, but noted women's historian Nancy Cott observes, 19th-century woman's rights advocates thought all women shared issues such as home, family, and childbirth. This assumption of commonality often ignored core differences, like income level and race, that separated women, Cott points out.[14]

The privileged interests of the woman's rights press become clear when contrasted with the situation of African-American women in the 19th century. Jacqueline Jones, in a widely respected history of African-American women, found that throughout the 19th century almost all African-American women focused on finding enough food, clothing, and shelter for themselves and their children. Until 1862, they sought freedom from slavery. After emancipation, almost all African-American women worked for pay, mainly as low-paid domestics or field hands. Concerns like voting and property rights were theoretical abstracts far outside their ken. James Oliver Horton, after examining ideas about women in African-American newspapers, points out that middle class African-American women in the 19th century received the same pressure to abide by the strictures of the Cult of True Womanhood as did their white sisters.[15]

The "Revolution"

The *Revolution* shows what privilege can reveal about the 19th-century woman's rights press. Although the newspaper lasted only from 1868 to 1870, it has a continuing fascination for historians because its publisher, Susan B. Anthony, and its editor, Elizabeth Cady Stanton, are two of the century's most famous advocates of woman suffrage. The publication favored divorce reform, better job opportunities and pay, unions for working women, and a larger role in organized religion, but it focused on woman's right to participate in the public sphere, most particularly the right to vote.[16]

Although the *Revolution* actively advocated reforms to help working women, the nature of the newspaper's birth undercuts these positions. After the Civil War woman's suffrage organizations planned to continue to campaign for both African-American and woman's suffrage, but influential backers, like newspaper publisher Horace Greeley, argued to delay any discussion of woman's suffrage until male African-American suffrage had been achieved. As a result in 1869, Elizabeth Cady Stanton and Susan B. Anthony, abandoning the campaign for African-American suffrage, formed a separate organization, the National Woman Suffrage Association, to campaign exclusively for women's issues including the right to vote. They founded their newspaper using funds donated by George Francis Train, who opposed the vote for African-American men and women.[17]

Anthony and Stanton's *Revolution* editorialized against the Fifteenth Amendment granting the right to vote to African-American men because it failed to enfranchise women. Editorials used contemptuous language to argue that women like the editors had more qualifications to vote than did many of the men the amendment would enfranchise. Wrote Stanton:

[I]f woman finds it hard to bear the oppressive laws of a few Saxon Fathers, of the best orders of manhood, what may she not be called to endure when all the lower orders, natives and foreigners, Dutch, Irish, Chinese and African, legislate for her and her daughters?... Think of Patrick and Sambo and Hans and Yung Tang, who do not know the difference between a Monarchy and a Republic, who never read the Declaration of Independence or Webster's spelling book, making law for Lydia Maria Child or Lucretia Mott or Fanny Kemble."[18]

Many late-20th-century readers would find this argument offensive, but this does not necessarily mean that the editors of the *Revolution* were racists. Historian David Fischer rightly admonishes historians to avoid the logical fallacy of presentism—that is, applying the values of today to the past.[19] However, that a radically liberal 19th-century newspaper would publish such copy may say a great deal about the historical roots of contemporary American racism. This is why studying privilege as a unit of analysis can contribute to historical knowledge.

New Research Questions
An interest in privilege discloses a new line of research questions. To understand privilege in the woman's rights movement, historians

must examine the interactions among the white, upper-income editors and the American women who were from the working class, women of color, and ethnic women.

University Publications of America has produced an inexpensive microfilm series: "Periodicals on Women and Women's Rights." The series includes the *Revolution, Una,* the *Lily,* the *Woman's Column* and 21 other titles. This microfilm publication of many of the woman's rights newspapers makes important primary sources easily available to a wide range of scholars.

In examining privilege, scholars need to keep one point in mind. Women's historian Ellen DuBois has warned revisionists of the history of the 19th-century woman's rights movement in fairness to acknowledge the movement's accomplishments. She argues that "the demand for the vote was the most radical program for woman's emancipation possible in the nineteenth century." In asking for the vote, women also asked for a "fundamental transformation of the family."[20] Historians should avoid denigrating the extent of the sacrifices made in the campaign for the vote or the ferocity of the battle, but they do need to document the relationship of the woman's rights press to all American women.

Scholars addressing this question could take as a guide the question posed by respected women's historian Nancy Hewitt. Paraphrased to apply to the woman's rights press, Hewitt's question is, Which did woman's rights editors put first? Were they loyal first to all those who shared their social class or loyal first to all those who shared their gender?[21]

This approach brings up other questions: How did the woman's rights press affect the status of all American women? Even if the press aimed to benefit mainly middle-class white women, did it have some trickle-down impact on other American women? When viewed in the context of all American women in the 19th century, how much effect did these relatively privileged newspaper editors and their demands have on the majority of American women? Given the severity of the battle they had to wage for the right to vote, how much were woman's rights editors obligated to acknowledge the needs of their African-American, immigrant and working-class sisters?[22]

Conclusion

Mass Communication historians should stop assuming the campaign for woman's right to vote served all womankind. Instead, they must discuss the woman's rights editors and their newspapers in relation to the needs of the many less privileged women of the 19th-century

America who did not share their social standing. Only then can history present a true understanding of the place of the woman's rights press in American history and its significance for all Americans.

Notes

1. See, for example, Birdsall S. Viault, *American History Since 1965* (New York: McGraw-Hill, 1989), 16.

2. Peggy McIntosh, "White Privilege: Unpacking the Invisible Knapsack," *Experiencing Race, Class and Gender in the United States,* ed. Virginia Cyrus (Mountain View, Calif.: Mayfield), 209-13.

3. Angela Y. Davis, *Women, Race and Class* (New York: Random House, 1981); Alice Walker, *In Search of Our Mothers' Gardens* (New York: Harcourt Brace Jovanovich, 1983), 8, xi; bell hooks, *Feminist Theory: From Margin to Center* (Boston: South End Press, 1984), 14; Elsa Barkley Brown, "Polyrhythms and Improvization: Lessons of Women's History," *History Workshop* 31 (spring 1991): 85-90.

4. Clint C. Wilson II and Félix Gutiérrez, *Minorities and Media: Diversity and the End of Mass Communication* (Newbury Park, Calif.: Sage, 1985); Jannette L. Dates and William Barlow, eds., *Split Image: African Americans in the Mass Media* (Washington, D.C.: Howard University Press, 1990).

5. Christine Stansell, *City of Women: Sex and Class in New York, 1789-1860* (New York: Alfred A. Knopf, 1986).

6. See for instance Sherilyn Cox Bennion, "The New Northwest and Woman's Exponent: Early Voices for Suffrage," *Journalism Quarterly* 54 (1977): 286-92; Bennion, "Woman Suffrage Papers of the West, 1869-1914," *American Journalism* 3 (1986): 125-41; Lauren Kessler, *The Dissident Press: Alternative Journalism in American History* (Beverly Hills, Calif.: Sage, 1984); Lynne Masel-Walters, "A Burning Cloud by Day: The History and Content of the *Woman Journal*," *Journalism History* 3, no. 4 (winter 1976-77): 103-10; Masel-Walters, "Their Rights and Nothing More: A History of *The Revolution*, 1868-1870," *Journalism Quarterly* 53 (summer 1976): 242-51; Masel-Walters, "To Hustle with the Rowdies: The Organization and Functions of the American Woman Suffrage Press," *Journal of American Culture* 3.1 (spring 1980): 167-83.

7. Maurine H. Beasley, "Women in Journalism: Contributors to Male Experience or Voices of Feminine Expression?" *American Journalism* 7 (1990): 39-54; Susan Henry, "Changing Media History Through Women's History," *Women in Mass Communication,* ed. Pamela J. Creedon (Newbury Park, Calif.: Sage, 1989); Catherine C. Mitchell, "The Place of Biography in the History of News Women," *American Journalism* 7 (1990): 23-32.

8. James W. Carey, "'Putting the World at Peril': A Conversation with James W. Carey," *Journalism History* 12, no 2 (summer 1985): 38-53; John Stevens and Hazel Dicken Garcia, *Communication History* (Beverly Hills, Calif.: Sage, 1980), 24; David Paul Nord quoted by Sybil Eakin, "Printing and Proselytizing: Communications History as Social History," *Clio Among the Media* 20, no. 2 (January 1988): 12-15.

9. Martha M. Solomon, ed., *A Voice of Their Own: The Woman Suffrage Press, 1840-1910* (Tuscaloosa: University of Alabama Press, 1991); Linda Steiner, "Evolving Rhetorical Strategies/Evolving Identities," *Voice of Their Own*, ed. Solomon, 183; Lana F. Rakow and Cheris Kramarae, *The Revolution in Words: Righting Women 1868-1871* (New York and London: Routledge, 1990).

10. Ann Russo and Cheris Kramarae, *The Radical Women's Press of the 1850s* (New York: Routledge, 1991); Masel-Walters, "To Hustle with the Rowdies."

11. Edward T. James, ed., *Notable American Women 1607-1950* (Cambridge, Mass.: Harvard University Press, 1971), 1:179-80, 3:342-43, 388-89, 1:444-45; Mari Boor Tonn, "The Una, 1853-1855: The Premiere of the Woman's Rights Press," *Voice of Their Own*, ed. Solomon, 48; Kathleen Barry, *Susan B. Anthony: A Biography of a Singular Feminist* (New York: Ballantine Books, 1988).

12. Susan J. Kleinberg, introduction to *Life and Writings of Amelia Bloomer, 1895*, D.C. Bloomer (New York: Schoken Books, 1975), v-xiv.

13. E. Claire Jerry, "The Role of Newspapers in the Nineteenth-Century Woman's Movement," *Voice of Their Own*, ed. Solomon, 29; Masel-Walters, "To Hustle with the Rowdies"; Barbara Welter, "The Cult of True Womanhood," in *Our American Sisters: Women in American Thought and Life*, eds. Jane E. Friedman and William G. Shade (Boston: Allyn and Bacon, 1973), 96-126; Gerda Lerner, "The Lady and the Mill Girl: Changes in the Status of Women in the Age of Jackson," *American Sisters*, eds. Friedman and Shade, 82-95; Steiner, "Evolving," 183.

14. Nancy Cott, *The Grounding of Modern Feminism* (New Haven: Yale University Press, 1987), 6-9.

15. Jacqueline Jones, *Labor of Love, Labor of Sorrow: Black Women, Work and the Family, from Slavery to the Present* (New York: Vintage Books, 1985); James Oliver Horton, "Freedom's Yoke: Gender Conventions Among Antebellum Free Blacks," *Feminist Studies* 12 (spring 1986): 51-76.

16. *Revolution*, eds. Rakow and Kramarae; Kessler, *Dissident Press*; Bonnie J. Dow, "*The Revolution*, 1868-1870: Expanding the Woman Suffrage Agenda," in *Voice of Their Own*, ed. Solomon, 78.

17. Robert L. Allen, *Reluctant Reformers: Racism and Social Reform Movements in the United States* (Washington, D.C.: Howard University Press,

1974), 139-149; Eleanor Flexner, *Century of Struggle: The Woman's Rights Movement in the United States* (Cambridge, Mass.: Belknap Press, 1975), 147-48; *Revolution in Words,* eds. Rakow and Kramarae, 14-15, 22; Kessler, *Dissident Press,* 76-77; Dow, "Revolution," 72; Masel-Walters, "Their Rights"; Barry, *Susan B. Anthony.*

18. Elizabeth Cady Stanton, "Manhood Suffrage," *Revolution,* 24 December 1868, 392.

19. David Hackett Fischer, *Historians' Fallacies: Toward a Logic of Historical Thought* (New York: Harper and Row, 1970), 135-40.

20. Ellen DuBois, "The Radicalism of the Woman Suffrage Movement: Notes Toward the Reconstruction of Nineteenth Century Feminism," *Feminist Studies* 3 (1975): 63-71.

21. Nancy A. Hewitt, "Beyond the Search for Sisterhood: American Women's History in the 1980s," *Unequal Sisters: A Multicultural Reader in U.S. Women's History,* eds. Ellen Carol DuBois and Vicki L. Ruiz (New York and London: Routledge, 1990), 1-14.

22. For more research questions, see Allen, *Reluctant Reformers,* 6.

9

The Woman Suffrage Press of the West

Sherilyn Cox Bennion

For the woman suffragist, the process of winning the right to vote was, to a certain extent at least, the process of evolving from outsider to insider. Although suffrage did not automatically open access to positions of power or dramatically change women's place in society, it allowed them to move into the political process in new and significant ways.

Scholars have advanced many different explanations for the early successes of the woman suffrage movement in the western United States. Wyoming led the way in 1869, followed by Utah in 1870. By 1900 Colorado and Idaho had joined them, and by the end of 1914 all women who lived west of the Rocky Mountains could vote. It has been suggested that a society less rigid and conventional than that of the East was more willing to try social experiments and that the frontier spirit promoted a sense of equality as women and men worked together to build a new civilization. Another theory is that political expediency led men to give women the vote. In some cases the motive may have been boosterism; suffrage might make an area known and bring settlers. Perhaps men were more chivalrous in the West or women more highly valued because of their scarcity. Men may have wanted to reward women for their strenuous efforts during the pioneer period. Probably all of these suggestions have merit, depending on the place and time in question.

While historians have examined and debated the reasons for the success of the woman suffrage movement in the West and have studied the progress of the movement both in individual states and in the region as a whole, only a few have looked at the publications that the suffragists founded, in which they discussed their ideas and goals. Historians have begun only recently to recognize the contributions of these periodicals in changing women from outsiders to insiders. Studies completed thus far usually focus on the suffrage periodicals of the East and base their discussion of suffrage ideas mainly on eastern sources, making the western women outsiders once again.[1]

This chapter identifies seven suffrage periodicals published in the West before 1900 of which copies survive.[2] At least five more appeared between 1900 and 1914. A few others must have existed, because early directories list suggestive titles like Washington's *Equal Rights Champion* of 1894 and label other periodicals, including California's *Homestead* of 1874, as suffrage papers, but all copies have disappeared. These publications were founded because the suffragists, considered outsiders by the conventional press and denied access by those who controlled it, resorted to establishing their own. They hoped to give the movement a voice, to expand its influence, and to win converts for the cause.

Women's rights periodicals are readily identifiable as part of the venerable tradition of alternative voices in the press of the United States. Certainly, they shared the traits one writer listed as characteristic of the dissident press: They were underdogs, at least until well into the 20th century; they held views that diverged from the mainstream; they wanted to effect social change; they were excluded from the traditional media marketplace, but their ideas gradually filtered into it.[3]

In an effort to illuminate the experiences and ideas of one group of American outsiders, this chapter looks first at the editors and their publications and then at the ideas they espoused. It tries to show the differences among the experiences of the suffragist editors, as well as their similarities, and attempts a tentative assessment of their influence.

The Publications

The West had no suffrage papers until 1869, about the same time that the most prominent eastern papers began. Although easterner Amelia Bloomer campaigned for women's political rights in the *Lily,* founded in Seneca Falls, New York, in 1849 after the landmark women's rights meetings there, the best-known eastern suffrage papers, the *Revolution* and the *Woman's Journal,* started in 1868 and 1870.

Emily A. Pitts, a 25-year-old schoolteacher who had moved to San Francisco from New York in 1865, started the West's first suffrage paper when she bought a half interest in the weekly *Sunday Mercury* in 1869. She transformed it, taking full control and renaming it the *Pioneer* later that year. Pitts explained the paper's motto, "DEVOTED TO THE PROMOTION OF HUMAN RIGHTS: LIBERTY, JUSTICE, FRATERNITY," by pointing out that she used "fraternity" only because "the paucity of our language...has no word to express the brotherhood and sisterhood of the race." Her "Salutatory" established the tone for the *Pioneer* and for the suffrage periodicals that followed it:

We defend the rights of women fearlessly and to the best of our ability. We shall insist upon woman's independence—her elevation, socially and politically, to the platform now solely occupied by man. We shall claim for her each privilege now given to every male citizen of the United States. In short, we shall claim for her the right of suffrage—believing that by this she will gain the position for which God intended her—equality with man.[4]

Pitts published the paper until September 1873, when she sold it to Mrs. C.C. Calhoun, citing ill health as the reason for her retirement. By that time Pitts had married August K. Stevens and begun listing herself in the paper as Emily Pitts-Stevens, sometimes with the hyphen, sometimes without. The new publisher promised to continue promotion of suffrage but ceased publication after only a few months.

During 1871 Abigail Scott Duniway, a pioneer suffrage leader from Oregon, visited Pitts Stevens and became Oregon editor for the *Pioneer,* serving in that position for several months before founding Oregon's first suffrage paper, the *New Northwest,* in Portland. She later wrote:

Before returning to Oregon I resolved to purchase an outfit and begin the publication of a newspaper myself, as I felt that the time had come for vigorous work in my own State, and we had no journal in which the demands of women for added rights were treated with respectful consideration.[5]

Duniway used the motto "FREE SPEECH, FREE PRESS, FREE PEOPLE" for most of the sixteen years that her weekly paper survived.

Neither the *Pioneer* nor the *New Northwest* was devoted exclusively to suffrage. Both contained general news, essays, advice, editorials, fiction, poetry, and advertising, but their main purpose remained promotion of women's right to vote. Every number carried reports from suffrage organizations and encouragement for supporters.

Duniway wrote poetry and fiction, as well as news columns and editorials, for her paper. In addition to the *New Northwest,* she published books of poetry, a novel, and her autobiography, *Path-Breaking.* She sold the *New Northwest* in 1887, reminding readers that she had warned them she would sever her ties with the paper unless they remitted payments more promptly. She also mentioned increasing calls in the lecture field that demanded her time, energy, and money.

Back in Portland after a sojourn in Idaho, she found financing and returned to journalism in 1891 with a publication called the *Coming Century,* a monthly magazine that continued into 1892. She may have intended the new periodical to be less preoccupied with women's rights than *New Northwest* had been, for she used the motto "DEVOTED TO

LITERATURE, POETRY, ART, SCIENCE, ETC." on the cover of the first number and even included a column of "Society Notes." However, she also published in this number her short story hailing a heroine who stood up to both father and husband and a history of the suffrage movement in Washington. An editorial stated that the time for arguments in favor of suffrage had passed; only "ways and means to hasten its advent" were needed.[6]

For the second number, Duniway changed the cover motto to "DEVOTED TO LITERATURE, ENLIGHTENMENT, LIBERTY" and to the inside masthead added a note that gave the campaign for equal rights top billing:

The Coming Century will fearlessly advocate equal rights for all, but its ample pages will afford room for the discussion of all other subjects of public interest whether pertaining to Liberty, Enlightenment, Equity, Religion, Law, Politics, Labor, Tax, Tariff, Temperance, Hygiene, Education, Literature, Art, Science, Business, News, Agriculture, Co-operation, Society, Amusement, Family and Home.[7]

This number also contained in its 32 pages announcements of the upcoming convention of the National American Woman Suffrage Association, a plea for women to replace "gush and sentiment" with "co-operation and system," a call for the establishment of a training school for women wage workers, a report of a suffrage convention in Washington, reprints of addresses on "the Matriarchate" by Elizabeth Cady Stanton and on "Higher Education of Women" by Helen F. Spalding, and other articles and letters that supported the advancement of women.

In 1895 Duniway became editor of another weekly, the *Pacific Empire,* published by Frances E. Gotshall, who informed readers in an introductory issue that she felt fortunate to have secured the services of Duniway, "the well known veteran journalist," without whose services she would hardly have dared to spread her sails. Duniway returned the compliment by approving of Gotshall's motto for the paper, ALIS VOLAT PROPRIIS, "She flies with her own wings," but suggested "She paddles her own canoe" might have been more appropriate. She also reminisced about the beginning of her journalistic career 25 years earlier, when, "full of hope and confidence," she had flung her banner to the breeze, "proclaiming 'Liberty throughout all the land, and to all the inhabitants thereof.'" That liberty still had not been secured, she continued, but progress had been made, and "now nobody doubts our ultimate success."[8]

In the *Pacific Empire,* Duniway followed her earlier pattern, with a lively mix of news notes, editorial comments, reprints from other publications, articles, and serial fiction, writing much of the paper's content herself. Gotshall guaranteed advertisers a prepaid subscription list of 1,000 subscribers, and Duniway's prominence undoubtedly helped attract readers. The back cover of the first regular issue featured an array of comments like this one from the *Portland Oregonian:* "Its reading columns exhibit the well-known characteristics of its editor, Abigail Scott Duniway, whose vigor as a writer never wanes."[9] During her two-year term as editor, Duniway assumed the presidency of the Oregon State Equal Suffrage Association, and the paper's increasing emphasis on suffrage reflected her preoccupation with suffrage campaigns in Oregon and elsewhere.

Colorado's first suffrage paper claimed on its masthead to be "The only paper in the State advocating Woman's Political Equality and Individuality." Caroline Churchill, its editor, used the title *Queen Bee* for both her paper and herself. In Minnesota, where she had run a millinery and dressmaking business from 1857 to 1862, "the longest five years" of her life, she had found a role model in Jane Grey Swisshelm, a crusading feminist and former Washington correspondent who edited a paper in St. Cloud.[10]

In 1869 Duniway left her daughter in the care of a married sister and set out for California to begin what she always called "a traveling business," which consisted of writing about her experiences, publishing her writings, traveling to sell them, and gathering material for new sketches in the process. She wrote and published two books before settling in Denver in 1879 and starting a monthly periodical called the *Colorado Antelope,* stating in the first number her belief that "every State in the Union should have a live feminine paper published at the Capital." The *Antelope* metamorphosed into the weekly *Queen Bee* in 1862, and Churchill continued it in that guise until at least 1895, often hiring women to do its mechanical work and teaching them skills, she said, that would keep them from being "obliged to wash or keep boarders when they are called upon to support their families." She published her autobiography, *Active Footsteps,* in 1909.[11]

Although she considered her paper the voice of the Colorado suffrage movement, Churchill never became part of the suffrage establishment there. Her explanation: "Popularity was not what she was looking for." Her methods were her own, she explained, and she "made no effort to curry favor."[12]

Churchill urged women to go to the polls in force, whether they could vote or not. In addition to suffrage, she crusaded for garbage removal, temperance, and improvement of the postal system. She opposed dance halls, tobacco, Catholics, and Mormons, always in colorful prose. Her autobiography, written in the third person, described the difficulty of founding a paper on the frontier and added, "Mrs. Churchill has performed a wonderful work under most difficult circumstances. It is not at all likely that another woman on the continent could under the same conditions accomplish as much."[13]

Washington's first suffrage paper was the *Alki,* published twice a month in Puyallup during 1895 and edited by Ida Le Fevre. The publication's name, an Indian word meaning "bye and bye" that the state had used in its motto, must have seemed particularly appropriate for a suffrage publication.

The number for April 15, 1895, demonstrated the existence of a woman suffrage network functioning among the western publications and often reaching out to include the eastern ones, as well. On its first page appeared a poem by Abigail Scott Duniway and a report of a reception in her honor. The poem, a tribute to suffrage leader Lucy Stone titled "Make the World Better," concluded:

> Let us up and to duty! Let us do our work well;
> And wherever the story of freedom we tell,
> We will make the world better, as Lucy Stone said,
> Who made the world better, then smiled and was dead.

Subsequent pages featured an appeal for subscriptions to the national *Woman's Tribune;* a report of a woman's election to the Oakland, California, board of education; and reprints from the *Seattle Press Times* of articles describing the organization of an antisuffrage society in Chicago, with replies from Washington state suffragists.

Like other suffrage periodicals, the *Alki* included columns of news notes and commentary. The number mentioned above listed officers elected in local suffrage societies, poked fun at the concern of newspapers in Tacoma and Seattle over "divided skirts," attributed England's "racial strength and accomplishment" to the "moral freedom" given English women, and boasted of the *Alki's* rapid growth. Fillers, occupying space between or at the end of articles, resembled abbreviated news notes. One read, "There are 139 convicts in the State penitentiary, at Salem, Oregon, and only two are women."

Many such items came from other suffrage publications. The editors not only read and clipped one another's papers, they met and conferred as they traveled to lecture at public meetings and to recruit supporters. The eastern suffragists also made many trips through the

West, and the western papers used their writings along with local material.

Next in time after the *Alki,* during 1897 and 1898, came a monthly paper in Reno, Nevada. Frances A. Williamson and her daughter, Mary L. Williamson, published the *Nevada Citizen,* "a journal devoted to the best interests of our commonwealth," with the motto "AS IN UNION THERE IS STRENGTH, SO IN ACTION THERE IS PROGRESS." Frances Williamson had spearheaded organization of the Nevada State Equal Suffrage Association in 1895, served as its first president, and used her paper, published at her own expense, as its official organ.

The *Nevada Citizen* not only supported woman suffrage but tried to help prepare women to use it effectively, stating the following as its object: "To promote the advancement of woman in the ethics of civil government, ordained in the Declaration of Independence and established by the Constitution of the United States of America."[14] The paper's content in its June 1897 number included an article on the history of the Constitution, part of a series called "Growth of the American Nation," and an editorial on "the nature of wealth and the laws which govern its production, exchange and distribution," as well as articles defending suffrage and lists of officers of both the Nevada State Equal Suffrage Association and the National American Woman Suffrage Association. The usual brief notices told readers that Jennie June Croly was writing a history of the women's clubs of the United States and that Mary E. Hubbard had been elected tax collector of Holden, Massachusetts.

Dress reform had been a continuing preoccupation of suffragists, and the adoption of bloomers—the long, full pantaloons named after women's rights advocate Amelia Bloomer—had given the establishment press a weapon for its campaign of ridicule. The *Nevada Citizen* refrained from counseling the adoption of such unusual attire, but a filler suggested more modest reform: "If ever a reform was needed, it is a rational form of dress for woman that will allow pockets. Man's ordinary apparel has seventeen pockets, and he has use for each. Yes, let us have pockets, equality in pockets."[15]

In addition to publishing their own papers, suffrage supporters also distributed columns to daily and weekly newspapers. Although this occurred more frequently after 1900, when campaigns became more professionally organized and more generously financed, an early suffrage history mentioned a column written for the *Rocky Mountain News* of Denver during the 1876–77 Colorado suffrage campaign by Mrs. E.L. Campbell, whose timidity led her to adopt a pen name, "Mrs. Schlachtfeld." Her timidity may have been more professed than real, for *schlachtfeld* is a German word meaning battlefield, and Campbell took an active part in the Colorado suffrage movement, speaking and distributing literature throughout the state.[16]

Many papers in addition to those devoted primarily to achieving woman suffrage included suffrage among their goals. An early one was the *Woman's Pacific Coast Journal,* a monthly founded by Carrie Fisher Young in 1870 after she moved her family by wagon from Idaho to San Francisco, seeking "apples, and grapes, and sunshine" and a chance "for papa to get well and strong."[17] She crusaded for temperance, health, and suffrage, with temperance and health receiving increasing emphasis as time went on, especially after Young changed the name of the publication to *Pacific Journal of Health* and opened, with her husband, the Nicasio Water-Cure in Marin County, north of San Francisco. The paper lasted until the fall of 1872. From 1882 to 1885, Young edited and published an Oakland paper called *Life Crystals,* but it devoted much less attention to suffrage.

A periodical published for 42 years by Mormon women in Utah also gave strong support to suffrage. Louisa Lula Greene founded the *Woman's Exponent* in 1872, but Emmeline B. Wells became editor in 1877 and stayed in that post until the *Exponent* ceased publication in 1914. Their territorial legislature had given Utah women the vote in 1870, but between 1882, when the federal Edmunds Bill denied wives of polygamous men the vote,[18] and 1896, when statehood restored it, Mormon women fought to regain suffrage. They saw it as a religious, as well as a political, cause and found no contradiction in supporting both suffrage and polygamy.

The *Woman's Herald of Industry and Social Science Co-operator,* published monthly in San Francisco from 1881 to 1884, served as the organ of the California Woman's Social Science Association, whose members aimed "to worship the *true* God" but had other goals ranging from learning how to live a pure and healthful life to determining how to progress without robbing the brain or purse of another. The *Herald* always supported suffrage; its editor, Marietta L. Stow, having suffered what she considered gross injustices at the hands of a discriminatory probate system, conducted a lifelong crusade on behalf of her sex, establishing a woman's church and a woman's political party, as well as the social science association and the *Herald.* In 1884, after founding the National Equal Rights Party and renaming her paper *National Equal Rights,* she announced that it would campaign for the party's presidential candidate, Belva A. Lockwood, and soon became the vice-presidential nominee herself. The *Herald* expired shortly after their spirited but unsuccessful political campaign.

Thus, from the earliest years of the struggles for woman suffrage in the West, publications of many kinds joined the crusade. The early ones, particularly, were highly individualistic. Even though they printed news of national suffrage leaders and organizations, they concentrated on the local scene, and they reflected the personalities of strong editors.

Rarely did the editors have independent incomes, so their papers battled for survival, as well as for suffrage. Subscribers, mostly middle-class women like themselves, had no funds to make donations beyond the price of a subscription, and editors had trouble collecting even subscription bills. They also found subscribers hard to come by, with low circulation revenues insufficient in most cases to support the papers. They used advertisements, but the limited readership and unpopular point of view made them an unappealing medium for businesses that sought a wide audience of prospective customers.

Although the editors intended to spread the gospel of suffrage to the unbelievers, the papers attracted principally readers already converted to the cause. This is not to say that they had little influence, for they kept readers informed of national and local developments, provided them with arguments for suffrage and answers to those who argued against it, encouraged them to persevere, and maintained links with others of like mind.

The Ideas

An examination of the western suffrage papers supports the proposition that the suffrage movement had no official ideology. A writer who looked at the statements and publications of eastern suffragists suggested that they developed a standardized repertory of arguments primarily in response to the arguments of their opponents, the so-called "antis."[19] The westerners, however, seemed not only to react to their critics but to assert as their fundamental premise the idea that justice demanded the extension of the vote—a natural right—to women. Certainly this contention, frequently and passionately asserted, underlay other arguments made in the western publications.

In *New Northwest* editorials with suffrage as their theme, for example, justice and natural rights themes were noted 123 times in a total of 207 mentions of ideas. A closely related note struck by editor Duniway was that lack of the franchise subverted egalitarian principles. It received 37 mentions.[20] Unfortunately, not enough numbers of other western papers have survived to make such numerical analysis meaningful for the group as a whole, but a reading of the available papers suggests the prevalence of Duniway's emphasis.

One way of looking at the ideas is to divide them into categories suggested by a historian who used California as a model. He categorized suffragists as "social feminists," who argued that enfranchised women would humanize society, protect the home and family through social legislation, and purify politics; "personal feminists," who focused on women's quest for dignity and independence; and "natural rights feminists," who emphasized equality and condemned taxation without representation.[21]

The ideas presented in the western suffrage papers could be placed into this framework, but only with the caveat that the editors in actuality showed little interest in developing logical systems or philosophical underpinnings for their beliefs. They sought to gather and present all possible justifications for suffrage, bolstering their contentions and answering their opponents with every idea at their disposal, combining and multiplying them almost indiscriminately. Inconsistency might result, as when one article stressed the need for equality and another in the same publication lamented that inferior men of other races had the vote while superior white women did not, but such juxtapositions did not seem to trouble the editors.

As campaigns became better organized and more carefully planned, supporters made a conscious effort to address certain kinds of messages to certain audiences, but before 1900 a more rough-and-ready attitude prevailed. Emphases, too, changed over time, but variations of the themes elaborated and stressed in the 20th-century suffrage papers had been around since Stevens and Duniway first took up journalism. A look at the papers shows how they presented and combined a wide variety of ideas.

In the West's first suffrage paper, the *Pioneer,* an article reported organization of the California Woman's State Suffrage Association and added a statement of belief by Emily Pitts Stevens that used themes reflecting social feminism, personal feminism, and natural rights:

We believe that those who still refuse to recognise [*sic*] the civil rights of woman strike at the foundation of equitable government...for women are taxed but not represented; authorized to hold property, but not to control it; permitted to form political opinions, but not allowed to use them. We believe that the feminine element is necessary to complete the harmony of life in government as in other departments. If our government is a protector and educator, then does it need the peculiar characteristics of woman.... Not the interests of woman alone, but the interests of all humanity are involved in this great question of Suffrage.[22]

Articles in the last of the 19th-century western papers, the *Nevada Citizen*, also combined a variety of ideas. Hardly an article or editorial mentioned only one. "The New Woman," an essay published in 1897, assured men that women did not seek "annihilation" of any of their "time-sanctioned spheres"; this would be "unwomanly, because unnatural." Women asked only that "the voice of the whole, not one-half of all citizens, speak through the ballot," which would build up "loftier and purer ideals of patriotism." Women had been referred to often as "the reserve force of the human family, but where is the economy of supporting a reserve force if it is never to be called into action," the essay asked.[23]

Even if called into action as part of the reserve force, women would remain womanly, still complementing the manly male, most suffragists insisted. Their publications repeatedly answered the "anti" argument that voting would render women unfeminine and lure them away from their natural sphere. Abigail Scott Duniway, a hard-working frontier farmer's wife before she became an editor, approved of "modesty, purity and other womanly attributes" and insisted that involvement in politics would not "taint" women.[24] The suffragists certainly meant no threat to men, they maintained, and no editor had the temerity to suggest that it would be desirable for women to become less feminine, although sometimes the papers defined femininity in a way to which their opponents might object.

The antis often used the Bible to support their contention that woman had a sphere separate and distinct from man's and should remain there. Pitts Stevens answered by quoting a Presbyterian minister who pointed out that 50 scriptural passages approved of praying and prophesying by women, while only two did not, and advised that the admonitions of the Apostle Paul be interpreted in the context of the times when they were given.[25]

Still, Pitts Stevens remained an ardent champion of the feminine woman. She agreed with an 1872 suffrage convention speaker that "there is nothing so beautiful as home life," even while she objected forcefully to limiting women's activities to the home and printed an article maintaining that only "superior brute strength" had kept them there, educated to be slaves, with a master who said:

And above all, REMEMBER, O! enslaved connubial echo of ourselves, to keep in that straight, narrow, barren, never turning lane, by our brute strength fenced in for you; by our superior wisdom for you at the entrance in gigantic capitals lettered, WOMAN'S TRUE SPHERE! at sides, lettered WOMAN'S TRUE SPHERE!! at the bottom, lettered, WOMAN'S TRUE SPHERE!!!! and at the gloomy end dropping short off into a gloomy grave, filled with smothered hopes, aspirations and longings for a life involving something beyond child bearing and housekeeping.[26]

According to this view, women could most effectively influence society for good when they escaped their traditional sphere. A writer in the *Alki* pointed out that "the time which the philanthropic woman spends in a round of charitable work had better be spent in helping to remove the causes which have made charitable institutions necessary."[27] More specifically, voting women would take the first steps toward doing away with prostitution, because self-respect and access to employment opportunities would follow the acquisition of political power. They also would improve the atmosphere not only of polling places but of politics generally and would take leadership in passing laws that would make homes and cities safer and cleaner.

Another reform often connected with woman suffrage was temperance. Some western suffragists, notably Duniway, insisted that the two should not be joined, that such cooperation invited the well-financed liquor interests to enlist in the ranks of the antis. She supported temperance and advocated education to achieve it but avoided linking it directly to suffrage. The well-organized suffrage campaigns of the 20th century, on the other hand, usually sought to recruit prohibition sympathizers and to utilize the organizational network of the Woman's Christian Temperance Union.

Experience in Wyoming, Utah, Colorado, and Idaho soon demonstrated that miraculous results did not follow automatically after women began to vote. However, suffrage supporters found positive outcomes of women's voting in those states and pointed them out in their papers. The president of the Nevada State Suffrage Association told those attending the 1897 state convention in a speech carried by the *Nevada Citizen* that suffrage had worked well in Wyoming, evidence that its adoption elsewhere would improve society. Under the heading "Woman Suffrage a Success," the *Alki* reprinted extracts from letters written by political leaders of three western states. The governor of Kansas wrote, "There has been no complaint"; the governor of Colorado, in a more positive vein, stated, "Their advent into political life will positively and permanently benefit all the people"; the chief justice of Wyoming asserted, "It has been tried and not found wanting."[28]

The contention that women would civilize the barbarous world of politics answered the fear expressed by the antis that participation in that world would degrade women, that the crowded, rough polling places would contaminate them. An early *Woman's Exponent* editorial, for example, predicted that women's presence would exert a refining influence on politics:

The fact that the motives of women are purer, their sentiments more refined and elevated than those of men, should be sufficient testimony that the right of suffrage ought to be conceded to them. Not that they may teach more wisdom by their superior intelligence, but that they may exert their more beneficient [*sic*] and chaste influences in endeavoring to purify the social atmosphere.[29]

The social benefits of suffrage might even include curing women of some of the bad habits that lack of responsibility had allowed them to develop, according to Carrie Fisher Young, editor of the *Woman's Pacific Coast Journal*. She lectured in Idaho in 1872, echoing what she had written in her paper when she said that "frivolity and extravagance among women could be remedied by making them responsible for their own debts and support." The first step toward this desirable end would be giving women the vote.[30]

Arguments for the vote as a means to economic justice emphasized a kind of personal feminism. Duniway particularly insisted that enfranchisement would cure the economic inequities between the sexes. She complained about the low wages paid women who had to work and stated that only political equality could ensure the equality of wages.[31] Such ills as women's exclusion from the professions and from high-paying jobs in general, their economic subordination in marriage, and their lack of opportunity for higher education could be alleviated by giving them the ballot.

Still, the natural rights arguments remained the firm foundation for all the others. Editors repeatedly invoked the ideals of the patriots of the country's revolutionary period to support their insistence that simple justice required that women vote. Phrases such as "government without consent of the governed" and "taxation without representation" appeared again and again.

Demonstrating their lack of concern with logical consistency, the editors overlooked arguments centered on equality for all when they pointed out women's superiority to many men who had the vote, including the foreign born and blacks. In the *Coming Century*, Duniway reprinted an interview with national suffrage leader Susan B. Anthony in which Anthony blamed naturalized citizens for defeat of suffrage in several states. Duniway added, "We have learned the hopelessness of appealing to the ballot[-]armed ignorance of foreign countries to secure the enfranchisement of intelligent American womanhood." The movement must appeal, she continued, to men who are "righteously and chivalrously indignant when American women are denied the exercise of their inalienable rights by the brutal ignorance of foreign votes." If editors noticed the conflict between the idea of voting as a natural right and the implication that not everyone could be trusted with it, they did not call it to their readers' attention, even though, as an officer of the Equal Suffrage Club of Puyallup, Washington, wrote, equality "is the great plan upon which our nation is founded."[32]

Conclusion

The editors of the western woman suffrage papers came to journalism not as a professional goal but as a means to the end of winning the vote for women. The early papers, especially, spoke for an outsider's point of view. Although they upheld the prevalent ideals of Victorian womanhood, they stepped outside societal norms to crusade for women's right to vote. Only in the 20th century, when capitulation of the last holdout states neared, could the publications claim to speak for a majority of the population.

As outsiders, the suffrage editors faced ridicule and harassment, of themselves and of their papers. The establishment press often used reports of suffrage meetings as an excuse to poke fun at the suffragists. In 1872, for example, the *San Francisco Chronicle* used the headline "Cluck, Cluck, Cluck" over its report of the state suffrage convention and began its description of the convention as follows:

With a pair of boots that almost reflected his own reflections the *Chronicle* reporter tramped into the hall of the suffragists. He was not quite prepared for so small a showing for so great a title. The Pacific Coast Woman Suffrage, Equal Rights, Patent Back-action and Universal Brass-heeled, Dolly Varden Convention had been advertised to consider grave questions of State, and take measures to prevent the further encroachment of the monster man upon the preserves of its constituency.[33]

Perhaps the greatest problem faced by the editors was obtaining the means to keep their papers going. They canvassed their communities looking for subscribers and advertisers, sometimes taking advantage of speaking engagements in other cities and states to plead for support. In their papers, they not only sought to recruit new readers but often offered premiums such as free subscriptions to other periodicals or, in the case of the *Woman's Exponent* of Utah, a portrait suitable for framing of Lucy Mack Smith, mother of Mormon prophet Joseph Smith. Such bonuses might go either to new subscribers themselves or to those who signed up specified numbers of new subscribers. Abigail Scott Duniway chided readers for their lack of support:

We do feel abused, and insist that we have a right to say so, when suffragists, many of whom, as in Washington Territory, have received their liberties mainly through these efforts, and many others, as in Oregon, who owe their property rights and whatever of fame they have gained to the influence of this journal, withhold from it their support. We confess that we do feel abused and outraged when they let their subscriptions expire unless personally solicited to renew them, and they often even then...make some other vain and vapid excuse to "let go."[34]

Despite such difficulties, the editors persevered. While their papers generally had short lives, suffragists maintained faith in the power of the press, and major campaigns brought new publications to celebrate "both the togetherness of this community and its apartness from larger society," as stated in an article about suffrage periodicals as community builders.[35]

It is impossible to demonstrate conclusively the total impact of the papers, but one can conclude with some degree of confidence that they played a major role and assess possible areas of influence. One goal of the papers was to win support for suffrage from the uncommitted or opposed. Because readers generally came from the ranks of those already converted, it is unlikely that the papers achieved notable success in this aim. Even the educational purpose of providing exposure to ideas and issues that the popular press overlooked or distorted probably did not function among the unconverted. Still, the suffrage papers gave the establishment press something to react to, and even a negative reaction at least kept the issue alive.

The fact that the movement could support publications at all must have lent it some substantiality in the eyes of the general public, and over time the public caught up with the suffragists, as their ideas penetrated mainstream thinking. Suffrage campaigns succeeded when they became mass movements among middle-class women. By adding the force of the printed word to the speeches and conversations of the suffragists and by providing ammunition for their proselytizing efforts, the papers promoted growth of middle-class support.

They also articulated and refined the ideas that became the bulwarks of the suffrage cause. The most basic and prevalent of these relied on the characterization of suffrage as a natural right whose extension to women simple justice required. The editors added to this natural rights appeal, according to their own preferences and the temper of the times, arguments that emphasized either women's need for dignity and independence or the benefits that enfranchised women would bring to society.

Perhaps most important—in both ideas and action—the papers provided suffragists a solid base from which to extend their efforts. A paper lent prestige to the cause among the committed and among the general public. It boosted morale and offered information and support, enabling readers to celebrate victories and move on after defeats. It urged action and suggested exactly what that action might be. It provided a means of personal and organizational communication among suffragists at local, state, and national levels. The papers led the way in the campaigns for suffrage wherever they were published. They helped develop ideas and organizations. They provided a forum for a cause espoused at first only by a few outsiders and helped them work their way toward full participation in the political life of their cities, states, and nation.

Notes

1. The standard histories of the suffrage movement, such as Eleanor Flexner's *Century of Struggle* (Cambridge, Mass.: Harvard University Press, 1975) and *One Half the People,* by Anne Firor Scott and Andrew MacKay Scott (Urbana: University of Illinois Press, 1982) concentrate on the national organizations and their work in the East. The multivolume *History of Woman Suffrage,* edited by Elizabeth Cady Stanton, Susan B. Anthony, Matilda Joslyn Gage, and Ida Husted Harper (1881-1922; New York: Arno and *The New York Times,* 1969) provides some details about the suffrage movements in individual western states. Beverly Beeton's *Women Vote in the West: The Woman Suffrage Movement 1869-1896* (New York: Garland, 1986) covers the entire region, and various articles and theses examine the coming of suffrage to individual western states. *A Voice of Their Own:The Woman Suffrage Press, 1840–1910,* edited by Martha M. Solomon (Tuscaloosa: University of Alabama Press, 1991), contains only one chapter on a western publication. Abigail Scott Duniway is the only western suffrage editor who has received more than passing attention.

2. The states included in this study, with years they adopted woman suffrage, are Arizona, 1912; California, 1911; Colorado, 1893; Idaho, 1896; Montana, 1914; Nevada, 1914; New Mexico, 1920; Oregon, 1912; Utah, 1870 and 1896; Washington, 1910; Wyoming, 1869.

3. Lauren Kessler, *The Dissident Press: Alternative Journalism in American History* (Beverly Hills: Sage, 1984), 16.

4. "Our Paper and Ourselves," *Pioneer,* 13 November 1869, 1; "Salutatory," *Sunday Mercury,* 24 January 1869, 2.

5. Stanton, Anthony, and Gage, *History of Woman Suffrage* 3:769.

6. "The Coming Century," *Coming Century,* 2 December 1891, 9.

7. Untitled note, *Coming Century*, 1 January 1892, 8.

8. "Publisher's Announcement," "Editor's Announcement," and "Salutatory," *Pacific Empire*, 16 August 1895, 1.

9. "Our Array of Backers," *Pacific Empire*, 3 October 1895, back cover.

10. "A Trip on the St. Paul, Minneapolis & Manitoba Railway," *Queen Bee*, 7 November 1888, 1.

11. Untitled editorial, *Colorado Antelope*, October 1879, 2; untitled note, *Queen Bee*, 2 July 1884, 1.

12. Caroline Nichols Churchill, *Active Footsteps* (Colorado Springs: Mrs. C.N. Churchill, 1909), 213-14.

13. Churchill, *Active Footsteps*, 81.

14. "Object," *Nevada Citizen*, June 1897, 2.

15. Untitled filler, *Nevada Citizen*, June 1897, 3.

16. Stanton, Anthony, and Gage, *History of Woman Suffrage*, 3:717-25.

17. "From Idaho to California," *Woman's Pacific Coast Journal*, June 1870, 23.

18. The Edmunds-Tucker Bill disenfranchised all women in Utah territory in 1887.

19. Aileen S. Kraditor, *The Ideas of the Woman Suffrage Movement, 1890-1920* (New York: Columbia University Press, 1965).

20. Other *New Northwest* arguments: that the ballot was needed for women's own protection, with 18 mentions; that enfranchised women would benefit society, 17 mentions; and that suffrage would enhance feminine qualities, 9 mentions. Lauren Kessler presented these figures in "A Siege of the Citadels" and "The Ideas of Woman Suffrage and the Mainstream Press," *Oregon Historical Quarterly* 84 (summer and fall 1983): 117-49, 257-75.

21. Ronald Schaffer, "The Problem of Consciousness in the Woman Suffrage Movement: A California Perspective," *Pacific Historical Review* 45 (1976): 469-93.

22. "Woman's State Suffrage Association," *Saturday Evening Mercury*, 14 August 1869, 1.

23. "The New Woman," *Nevada Citizen*, June 1897, 3.

24. "An Overshadowing Question," *New Northwest*, 23 January 1879, 2.

25. "Progress," *Sunday Mercury*, 10 July 1869, 1.

26. "Convention Proceedings," *Pioneer*, 27 June 1872, 8; Prentice Mulford, "Brute Strength, Man's Wisdom. Mr. Axtell's Wisdom. Women Content with Shopworn Sops! Woman's Sphere," *Saturday Evening Mercury*, 4 September 1869, 1.

27. "'Woman's Wisest Policy' Reviewed," *Alki*, 15 April 1895, 3-4.

28. "Address of State President, Mrs. Elda A. Orr," *Nevada Citizen*, December 1897, 4; "Woman Suffrage a Success," *Alki*, 15 April 1895, 5.

29. "Why Women Should Vote," *Woman's Exponent,* 1 August 1872, 36.

30. A newspaper report of her speech is quoted in T.A. Larson, "The Woman's Rights Movement in Idaho," *Idaho Yesterdays,* spring 1972, 4.

31. "Opportunities for Working Women," *New Northwest,* 5 November 1875, 2.

32. "No Need to Worry," *Coming Century,* 2 December 1891, 9; "Organized Opposition," *Alki,* 15 April 1895, 8.

33. "Cluck, Cluck, Cluck," *San Francisco Chronicle,* 19 June 1872, 3.

34. "Record of a Year's Work," *New Northwest,* 16 December 1886, 1.

35. Linda Steiner, "Finding Community in Nineteenth Century Suffrage Periodicals," *American Journalism* 1 (summer 1983): 4. This article uses eastern suffrage periodicals to support the idea that the papers created and sustained a sense of community among their readers.

10

The "Mormon Problem" and the Press

David A. Copeland

Because we hold it for a "fundamental and undeniable truth," that religion, or the duty which we owe to our creator, and the manner of discharging it, can be directed only by reason and conviction and not by force or violence. The religion, then, of every man, must be left to the conviction and conscience of every man; and it is the right of every man to exercise it as these may dictate. This right, is, in its nature, an unalienable right.

—James Madison, 1785[1]

When James Madison, the Bill of Rights author, applied the above thoughts on religious freedom to parchment, he was merely recording the feelings of most Americans in the formative days of the United States.[2] This "unalienable right" of worship eventually transformed itself into the first clause of the First Amendment of the Bill of Rights. That clause, taken at face value, appears straightforward and easy to understand. "Congress shall make no law respecting an establishment of religion, or prohibiting the free exercise thereof,"[3] but interpreting the limits of free exercise and restrictions on establishment has kept the courts busy since the first exercise clause case, *Reynolds v. United States*,[4] was decided by the United States Supreme Court in January 1879.

The *Reynolds* case asked the Court to decide whether the practice of polygamy, as practiced by members of the Church of Jesus Christ of the Latter-Day Saints, better known as Mormons, was a form of the free exercise of religion protected by the First Amendment. A unanimous Court ruled that plural marriages, even if they were perceived to be part of the exercise of religion, violated part of a valid congressional law, the Morrill Act, and could not be permitted. There can be no doubt that the Mormons, founded by Joseph Smith in the 1820s, evoked hostility from the communities in which they lived. Mormons were immediately considered outsiders because of their religious practices, which included strenuous efforts to proselytize "gentiles" (non-Mormons),[5] varied from the accepted tenets of mainline American religions. Most Mormons in the formative years of the religion had come from mainstream American religions, but now they accepted values that were superstitious and repugnant to most Americans.

Mormonism took on un-American connotations in the 1830s because of its claim of divine revelations and because Mormons were seen as agitators of Native American and slave populations.[6] Only outsiders—enemies of the United States—would attempt to stir up and befriend these two groups, especially the Indians. Mormons were, as a Missouri writer described them in 1837 a "mass of human corruption," a "tribe of locusts, that still threatens to scorch and wither the herbage of a fair and goodly portion of Missouri by the swarm of emigrants from their pestilent hive in Ohio and New York."[7]

When the Mormons unveiled polygamy as a part of their religious practice in 1841, they further enhanced their outsider status. Polygamy had long been considered anathema by American religious beliefs and by law. Because of their religious practices and the perceptions of them portrayed in the writings of the day, Mormons were herded along a bloody trail from New York to Illinois, to Missouri, and eventually to the "State of Deseret," Utah. As outsiders to American values and beliefs of the period, Mormons were pushed outside the borders of the United States into Mexican territory and attacked by the American press.

For the Supreme Court, the Mormon question in *Reynolds* turned on laws that, it said, were "made for the government of actions, and while they cannot interfere with mere religious belief and opinions, they may with practices."[8] The Morrill Act limited practice; that decision remains constitutionally valid.[9] For America's press, "The Mormon Problem," as many papers referred to the Mormons and their peculiar religious practices, was how to deal with this religious group, its illegal practice, and the fear that Mormans and polygamy raised in many Americans.

An investigation into the way America's press treated Mormons is important because the press, more than any number of Supreme Court decisions, reveals the true sentiments of America concerning Mormons.[10] Such a look at the press and its dealings with Mormons also affirms John Lofton's findings that, "except when their own freedom was discernibly at stake, general circulation newspapers have tended to go along with efforts to suppress deviations from the prevailing political and social orthodoxies of their time and place rather than to support the right to dissent."[11] The slant of articles, the number of times Mormon issues appear in the papers, the frequency with which papers publish stories about bigamy trials, and the editorial biases speak to American prejudice and press callousness to First Amendment rights that do not directly affect them. There was little doubt that among 19th-century American "gentiles," Mormon polygamy was religious anathema and morally corrupt. This chapter will describe the American opinion of Mormons and the press at the same time. The goal is not to determine whether Reynolds was deserving of First Amendment protection but to observe the press's reaction to the Supreme Court decision and Mormons in general: how the 19th-century American press generally applauded the unanimous decision against Mormons and viewed condescendingly a group that supported concepts mainline America rejected. That the press reacted negatively to an outsider group like Mormons explains much about the press's resistance to support of First Amendment rights and why many of these groups found it necessary to create their own news sources. To observe the press's reaction to Mormons, polygamy, and *Reynolds v. United States*, representative daily papers from the nation will be reviewed. The *New York Times* represents the Northeast; the *Chicago Tribune*, the Midwest; the *Atlanta Daily Constitution*, the South and the *San Francisco Chronicle,* the West.[12] Papers will be searched to see the reaction to *Reynolds*, handed down on January 6, 1879, and the subsequent treatment of Mormons throughout the year.

The Mormons and Polygamy

Mormonism, as a religion, was the progeny of Joseph Smith.[13] In 1820, Smith claimed a series of heavenly visitations from God and Jesus that told him all existing churches were in error. The truth, Smith was told, would be revealed to him at a later date. That revelation, upon which Smith founded his new religion, came, he claimed, as a set of golden tablets he unearthed and later translated into English from a hieroglyphic text that spoke of God's prophet, Mormon, and his son, who had come to North America and triumphed over evil.

Smith published the tablets' translation as the Book of Mormon in 1830, basing the Latter-Day Saints on that translation and the Bible. By the 1840s, Smith's religious amalgamation acquired a following, but unrest followed wherever the Mormons went. Persecution forced the Mormons to move from state to state, but they established themselves in Illinois long enough to build the city of Nauvoo into an establishment of 10,000 people. It was in Nauvoo that Smith and his brother, Hyrum, were arrested after Smith ordered the dissident Mormon newspaper, the Nauvoo *Expositor*, destroyed.[14] The two brothers died when an angry mob broke into the jail in Carthage and gunned them down. The majority of the Mormons then moved westward under the guidance of Brigham Young settling in the Mexican territory of Utah in 1847. They named their new home the State of Deseret.

Of all the Mormon practices, the one that most angered their opponents was that of multiple marriages. Smith introduced this concept of plural marriages sometime in 1841 after he had received a "revelation from God," saying, "if he have ten virgins given unto him...he cannot commit adultery, for they belong to him, and they are given to him, therefore is he justified."[15] The Mormons did not make their practice of plural marriages publicly known until 1852, and the practice became a problem for the United States because the country had acquired Utah from Mexico in 1850.

Americans reacted vehemently to the practice of polygamy. Many saw it as an evil as abhorrent as slavery. In that context, Congress turned its attention from the Civil War just long enough in 1862 to pass the Morrill Act, which included this language concerning polygamy:

[E]very person having a husband or wife living, who shall marry any other person, whether married or single, in a Territory of the United States... shall...be adjudged guilty of bigamy, and, upon conviction thereof, shall be punished by a fine not exceeding five hundred dollars, and by imprisonment not exceeding five years.[16]

America's postwar presidents, Grant and Hayes, condemned polygamy and the practices of the Mormon church. Even though Congress made polygamy illegal in the territories with the Morrill Act and presidents condemned the practice, the Civil War and Reconstruction absorbed most of the nation's energy in the years following the outlawing of polygamy. More than a decade passed before any Mormon polygamy case came before the courts. When George Reynolds, a personal secretary to Brigham Young, agreed to carry his plural marriage to court, the Mormons and the nation had a "test case" to determine the validity of the polygamy law versus the religion clauses of the First Amendment.

Reynolds v. United States

On August 3, 1874, Reynolds married Amelia Jane Schofield; he had married Mary Ann Tuddenham on July 22, 1865.[17] The government charged Reynolds with violating the Morrill Act in October. In order to gain a conviction, the government subpoenaed Reynolds's second wife. Faced with being the wife of a bigamist or with being considered a woman living in an immoral relationship as a concubine, Amelia Jane testified to the plural marriage of her husband. The result was Reynolds's conviction for violating the Morrill Act. He appealed to the United States Supreme Court on a writ of error, and the Court accepted the case and heard arguments in November 1878.

In deciding the legal and religious ramifications of the case, Chief Justice Waite focused upon what provided the "true distinction between what properly belongs to the church and what to the state."[18] As a result, the unanimous Supreme Court decision said that "Congress was deprived of all legislative power over mere opinion, but was left free to reach actions that were in violation of social duties or subversive of good order."[19] The actions of the Mormons, the Court declared, were controllable. Plural marriages could be a religious belief but not an action:

Laws are made for the government of actions, and while they cannot interfere with mere religious belief and opinions, they may with practices. Suppose one believed that human sacrifices were a necessary part of religious worship, would it be seriously contended that the civil government under which he lived could not interfere to prevent a sacrifice? Or if a wife believed it was her duty to burn herself upon the funeral pile [sic] of her dead husband, would it be beyond the power of the civil government to prevent her carrying her belief into practice?[20]

Reynolds's lawyers countered by pointing out that polygamy was not prohibited by any moral code like the crimes of murder or theft. The belief in plural marriage and the practice of it were in no way offensive to the citizens of the Utah territory. Those citizens, the lawyers said, felt this was another example of legislative excess as the federal government attempted to control actions protected by the religion clauses of the First Amendment. Reynolds's lawyers took a different view of "unalienable right" and "Wall of Separation," as viewed through the free exercise of religion:

One who commits or abstains from an act under a belief that it is God's will that he should do so, is free from guilt.... [H]e cannot be criminally responsible, since guilty intent is not only consciously absent, but there is present a positive belief that the act complained of is lawful, and even acceptable to the Deity.[21]

The Court, however, said that if Utah belonged to the United States, its citizens would live by United States law. That meant that no plural marriages would be allowed. Chief Justice Waite asked, "Can a man excuse his practices to the contrary because of his religious belief?" The Chief Justice provided his own answer: "To permit this would be to make the professed doctrines of religious belief superior to the law of the land, and in effect to permit every citizen to become a law unto himself. Government could exist only in name under such circumstances."[22] The practice of polygamy was illegal, and no amount of protestation under a First Amendment rationale would change that fact. The testing of the Morrill Act ended, and Reynolds began his two-year prison sentence.

The Press Deals with Mormons, 1830-78

America's press found plural marriages "odious" and considered polygamy a detested crime. In 1878 and 1879, the *New York Times* published 87 stories about plural marriage court cases, and the count did not include coverage of Reynolds. But America's press coverage of the Mormons did not begin with *Reynolds v. United States*. Joseph Smith's golden tablets evoked press notice in Palmyra, New York, in 1829. The town's paper, the *Reflector*, made derogatory references about Smith's "Golden Bible."[23] With the murder of Smith and his brother Hyrum, the press launched an informational deluge about the Latter-Day Saints. The murders received front-page coverage in hundreds of United States papers.[24] The accounts of the accused Mormon-murderers, even in religious newspapers, allowed the readers to feel as though they were a part of the trial scene. "Every body almost attending court comes armed to the teeth, and frequently muskets and rifles will be seen taken out of wagons with as much deliberation as if they were attending a militia muster instead of attending a court of justice."[25]

The national reaction to Mormons, specifically plural marriages, manifested itself in the Republican platform in the 1856 presidential election. As the party constructed the platform for its candidate, John C. Frémont, it called for the eradication of the "twin relics of barbarism," slavery and polygamy, and in effect declared war on both.[26] The nation turned its attention to the issue of slavery, spent four years in war and another twelve in Reconstruction, before focusing upon the second of the relics, polygamy. Yet even in the midst of the threats of civil war, the Nashville *Daily News* could turn away from the national attacks on slavery to slander Mormons:

[T]he Mormons call their wives their cattle; they choose them pretty much as they choose their cattle.... Incest is common. Sometimes the same man has a daughter and her mother for wives at once. The ill-assorted children—the offspring of one father and many mothers—run about like so many wild animals ... and are fit to steal, rob and murder emigrants.[27]

In the middle of the Civil War, the Morrill Act of 1862 provided the legislation the country needed to see to it that polygamy might perish like slavery. After freeing itself of the Civil War and Reconstruction, the country began its move toward polygamy's eradication.

Even though the nation knew of the Mormon practice of polygamy and universally detested it, Mormons were for the most part tucked safely away from view in the Utah Territory. But even before the Civil War, the press warned that "the Mormons are preparing to emigrate."[28] As the Mormons carried their religion outside the territories, polygamy became more of a problem. The *New York Times* related Mormon movements on a regular basis, even before the Reynolds Supreme Court decision, much like troop movements.[29] When the Court heard arguments in the case, beginning November 14, 1878, the coverage and printed assault on Mormons commenced in earnest. On November 15, the *Times* reported the case from the Supreme Court, giving the arguments presented by Reynolds's lawyer Ben Sheeks and by Attorney General Charles Devens. Devens's rebuttal was termed "eloquent and impressive," and an editorial of November 16 titled "Is Polygamy a Crime?" presented the issue at stake in the case. "Has the United States any constitutional right to prohibit polygamy in the Territories?" The Mormons, the editorial maintained, felt that it was no one's business if a man had one or 20 wives so long as his actions were based upon honestly held religious beliefs. The *Times*, however, felt that such claims for religious protection were outweighed by morals and national conviction:

If polygamy is a crime against moral order and the well-being of society, no amount of alleged religious consecration can, or should, sanctify it. And, if it be once admitted that any form of religious faith may be allowed to shield practices which are not crimes because they are not committed with evil intent against the rights of others, then the door is open to an infinite variety of evilness.

The press and Americans saw the question of Mormons and polygamy as an issue beyond First Amendment rights. In fact, no amount of First Amendment dickering could legitimize polygamy in the eyes of non-Mormon America. With the case presented to the Supreme Court, the nation waited for the only possible decision: the affirmation of Reynolds's guilt. That decision came in January 1879.

Cutting Out the Mormon Cancer: 1879

When the Court's decision in *Reynolds* was announced on January 6, the country anticipated the outcome. The Supreme Court decision against polygamy "will surprise no one—not even the Mormon hierarchy," the *San Francisco Chronicle* said in its editorial of January 8. Throughout 1879, the newspapers followed Mormons and polygamy.

Often they reported the further events that unfolded after the Reynolds decision. At other times, the papers printed editorials concerning the continuing saga of controlling polygamy in Utah and removing it from America. Rarely did letters appear, but when they did they were as negative as the editorials. In New York, the continued arrival of European immigrants, who were often Mormon converts,[30] concerned the editorial staff of *New York Times*. Twenty-five million Europeans arrived in America from 1815 to 1890, and most of them came through New York. Immigrants, especially those who advocated a practice as abhorrent and illegal as polygamy, represented a danger to the country, the *Times* intimated, when it claimed that the Mormons were attempting "to secure a permanent foundation for their little empire" by importing converts.[31] In San Francisco, the Mormons were a threat to the linkage of East and West because the railroad's connection of the two regions passed through the Utah Territory, according to the San *Francisco Chronicle*. In Georgia, the *Atlanta Daily Constitution,* among all other papers, dealt most favorably with the Mormons until the murder of a Mormon missionary. The papers did not let the Mormon problem die in 1879.

When the *New York Times* broke the story of *Reynolds v. United States* on January 7, it did so in its general coverage of the Supreme Court. The case was not even the first listed. The report presented only the facts and drew no inferences. In San Francisco, the *Chronicle* did the same and on January 11 ran the full text of the decision as it "relates to the prisoner's plea of religious belief and to the constitutional power." The *Chicago Tribune*'s article was written in a similarly objective fashion. In the *Tribune*'s words:

This Court, in a long and carefully-prepared opinion, delivered by the Chief Justice, holds that polygamy is not under the protection of the clause of the Federal Constitution which prohibits interference with religious belief; that a plea of religious conviction is not a valid defense; that Congress did not step outside the limits of its constitutional powers, in passing the law for suppression of polygamy in Utah.[32]

Even though each paper reported the facts of the trial in an unbiased manner, editorials accompanied the decision or followed it by a day. These editorials revealed the feelings of the press toward Mormons. With the decision, the consensus among the press and nation was that Mormonism might survive, but "this degrading practice [of polygamy] cannot be very long-lived."[33] The press wasted no time in applauding the unanimous Supreme Court decision as one that would protect the nation.

Of all the initial reactions to *Reynolds*, none was more caustic than that of the *San Francisco Chronicle*. Its page-one opinion on the Mormons following the announcement of *Reynolds* referred to polygamy as "the Mormon ulcer, fattening itself on the intermural basin." But even a Supreme Court decision, the paper stated, might not be enough. The *Chronicle* speculated that the only way to solve "the Mormon Problem" might be by the sword "to cut at last the Mormon cancer out of our sunset shoulder."[34]

Reynolds called into question Congress's right to create a law that might violate the religious clauses of the First Amendment, and the initial editorials addressed the problem. The *New York Times, San Francisco Chronicle,* and *Chicago Tribune* did dispute the decision. "It is to the credit of the American people that the highest judicial tribunal of the nation has decided, with the unanimous concurrence of the Judges, that polygamy is unlawful in the Territory of Utah as well as in other portions of this country," the *Tribune* declared.[35] The *Times* addressed the issue more directly:

It was alleged that the Constitution of the United States expressly prohibited any interference with polygamy, as a religious rite, in the clause which declares that "Congress shall make no law respecting an establishment of religion, or prohibiting the free exercise thereof." ...George Reynolds, in his defense, claimed that the United States statute of 1862 was a direct contravention of the above-quoted clause of the Constitution.... [It] merely extended over the Territories the common law in relation to bigamy which exists in every state in the Union.[36]

The *San Francisco Chronicle* saw the argument as one of fundamental rights in society. Society disdained polygamy; its practice by Mormons, therefore, had no First Amendment rights. "[T]he right of Congress to legislate for the protection of the fundamental principles of society," the *Chronicle* said, "cannot be abridged by the Mormon claim of religious belief, any more than it could by the claim of certain other religious beliefs that human sacrifices are necessary."[37]

Editors of these papers expressed no doubts that the Mormon claim of First Amendment protection for plural marriages was unjustifiable. The *New York Times* went on to drive home the point with another editorial six months later. In an editorial titled "Law and Conscience," the paper paralleled the actions of murder and polygamy as evil actions that some were trying to sanction under the guise of religious exercise.

The right of individual and religious opinion is just now very strenuously insisted upon in this country. Anything may be done in the name of religion. In Pocassett, Mass., for example, a child was killed by its father, who insisted that he had received a divine command to offer up his offspring as a sacrifice. In Utah, the Mormons contend that they have divine warrant, if not divine injunction, to marry as many wives as each man may choose to take unto himself....

According to the laws of the land, the Freemans, of Pocasset[t], are guilty of murder. The Utah Mormons, under the law are amenable for the crime of polygamy.... The plea of the Mormons is precisely like that of the Pocassett murderers.... [P]olygamy is commanded by divine revelation; that the Constitution forbids the enactment of any law prohibiting the free exercise of religion, and that legal interference with polygamy, as practiced by the Mormon Church, is an unconstitutional invasion of the rights of conscience....

This is precisely the argument, with a change of terms, which would be advanced by the Pocassett child slayers.... Such delusions as these can only be cured by an application of the severest remedy.[38]

As the newspapers in New York, Chicago, and San Francisco applauded *Reynolds* and condemned polygamy, Atlanta readers were treated to a watered-down version of the above. How could the purveyors of the first removed branch of the "twin relics of barbarism" be totally hostile to the purveyors of the second? Even if Southerners detested polygamy, the temperament of a nation twenty years prior made Southerners and Mormons strange bedfellows in the 1870s. Republicans and others in 1850s America had cast the basis of southern society, slavery, into the pot with Mormon polygamy. The South detested the manner in which the rest of the nation had attempted to dictate its way of life, and consequently, southern congressmen joined together to filibuster against the first attempts to pass the Morrill Act prior to the Civil War. Its passage could have led to limiting slavery, as well as polygamy, in the territories,[39] so it was not totally out of character for the *Atlanta Daily Constitution* to offer caution in its initial remarks concerning *Reynolds* and polygamy.

The Atlanta paper first acknowledged the *Reynolds* decision on January 10. Its editorial carried a sympathetic plea for the innocent women and children who would be hurt by the enforcement of the Morrill Act.

Were this law fully enforced, a good part of the Mormon population would be sent to prison, their children declared illegal, their wives concubines, and their property seized in judgment of fines against them.... The problem involves the stoppage of polygamy without the infliction of unnecessary hardship, and this includes questions very difficult of treatment. For example, shall plural wives of to-day [*sic*] and their offspring be cut off from sharing in the estates of their Mormon husbands? They are the victims of polygamy, and the law as it stands is merciless towards them.[40]

The *Daily Constitution* understood the trials that many Mormons were about to face, since it represented Southerners who had experienced the hardships of the expurgation of one of the "twin relics." Although the paper had to put its empathy aside and admit "polygamy must be discountenanced" and its "growth at least, must be stopped," the *Daily Constitution* offered a solution to the dilemma that would protect its victims. Let those who are already a part of a plural marriage continue, and then in the case of further plural marriages, "[l]et the law in such cases be enforced to the letter."

Two weeks later, the paper supported its position in another editorial: "60,000 women are in danger of becoming husbandless in one blow, and several times that number of innocent children legally fatherless."[41] The editorial did not lay blame for "The Mormon Problem" on Joseph Smith, Brigham Young, or any of the Latter-Day Saints. Instead, it blamed the country for its permissive attitude:

The country is brought face to face with a problem of gigantic proportions as a natural and just penalty of its neglect in the past. It has permitted polygamy to go on gathering strength, until it has become uncertain whether the evil has not become permanent and impregnable.... The further we go in this matter, the more fully we see what a maze of difficulties our remissness in the past has gotten us into.[42]

With this editorial, however, the southern newspaper began to divorce itself from "twin relic" status. "We have permitted an institution to grow up in the heart of the country that is an offense to all civilized society; we freely admit the wickedness of polygamy; we heartily desire its extinction."[43] The *Daily Constitution* wanted to bring polygamy to an end, but it wanted to do it at the least expense to those this law would harm.

The Mormon problem for all purposes dropped from the *Atlanta Daily Constitution*'s pages and interests for seven months after its January editorials. It arose again following the July 21 Whitfield County, Georgia, murder of Mormon missionary Joseph Standing. Standing, who worked with the Cherokees, was, according to Mormon testimony, abducted and shot in the head as he attempted to escape his captors.[44] Outraged at this event, the editorial page of the *Constitution* declared:

The last exhibition of mob violence in Georgia, the killing of Joseph Standing, the Mormon, was absolutely and utterly without excuse, and should be condemned and punished. The governor has ordered his proclamation for reward for the capture of these murderers, and chances are that they will be brought before the courts.[45]

Outrage turned into disgust for Standing when a page-one story on Sunday, August 24, revealed "the other side of the story" concerning the Mormon missionary. In a "special" to the paper entitled "A Lustful Lout," the *Constitution* reported the account of a man, supposedly of God, who converted the wife of the man with whom he was boarding and his two daughters to Mormonism, and impregnated one of the daughters. In addition, the article alleged:

[W]e are pained to say that his intimacy with women was not by any means confined to this one family. Some three or four, if not more, young ladies living in the vicinity of Varnell's station, whose names we prefer not now to mention, met with their ruin by this man; one of the young ladies is the daughter of one of the murderers. Nor does this tale stop here, as he has caused trouble in several families by being too intimate with their wives, and trying to get them to adhere to the Mormon faith and persuading them to emigrate to the Mormon country.

Although the *Constitution*'s position on Mormons after the death of Standing changed to disgust for the group, the paper originally had proposed temperance for the Latter-Day Saints in the weeks following the *Reynolds* decision. That call for temperance held little sway with the other papers. As the major Mormon events of 1879 unfolded, the papers continued their attack aimed at the eradication of polygamy. At times, however, it seemed the eradication of Mormonism was the aim. On January 20, Mormons, led by Brigham Young's two daughters, marched to the Capitol to speak to the House Judiciary Committee on behalf of the women and children soon to be without legal husband or father. A *Chicago Tribune* letter addressed this problem of being "outcasts" and "illegitimate": "To all the world beside they are that now, and no more disgrace, nor as much, would attach to those women when separated from their so-called husbands."[46] The *New York Times* was even more hostile than the Chicago letter writer: "[T]hese whining hypocrites implore us not to take away their women, brand them with dishonor, and declare their offspring illegitimate."[47] While the *New York Times* and *Chicago Tribune* were reporting on Mormon activity in the East, the *San Francisco Chronicle* kept tabs on western action. Mormons all over Utah met to denounce the Supreme Court justices as "hellhounds," and to affirm that polygamy would continue.[48]

By summer, Mormons had gathered 20,000 signatures to send to President Hayes asking for a way around *Reynolds*. The *San Francisco Chronicle* was fearful that Hayes and the cabinet might seriously consider the proposal. "No Christian Cabinet in the world would for a moment entertain such a prayer...yet...Mr. Hayes and his Cabinet really entertain the polygamist petition." The *Chronicle* continued, "It is humiliating to be forced to write, but there is the fact; and in these stupid times...it will not be surprising should the Cabinet recommend that Reynolds' sentence be considerably weakened ... if not altogether changed under the President's pardoning power."[49] The *Chicago Tribune* had more confidence in the president: "Executive interference to save this polygamist would undoubtedly be construed as an intimidation that the law will be treated as a dead-letter."[50]

The worry at the *San Francisco Chronicle* and *Chicago Tribune* arose because Reynolds's lawyers had petitioned the Court concerning the sentence, which required service at hard labor. The Morrill Act never mentioned the terms of the prison sentence, and many Americans feared that this oversight might be reason enough to overturn the sentence. Their fears subsided when the *New York Times* reported on June 19 that Reynolds had reached the federal penitentiary in Omaha.[51] Reynolds did not stay in the Nebraska prison, however. Without warning, the government sent Reynolds to the federal prison in Utah, and the fears that Democrats or Republicans had struck a deal with the Latter-Day Saints rose. The *New York Times* reminded its readers of Mormon claims: "This is an unexpected turn of affairs, in view of the boast of Brigham Young, repeated since by Mormon leaders, that Mormon money could bribe any officer of the federal Government, from a Territorial Judge to the presidential chair."[52]

The politics—and economics—of the Mormons in Utah affected the way the *Chronicle* looked at the Mormon problem as much as a dislike for polygamy. The paper made that fact quite obvious from the start. California's rapid growth after the gold rush of 1848-49 led to statehood in 1850. With the completion of the transcontinental railroad in 1869, the *San Francisco Chronicle* was very much aware that the days of Reconstruction had given way to a Democratic Congress that might be willing, for the sake of the party, to grant Utah statehood for the promise of a Democratic vote in the next election.[53] On the day before former President Grant visited San Francisco, the *Chronicle* ran an editorial on the potential alliance between Democrats and Mormons:

The latest plan of our polygamous neighbors of Utah to get that Territory into the Union as a State, is for an alliance with the Bourbon Democracy...by the addition of two Senators to their strength in the Senate and three electoral votes in the next Presidential election. The Democrats on their part are expected to concede the question of polygamy to the new State.[54]

The *Chronicle* feared the power that states' rights would give the Mormons. The economic repercussions to California could be disastrous if the Mormons ever decided to shut down the portion of the railroad that passed through Utah in order to gain a bargaining chip for plural marriages. Speaking in allegorical terms, the *Chronicle* referred to the Pacific Railway as the "shaft" of the arrow and its "chief feather" as Salt Lake City. Mormons controlled Californians' welfare and "the most important mining region on the planet."[55]

Because Utah and the Mormons played such a vital role in the welfare of California, the *San Francisco Chronicle* was willing to urge war to ensure the rail lines would remain open.[56] The *Chronicle* also feared the ever-increasing spread of Mormons into other territories and the possibility of their emigration into California. Consequently, the newspaper printed numerous controversial accounts concerning Mormons. In one of them, Idaho resident James Dwiggins was run off his property by his Mormon son-in-law and left naked to be butchered by Idaho Indians. Dwiggins chose to face the Indians instead of a Mormon lynch mob. Dwiggins's wife, who moved to San Francisco, forfeited the property to her son rather than become a Mormon.[57] In October, the *Chronicle* published "Mormon Mysteries Revealed," a "full expose of the 'sealing' process in the Salt Lake City Endowment House." Included in this revelation were the promises made at marriage. "You swear to obey the Mormon laws in preference to the laws of the United States on pain of having your throat cut from ear to ear and your tongue cut out" headed the list.[58] More than any other newspaper, the *San Francisco Chronicle* feared the potential for disaster that the Mormons could inflict upon its home state. Polygamy and the *Reynolds* case provided the perfect tool to attack the group legally.

As the gateway to America for European immigrants, New York City and the *Times* understood the potential benefits—and harm—that immigrants held for the country. From 1815 to 1860, 10 million Europeans entered America; another 15 million, again mostly through New York City, followed in the next thirty years. Eighty percent of these immigrants remained in the Northeastern part of the United States, and New York City was forced to find a way to welcome, register, and relocate these newcomers.[59] By the 1850s, foreigners accounted for half of the city's population, and a growing backlash against them known as nativism began to focus on the religion of the immigrant. Roman Catholics, considered conspirators in plans to rid the world of Protestants "on the ancient and profligate altar of Rome," were described as "inferior in intelligence and virtue to the American people."[60] Jews were the special target of hatred. Signs such as "No Jews or Dogs Admitted Here"[61] were not exceptions.

Considering these forms of bigotry, the city's negative reaction to the arrival of European Mormons was not surprising. What set Mormons apart from Jews or Catholics was that Mormons wanted to proselytize the nation's citizenry and advocated breaking federal law and social decency with the "disgusting feature of their faith," polygamy.[62] The *New York Times* saw in the microcosm of immigration into New York City the potential danger for the nation and warned, "[T]hose who think that the Mormon leaders are depressed, or relaxing their efforts, to secure a permanent foundation for their little empire, deceive themselves."[63] The emigration from Europe of Mormons, converted by missionaries, only added more troops for the fight, the *Times* speculated, so it reported the arrival of these immigrants in methodic fashion.

When ships from Europe arrived, the *New York Times* ran stories such as "The First Batch of Mormons," which reported 138 Mormons on a boat with 315 immigrants.[64] That the *Times* ran these reports with the focus on Mormons is significant. It supports the assertion that Mormons were a danger to America greater than that of any other immigrant group. In June, the *Times* proclaimed "Mormon Recruits" in its headline, but Mormons were anything but the majority of those on board. "Eleven hundred and six immigrants were landed at Castle Garden yesterday.... One hundred and twenty-eight of the *Wyoming*'s passengers were Mormon converts."[65] As if the Mormons, who comprised less than 12 percent of the passengers were the only ones on the *Wyoming,* the account commented only on the Latter-Day Saint immigrants. "Several of the women were good-looking.... No man among them had more than one wife.... They report three more batches as about to sail."[66] That last "batch" of Mormons arrived in New York on October 28, 1879, and the *Times* announced it the following day.

As the *New York Times* kept its head count on Mormon immigrants, it supported President Hayes's plan to request European aid to curtail Mormon emigration. In August, the paper reported a circular from the United States government to European governments asking that they keep Mormons from leaving their respective countries. The *Times*, however, knew the likely result of the request. "The offensive ulcer which they have so long cultivated must be removed, sooner or later. We have not much faith in the efficacy of diplomatic circulars sent forth to invoke the aid of foreign Governments."[67] The United States did not carry enough political clout in the world in 1879 to restrict Mormon immigration, and these immigrants, the *Times* figured, comprised the greater part of the estimated 200,000 Mormons in America.[68] As the *Times* reported, "Very few [Mormons], except the children born near Utah, are Americans, most of the adults having immigrated from Great Britain, Sweden, and the North of Europe."[69] Emigrating to America was one thing for Europeans; it was quite a different thing to bring and promote an outlawed practice like polygamy. That was a hostile act, not unlike an military invasion. The *New York Times* approached the Mormons in just that fashion.

Conclusion

James Madison may have seen the exercise of religion as an unalienable right in 1785, but America's newspapers in 1879 viewed the polygamy practiced by Mormons as an "ulcer" or "cancer" that justifiably must be removed. The fact that the Supreme Court agreed in *Reynolds v. United States* only supported the newspapers' outburst of disgust concerning polygamy and Mormons throughout the year. In 1879 the prevailing opinion was that Congress had the right to provide legislation for the best interests of society. That meant snuffing out the "odious" practice of polygamy, even if that abridged the religious belief in plural marriages that Mormons held as protected by the First Amendment. In addition, regional fears—both economic and political— added to the general dislike of Mormons. The fear that Mormons in Utah might cut off California from the rest of the nation spurred the *San Francisco Chronicle* to call for war, if necessary, to bring the Mormons into line. The *Chronicle* preferred the eradication of the Mormons to ensure railroad stability for itself and the Union Pacific. By 1879's end, "the peculiar institution of Mormonism," according to the paper, was worthy of sending the nation into war just as the "peculiar institution of slavery" had been in 1860.[70] The *New York Times*, because of the tremendous influx of immigrants and the potential threat Mormon immigrants provided, promoted stiff controls on the Mormons as well, but the *Times* proposed a strong treatment of cauterization rather than an all-out war. Quoting Dr. O.W. Holmes, the paper advocated a medical method recalled from earlier days—the application of the cauterizing iron. A mysterious disease at a girls' school quickly disappeared when the wise, old doctor produced the glowing iron rod. The *Times* felt *Reynolds* was the first application of the iron to the Mormons but proposed that "a few more such wholesome applications...will bring the law-breakers to their senses."[71] The mainline press of the 19th century simply refused to accept this group outside traditional beliefs.

Even though America opposed polygamy, it could not eliminate it even with the federal legislation.[72] Utah eventually outlawed the practice, and the territory became the 45th state in 1896. One hundred years after *Reynolds*, however, the best estimates counted 35,000 polygamists living in the western United States,[73] and as recently as April 1991, a practicing polygamist of 21 years with nine wives appeared on national television to say, "I know of no law that I'm violating."[74] The American press of 1879 wanted polygamy excised from the fabric of the nation. Mormon claims of First Amendment protection were irrelevant, and, consequently, the press tossed such claims aside as soon as the *Reynolds* was handed down. As the *San Francisco Chronicle* said:

All their high talk about such a law interfering with the right of conscience and religion is chaff and nonsense, and the hypocritical cant of a pack of infamous scoundrels, who, for more than a quarter of a century, have been using the name of religion to face this and darker crimes.[75]

Polygamy survives without First Amendment protection, and *Reynolds* remains on the books as a valid interpretation of the Constitution. In the 19th century, Mormonism and polygamy were calls to banishment by America's government and by the majority of America's people. Being outside the mainstream of American beliefs and practices, as Latter-Day Saints learned, meant being an outcast to America's press as well.

Notes

1. James Madison, "A Memorial and Remonstrance on the Religious Rights of Man," in The *Papers of James Madison*, ed. Robert A. Rutland and William M.E. Rachal (Chicago: University of Chicago Press, 1973), 8:298.

2. As Madison and the other Constitutional Convention delegates carried the document back to their respective states for ratification in 1787, the call for a Bill of Rights arose immediately. In fact, had not the promise of one been given, the two largest states—Virginia and New York—would have balked at ratification. Virginia had passed "An Act for Establishing Religious Freedom," as written by Thomas Jefferson, in 1786, and religious freedom was utmost in many Americans' minds. Only a century had elapsed since the Act of Toleration's passage in England gave dissenters the right to openly practice their religion. Americans feared the possibility of a state church for the new

country. Congregationalism, the principal church of New England, and Anglicanism, the dominant church of the South in the colonial period, were likely choices. Madison corresponded with a number of religious leaders. One of them, John Leland, reminded Madison that as the Constitution presently stood, "Religious Liberty, is not sufficiently secured.... [I]t is Very Dangerous leaving Religious Liberty at their [the branches of government's] Mercy." "John Leland's Objections to the Constitution without a Bill of Rights" (1788), reproduced in William R. Estep, *Revolution within the Revolution* (Grand Rapids: Williams B. Eerdmans, 1990), 201. Jefferson also reminded Madison "[A] bill of rights is what the people are entitled to against every government on earth."

3. U.S. Constitution, amend. 1.

4. *Reynolds v. United States,* 98 U.S. 145 (1879).

5. Mormonism, born in a period of religious fervor and revival, had enough of its roots buried in Christian traditions that it appealed to some people who were disillusioned with mainline denominations. The move to Mormonism was not initially a radical step since many Americans were looking forward to a return and rule of Jesus on earth. The total devotion that Mormonism required appeared to be the proper avenue to ready oneself for that event. Since Mormons lived in relatively closed communities, they provided for all the needs of those in the group, much as the communal societies of the period like those at Oneida, New York. Unlike some other groups that were frowned upon by mainline Protestants, for Mormons proselytizing was an integral part of their religion. Much of this missionary zeal came from Mormonism's concept of celestial heaven. Works played an essential part in reaching this highest of three heavens, so becoming a missionary took on nearly mandatory characteristics.

6. Leonard J. Arrington and Davis Bitton, *The Mormon Experience: A History of the Latter-Day Saints* (New York: Alfred A. Knopf, 1979), 46-50.

7. Alphonso Wetmore, *Gazetteer of the State of Missouri* (St. Louis, 1837), 94-96, quoted in Arrington and Bitton, *The Mormon Experience,* 47.

8. Wetmore, quoted in Arrington and Bitton, *The Mormon Experience,* 166.

9. After the Morrill Act, other legislative acts were passed to continue the effort to abolish polygamy. The Edmunds Act of 1882 made cohabitation a crime. The Edmunds-Tucker Act of 1887 dissolved the incorporation of the Mormon Church. The Idaho Test Oath Act of 1887 made voters swear they were not polygamists. For exposition of these acts see Ray Jay Davis, "The Polygamous Prelude," *American Journal of Legal History* 6 (1962): 1-12. The *Reynolds* decision has been used against Mormons who continue to practice polygamy. See *Potter v. Murray City,* 760 F. 2d 1065 (10th Cir.), *cert. denied,* 106 S.Ct. 145 (1985).

10. Newspapers of the 1870s and 1880s replaced the old party-line stances that had been the basis of editorials and reporting with crusades against political, social, and moral injustices. This transformation was a reflection of larger changes in society following the Civil War. While the Supreme Court was interested in preserving the law under the Constitution, newspapers of the period were interested in making money and selling newspapers. Daily circulation increased by one million from 1870 to 1880, from 2.6 million to 3.56 million, surpassing the growth of America's population for the same period. Newspapers also increased staffs to better cover news, but editors and owners knew that covering stories that played to the tenor of the nation were needed. Because of the social and moral climate of the period, stories about polygamy and those who practiced it—specifically Mormons—better reflects society's interests than a single Supreme Court ruling. As can be seen by reading the papers, these stories were often harsh in their treatment of Latter-Day Saints. See Frank Luther Mott, *American Journalism*, 3rd ed. (New York: Macmillan, 1962), 411-15; Ted Curtis Smythe, "The Press and Industrial America 1865-1883," *The Media in America*, 2nd ed., ed. Wm. David Sloan, James G. Stovall, and James D. Startt (Scottsdale, Ariz.: Publishing Horizons, 1993), 214-27; ed. Mark A. Noll and others, *Christianity in America* (Grand Rapids: William B. Eerdmans, 1983), 296-320. Newspaper circulation figures from S.D.N. North, *History and Present Condition of the Newspaper and Periodical Press of the United States, With a Catalogue of the Publications of the Census Year* (Washington, D.C., 1884), 187.

11. John Lofton, *The Press as Guardian of the First Amendment* (Columbia: University of South Carolina Press, 1980), 279.

12. Newspaper selection was made for the following reasons. The *New York Times* is indexed through the period. The indexing, along with its complete national coverage made it a logical choice. The selection of the *Chicago Tribune* and *Atlanta Daily Constitution* was made simply because they represented two regions of America. *The San Francisco Chronicle* was the western choice because of its availability and because the San Francisco area was the most important region of the state. By selecting these four papers, a cross section of the nation could be achieved. The newspapers from Salt Lake City would certainly say more about Mormons and polygamy than any other papers in America; however, they would not give a true representation of the nation. The Mormon paper, the *Deseret News*, tended to ignore any negative press Mormons received in the "gentile" press. Also, the Salt Lake *Tribune*, a non-Mormon publication, gives the sentiment of non-Mormon Utah residents instead of the nation at large.

13. Sources on Smith and the Latter-Day Saints are numerous. Among them are Donna Hill, *Joseph Smith, the First Mormon* (Garden City: Doubleday, 1977); Leonard J. Arrington and Davis Bitton, *The Mormon*

Experience. A History of the Latter-Day Saints (New York: Alfred A. Knopf, 1977); Jan Shipps, *Mormonism: The Story of a New Religious Tradition* (Urbana and Chicago: University of Illinois Press, 1985). For the collected writings of Smith, see Robert L. Millet, ed., *Joseph Smith: Selected Sermons and Writings* (New York: Paulist Press, 1989).

14. Loy Otis Banks, "The Role of Mormon Journalism in the Death of Joseph Smith," *Journalism Quarterly* 27 (1950): 268-81, argues that Smith was gunned down because he ordered "an apostate journal published by dissenting Mormons" shut down and its press and type destroyed. The *Expositor* printed one edition on June 7, 1844, in which it challenged many of Smith's doctrines for the Mormons. Smith was arrested, along with his brother Hyrum, on June 24. Three days later, between 150 and 250 men broke into the Carthage, Illinois, jail where the two were incarcerated and filled the jail cell and the two Mormons with bullets.

15. *The Doctrine and Covenants, of the Church of Jesus Christ of the Latter-Day Saints Given to Joseph Smith, Jun., the Prophet, for the Building Up of the Kingdom of God in the Last Days* (Salt Lake City: Deseret News Company), 1880; reprint, Westport, Conn.: Greenwood Press, 1971), 473 (page citation is to the reprint edition).

16. The Morrill Act of July 1, 1862, was a significant piece of legislation. It set apart lands for the sites of colleges and provided funds for their establishment.

17. Erma Linford, "The Mormons and the Law: The Polygamy Cases," *Utah Law Review* 9 (1964): 332.

18. *Reynolds v. US*, 163.

19. *Reynolds v. US*, 164.

20. *Reynolds v. US*, 166.

21. Brief for Plaintiff in Error, *Reynolds v. United States* 98 US (8 Otto) 145 (1879), 54- 57.

22. *Reynolds v. US*, 166-67.

23. Edwin Brown Firmage and Richard Collin Mangrum, *Zion in the Courts* (Urbana and Chicago: University of Illinois Press, 1988), 50. Mormons found themselves involved in litigation wherever they went, and the newspapers, through their coverage in the years prior to the Carthage murders, gave Smith some national standing and helped create a negative image of Mormons (52-58).

24. Banks, "The Role of Mormon Journalism in the Death of Joseph Smith," 280.

25. *Biblical Recorder* (Raleigh), 5 July 1845.

26. Linford, "The Mormons and the Law," 312; Firmage and Mangrum, *Zion in the Courts,* 129.

27. *Nashville Daily News*, 25 March 1860.

28. *Biblical Recorder* (Raleigh), 21 January 1858.

29. See, for example, "Mormons in New York," 26 November 1875, and "Mormons Arrive in New York City," 6 June 1876.

30. The Mormons, in their proselytizing efforts, sent missionaries to western Europe. Mormon converts were promised land in Utah if they emigrated to the United States.

31. *New York Times*, 16 April 1879, 4.

32. *Chicago Tribune*, 7 January 1879, 2.

33. *New York Times*, 8 January 1879, 4.

34. *San Francisco Chronicle*, 7 January 1879, 1.

35. *Chicago Tribune*, 8 January 1879, 4.

36. *New York Times*, 8 January 1879, 4.

37. *San Francisco Chronicle*, 8 January 1879, 2.

38. *New York Times*, 4 June 1879, 4.

39. Firmage and Mangrum, *Zion in the Courts,* 131-32.

40. *Atlanta Daily Constitution*, 10 January 1879, 2.

41. *Atlanta Daily Constitution*, 26 January 1879, 2.

42. *Atlanta Daily Constitution*, 26 January 1879, 2. At this time, Congress was debating two bills, one proposed what the *Atlanta Daily Constitution* proposed—legitimization of children and wives currently part of polygamous marriages. The other, which eventually became law as the Edmunds Act of 1882, disqualified polygamists from jury duty and made cohabitation a crime.

43. *Atlanta Daily Constitution,* 26 January 1879, 2.

44. *Atlanta Daily Constitution,* 7 August 1879, 1.

45. *Atlanta Daily Constitution,* 5 August 1879, 2.

46. *Chicago Tribune*, 21 January 1879, 12.

47. *New York Times*, 22 January 1879, 4.

48. *San Francisco Chronicle*, 28 January 1879, 3.

49. *San Francisco Chronicle,* 15 June 1879, 4.

50. *Chicago Tribune*, 17 June 1879, 4.

51. The Court heard the arguments concerning the sentence in the middle of June and ruled that the sentence of the district court be set aside and "a new one entered on the verdict in all respects like that before imposed, except so far as it requires the imprisonment to be at hard labor" (*Reynolds v. US* 169).

52. *New York Times*, 15 September 1879, 1.

53. The 1876 presidential election put Rutherford B. Hayes in the White House by one electoral vote although his Democratic opponent, Samuel J. Tilden, won the popular election by 250,000 votes. Had Utah been granted statehood, its electoral votes for the Democrats would have swung the election. The upcoming 1880 election would be just as tightly contested. Republican James A. Garfield did defeat Democrat Winfield S. Hancock by four-tenths of a percentage point of the popular vote. Figures from *Historical Statistics of the*

United States, Colonial Times to 1957 (1961) and the U.S. Department of Justice printed in John M. Blum, *The National Experience: A History of the United States since 1865* (San Diego: Harcourt Brace Jovanovich, 1985), 939.

54. *San Francisco Chronicle*, 20 September 1879, 2.

55. *San Francisco Chronicle*, 7 January 1879, 1.

56. *San Francisco Chronicle*, 7 January 1879,1.

57. *San Francisco Chronicle*, 16 January 1879, 4.

58. *San Francisco Chronicle*, 3 October, 1879, 2.

59. Sean Dennis Cashman, *America in the Gilded Age*, 2nd ed. (New York and London: New York University Press, 1988), 95, 101-02.

60. William G. Brownlow, *Americanism Contrasted with Foreignism, Romanism and Bogus Democracy* (1856), quoted in Blum, *The National Experience*, 313.

61. Cashman, *America in the Gilded Age*, 112.

62. *New York Times*, 14 August 1879, 4.

63. *New York Times*, 16 April 1879, 4.

64. *New York Times*, 2 May 1879, 8.

65. *New York Times*, 5 June 1879, 3.

66. *New York Times*, 5 June 1879, 3.

67. *New York Times*, 14 August 1879, 4.

68. Even though Mormonism was an American faith, its appeal in the United States was limited to Christians dissatisfied with that faith as practiced by mainline denominations. Economic, social, and political factors in Europe—combined with the Mormons' promise for free land and the chance for a new beginning in America—made the Mormons' work of proselytizing more successful in Europe. Between 1840 and 1900, church historian Sydney Ahlstrom estimates that 90,000 Europeans converted to Mormonism entered the United States. See Sydney E. Ahlstrom, *A Religious History of the American People* (New Haven and London: Yale University Press, 1972), 507 n4.

69. *New York Times*, 10 December 1879, 4.

70. *San Francisco Chronicle*, 25 December 1879, 2.

71. *New York Times*, 4 June 1879, 4.

72. In addition to the Edmunds Act of 1882 and other legislative enactments, the Supreme Court ruled again on polygamy in *Davis v. Beason*, 133 US 333 (1890). The Court affirmed *Reynolds*. "However free the exercise of religion may be, it must be subordinate to the criminal laws of the country" (342-43).

73. *Time*, 19 May 1975, 74, 72. Polygamist family from Utah, interview by Paula Zahn, *CBS This Morning*, 15 April 1991.

74. Polygamist family from Utah, interview by Paula Zahn, *CBS This Morning*, 15 April 1991.

75. *San Francisco Chronicle*, 8 January 1879, 2.

11

The Peace Advocacy Press

Nancy L. Roberts

"Dear Sir, I am converted to Peace principles, and I attribute it to the reading of your paper," a Georgia minister wrote to the editor of the Quaker *Messenger of Peace* in 1879. Meanwhile, another reader admonished the editor of the *Herald of Peace* that his paper "ought to be named the *Herald of War*. It stirs up so much strife and controversy."[1]

As these examples hint, the press was a provocative agent in 19th-century U.S. peace advocates' program to change public opinion. Throughout U.S. history, of course, numerous alternative periodicals have given voice to cultures and viewpoints not expressed in the mainstream press. This alternative press tradition includes many vigorous social movement advocacy publications which have challenged the dominant culture to consider new ideas and issues and to foment change. Important 19th-century examples include the periodicals of abolitionists, evangelicals, temperance activists, woman suffragists—and of peace advocates, the subject of this study.

This research suggests that modern advocates' conception of journalism as a form of activism in its own right, comparable to public speaking and interpersonal communication, is hardly new. Like their 20th-century counterparts, 19th-century peace advocates also emphasized the significance of writing as a form of activism and the power of the press to change public opinion. And while early 20th-century (pre-*Masses*) reformers and radicals tended to approach their causes with the utmost gravity—to do otherwise, they feared, could call into question their commitment to the cause—so did 19th-century peace advocates communicate their ideas in a sober, didactic, sometimes boring way. Yet they also aimed to be attention-getting, interesting, and even entertaining.

The most central reform movement in U.S. history is peace advocacy.[2] Beginning early in the 19th century with the development of the first organized peace societies, countless reformers and radicals have worked for the realization of world peace, in innumerable ways. Some have been propelled by religious convictions, particularly those members of the historic peace churches, the Quakers, the Mennonites, and the Church of the Brethren. Many more have striven for peace through nonsectarian affiliations such as the American Peace Society (started in 1828), the League of Universal Brotherhood (1846), and the Universal Peace Union (1866).

Scholars of diplomatic, military, and political history have dominated the field of peace history. Working essentially within the framework of these perspectives, they have paid scant attention to the peace press.[3] Those historians who have studied the 19th-century advocacy press have directed their attention to the publications of reformers such as evangelicals,[4] feminists,[5] abolitionists,[6] and temperance advocates.[7] Yet peace advocacy, certainly in the antebellum period, was common—and often correlated with advocacy of other reforms such as abolition and women's rights.[8]

19th-Century Peace Advocacy Movements and Their Presses

The history of peace advocacy in the United States is complex, with many overlapping developments, organizations, and publications. This simplified account focuses on the history of nonsectarian and religious groups which were of primary importance, especially through their sponsorship of peace advocacy periodicals, tracts, and pamphlets.

In 1815 the modern, nonsectarian American peace movement was born. The years 1815–16 saw the simultaneous, independent emergence of major peace societies in the United States and Britain.[9] The immediate catalyst for the formation of these societies was the century of European conflict which culminated in the continental wars of the Napoleonic period and their extension to the Americas in the War of 1812.[10] Like the philanthropic reforms of the early 19th century, the peace movement's intellectual roots lay in the 18th-century Enlightenment. These humanitarian, patriotic reformers founded nondenominational organizations whose membership was overwhelmingly Protestant. Historian Charles DeBenedetti describes them as "typical romantic reformers, individualistic yet organized, rationalistic yet sentimental, personally conservative yet socially radical, humanly optimistic yet scripturally literalist."[11] Well-educated, most were middle-class, Congregationalist or Unitarian gentlemen of the urban Northeast. Many were clergy, teachers, and professional men.[12]

They founded organizations such as the New York Peace Society (1815)[13] and the Massachusetts Peace Society (1815),[14] initiating a continuous American peace movement. By 1819, 17 regional peace societies from Maine to Georgia and from Rhode Island to Indiana, had sprung up.[15] By the end of 1821, the Massachusetts Peace Society had distributed, with its auxiliaries, a total of 7,155 copies of its periodical, the *Friend of Peace*.[16]

In 1828 the American Peace Society (APS) was formed, absorbing many of the smaller state and regional peace organizations.[17] The APS and other peace advocacy associations can be considered part of a social movement, which C. Wendell King has defined as "a group venture extending beyond a local community or a single event and involving a systematic effort to inaugurate changes in thought, behavior, and social relationships."[18]

Alexis de Tocqueville observed during his visit to the United States in the early 1830s that some of the most significant U.S. associations were those of social movements, many of which "recognized that communication was essential in maintaining their cohesion" and accomplished this by the publication of pamphlets and newspapers.[19] Typical was the APS, which tried to change public opinion through its periodicals such as the *Advocate of Peace*, the *Calumet*, and the *Harbinger of Peace*. The APS also published tracts, encouraged peace sermons in the churches, and sponsored peace essay contests in colleges, sometimes leading to the formation of student peace societies such as those at Amherst, Dartmouth, and Oberlin.

The APS aimed "to reach the public mind only through the ordinary channels of influence," seeking "reform with as little agitation as possible." It wished "to effect a peaceful change on this subject by the moral suasion of the gospel addressed to the community in ways to which they are already accustomed." Thus, the APS first sought the sanction of the "highest ecclesiastical bodies," and instructed its agents "invariably to act in concert with pastors."[20] This strategy also suggests that peace advocates sought to cultivate respectability as a means of winning society's acceptance. In 1837, inspired by the nonresistance ideas of John Humphrey Noyes, the Christian perfectionist founder of the upstate New York Oneida Community, William Lloyd Garrison became the leader of the new radical group, the New England Non-Resistance Society, which splintered from the APS during the debate over war as a potential means to end slavery.

During the Civil War, peace advocates were divided over the issues of war and abolition and the American Peace Society declined. Wartime pacifism became largely the lonely province of the three traditional peace sects (the Mennonites, Brethren, and Quakers) and some newer, millenarian nonresistant sects, such as the Seventh-Day Adventists and the Christadelphians. Following the war the APS was revived, reclaiming its traditional, middle-of-the-road character that allowed for "defensive" war.

In 1866 a new nonsectarian organization, the Universal Peace Union (UPU), was founded. In reaction to the APS's pro-Civil War position, the UPU took a much less compromising position on violence, following Garrisonian nonresistance. Alfred Love led the group from 1866 until his death in 1913.[21] Together, the American Peace Society and the Universal Peace Union represented the two points of view whose polarity had led to the decline of the APS in the antebellum years.

In the post-Civil War years, these groups were significant peace societies. Curiously, despite the important inspirational effect of the Quakers' historical peace testimony on early peace advocacy writers (both conservative and radical), the Quakers themselves had little to do with any of the nonsectarian peace groups.[22] In 1867, in response to the Civil War, the Quakers founded the Peace Association of Friends in North America, whose major publication was the *Messenger of Peace.*

Also considered a part of the peace movement in the second half of the 19th century were various groups which organized to codify and support specific methods of peace-seeking, such as arbitration and international law and organization.[23]

At their birth, peace societies immediately saw a need for publications to cover the peace issues that were left out of mainstream and religious newspapers.[24] Exploiting advances in printing and transportation, many groups, such as religious ones, diffused their propaganda as tracts,[25] which they distributed free of charge or for a nominal sum. While tracts were a significant component of the 19th-century peace advocacy press, this study focuses on the peace periodical press. As Merle Curti has noted, of all the official peace publications, "the periodicals themselves are the most important printed materials, as they contain the annual reports and many of the sermons and addresses which ... circulated in tract form."[26]

Just as peace advocacy took a variety of forms, from absolute pacifism to a moderate position allowing for "defensive" war, so did the peace advocacy periodical press express a kaleidoscope of viewpoints, from the fairly conservative position of the American Peace Society and its regional antecedents and affiliates (allowing for "defensive war"), to the radical, thoroughgoing pacifism of the New England Non-Resistance Society.[27] Most visible, widely circulated, and comparatively prominent were the publications of the broadly based nonsectarian Christian humanitarian peace organizations, such as the American Peace Society's *Advocate of Peace*, *Calumet*, and *Harbinger of Peace*, and the publications of its regional forerunners and affiliates, such as the Connecticut Peace Society's *American Advocate of Peace*, the Massachusetts Peace Society's *Friend of Peace*, and the Pennsylvania Peace Society's *Advocate of Peace and Christian Patriot.*

Less visible than these periodicals, at least in the antebellum years, were the expressly religious publications of the historic peace churches. The Mennonite press was still in its infancy in the 1850s; moreover, Mennonites were separatists who did not aim to proselytize the outside society.[28] A regular Quaker weekly press first appeared in October 1827 with the publication of the Philadelphia *Friend*. Although in the years before mid-century Quaker periodicals devoted considerable attention to peace issues, the amount of space given to such issues was a small amount of the total and pacifism was discussed mainly in religious terms. So while the nonsectarian peace organizations confessed their indebtedness to the Quaker peace witness, American Quakers themselves, for a variety of reasons, were socially isolated during this period. Largely reluctant to collaborate with their admirers, the Quakers gave them "a certain slightly condescending approval."[29] Meanwhile, the German Baptist Brethren produced "no literature dealing even incidentally with the subject of their peace testimony before the middle of the 19th century."[30]

Analysis of a Sample of Peace Advocacy Periodicals
Method

To bring the peace advocacy press into greater relief, this study analyzes ten of the 19th century's most important, comparatively high-circulation publications of prominent nonsectarian peace advocacy organizations such as the American Peace Society and the Universal Peace Union, as well as two Quaker publications (to represent the religious-based peace advocacy of the historic peace churches). The sample varies in geographical and philosophical origins. Complete files of the following periodicals at the Swarthmore College Peace Collection were examined, representing the period ranging from 1815 to 1913:[31]

- The *Friend of Peace*, the organ of the Massachusetts Peace Society, a quarterly published and edited by Noah Worcester in Boston and Cambridge, Mass., 1815–27.
- The *Advocate of Peace and Christian Patriot*, issued monthly by the Pennsylvania Peace Society in Philadelphia, 1828–29.
- Three successive periodicals of the American Peace Society: the *Harbinger of Peace* (a monthly duodecimo published in New York and edited by William Ladd, May 1828–April 1831); the *Calumet* (two octavos issued bimonthly from New York and edited by William Ladd, 1831–35); and the *Advocate of Peace*, issued mainly from Boston, which from 1837 superseded the *American Advocate of Peace* (1834–36), which had been founded as the quarterly organ

of the Connecticut Peace Society in Hartford.[32] (The *Advocate of Peace* has been continued since 1910 in *World Affairs*.)
- Three periodicals of the Universal Peace Union: the *Bond of Peace* (published monthly in Philadelphia, 1868–74); the *Voice of Peace* (published monthly in Philadelphia, 1874–82); and the *Peacemaker* (published in Philadelphia, 1883–1913, with frequency and title variations).[33]
- Two Quaker periodicals: the *Messenger of Peace*, published by the Peace Association of Friends in America,[34] New Vienna, Ohio, (1870–77) and Richmond, Indiana, (1887–90), with title variations, and edited by Daniel Hill; and the *Herald of Peace*, published semimonthly in Chicago (1868–89).

Purpose and Audience

The peace press's audience ranged from the uninitiated to those who were committed members of peace organizations. Editors aimed to build and maintain their geographically dispersed communities of conscience while attracting and educating new converts. This two-fold audience also characterizes some other 19th-century social movement advocacy publications, such as those of the woman suffrage movement. It is a challenging task to reach such a dual audience; as Martha M. Solomon has observed, "the job of gaining new members while maintaining a consistent sense of group identity...requires unusual rhetorical acumen."[35]

Occasionally the peace publications themselves hint how they further defined that audience.[36] The peace press sought especially to maintain its loyal following and build internal cohesion. Much content was directed to those who were already members. Morale was built in several ways, often through the cataloguing of each incremental gain for the cause of peace. Even the smallest acknowledgment of their arguments conferred by mainstream society was presented as occasion for rejoicing. For example, the first annual report of the Massachusetts Peace Society, published in the *Friend of Peace* in 1817, noted, "All human institutions are stamped with imperfection; and the best of them are capable of being improved by time and experience." The report continued:

Considering the circumstances under which the Massachusetts Peace Society originated, the smallness of its funds, and the powerful prepossessions it had to encounter, it was not to be expected that the first Report of its officers, would contain a list of facts either very numerous, splendid, or interesting.

Despite this disclaimer, the report noted many small achievements, including the distribution of six numbers of the *Friend of Peace*, as well as other publications to "several Colleges in New-England."[37]

In a regular column called "Auspicious Occurrences," the *Friend of Peace* frequently noted the founding of other peace societies and their publications,[38] along with such far-flung intelligence as the news that a Catholic paper in France had praised the work of the Massachusetts Peace Society.[39]

A similar column was the *Advocate of Peace*'s "Auspicious Movements," which reported, for instance, the "omen of much promise to our cause" that the secretary of the American Peace Society had "been invited to attend discussions appointed by some ecclesiastical bodies on questions of great importance to the cause of peace."[40] Other peace periodicals carefully and frequently noted the growth of the peace movement, both in the United States and abroad.[41] And individual publications ran articles that pointed out the direct salutary effects of reading their pages.[42]

Also, doubtless to build morale as well as to attract new partisans, laudatory letters to the editor were often printed. The letters published were almost invariably positive; the *Friend of Peace* once admitted censoring part of a letter which expressed certain sentiments about "the Editor...which could not with propriety be published in this work."[43]

Such a uniformly positive, movement-building tone minimized any internal discord that might have existed. Thus, during the antebellum period, which saw considerable dissension within the American Peace Society over aims and purposes of the peace movement relative to slavery, the *Advocate of Peace* reported only that there was "some diversity of views among our own members."[44]

Editors frequently tried to gauge the positive effects of their communication. Much of the evidence they gathered was anecdotal. "Our cause is rapidly gaining ground," the *Harbinger of Peace* announced confidently in 1829. "Contributions to our paper are more frequent, and, on all hands, we hear complaints that our book is too small, and that it ought to be twice or thrice as large."[45] Likewise, the *Calumet* in 1832 claimed that "The friends of Peace are scattered throughout almost the whole of Christendom.... Our influence extends to Europe."[46]

Overview of Content

Typical of its contemporaries, the *American Advocate of Peace* aimed

1st, to extended discussions of the most important topics connected with the cause of peace; 2d, to brief Critical Notices of current publications as they come within the application of our principles, with the design of promoting, in this respect, in a Christian country, a pure and Christian Literature; 3d, to intelligence concerning the progress of pacific principles and the civil and political affairs of nations.[47]

Likewise the *Voice of Peace* sought "to proclaim ripe and fresh arguments for peace. To offer Letters, Essays, Stories, Speeches and information on the most practical means for its establishment," with "kindred subjects...only find[ing] a place when they are for those things that make for peace."[48]

Considerable content consisted of didactic essays. Characteristic examples included facts and statistics to prove war's immorality and waste, for example, "The Delusions and Suicidal Results of War"; arguments illustrating the incompatibility of war with Christian principles, such as "Is Peace Consistent with Christianity?"; and practical suggestions for reform, such as "The Object of Peace Societies Practicable."[49] Poetry was fairly common among the later-dated publications[50] and moralistic fiction also appeared occasionally.[51] Such content, paralleling that available in contemporary mainstream newspapers and magazines (to which readers were accustomed), was a reader-attracting strategy also employed by the woman suffrage press, the temperance press, and, perhaps to a lesser degree, by the antislavery press.[52]

Also, the *Bond of Peace*, the *Herald of Peace*, the *Voice of Peace*, and the *Peacemaker* published special children's sections, offering essays, poems, and stories to help teach youngsters about peace,[53] as did the temperance press.[54]

Appearance, Advertising, Economics, and Circulation

These periodicals range in size and appearance, from the comparatively modest *Harbinger of Peace* measuring five by eight inches and the *Friend of Peace* at six by nine and a half inches, to the *Herald of Peace* at nine by twelve inches. Throughout the sample, the number of per-issue pages and advertisements, as well as illustrations, increases with time, doubtless reflecting developments in technology as well as, in some cases, the relative success of the organization with which each periodical was associated. By the 1870s and 1880s, advertising was plentiful, often filling several pages and touting general-interest products including books and periodicals, health nostrums, and household appliances and supplies. (Advertising was similar in scope and kind among at least one other contemporary social movement periodical, the temperance movement's *Union Signal*.)[55]

Despite the varying timespans and organization fortunes represented by these periodicals, the cost of annual subscriptions remained fairly consistent. Throughout the period studied, $1.00 per year was a typical price, starting with the *Friend of Peace* even before 1820. The extremes are represented by the *Messenger of Peace*, charging 50 cents (1879) and the *Herald of Peace*, $1.50 (1868). Compared to the prevailing rates for other U.S. magazines, the peace publications were inexpensive.[56] This likely stems from the typical advocacy editor's desire to achieve a wide readership, even before profitability, as well as their comparatively fewer pages.

Like many other social movement-reform publications in U.S. history, the peace press ran in the red.[57] Like so many of their contemporaries, editors such as Noah Worcester and William Ladd worked without salary, publishing their papers at their own risk and expense.[58] Besides subscription (and advertising) revenue, income from job printing and donations provided necessary funding. Appeals for funds were common, and lists of the donors and the amounts they paid or pledged, were published regularly.[59]

Circulation data indicate that while audiences for these periodicals did not rival in size those for the penny press, neither were they inconsequential. For instance, in 1850 the *Advocate of Peace* had a circulation of 3,000.[60] Circulation figures generally reached 1,000 to 2,000 or more, fairly typical of mainstream magazines in the pre-1850 period.[61] Furthermore, many copies were passed along; their publishers made a point of getting them into libraries and to opinion leaders (as indicated by their regularly published subscription lists).

Views of Reform and Journalism

In the pages of the peace press, advocates wrote candidly of their purposes, both as reformers and radicals, and as writer/journalists. The characteristic 19th-century belief in rationality reigned.[62] As the American Peace Society claimed in the *Calumet*, "Past experience also teaches us, that delusions...have been dissipated by the light of truth."[63] The peace advocacy press set out to illuminate that truth, to marshal and publicize all the rational arguments in favor of its cause. Just as their antislavery counterparts held "that the press was one of the most powerful agencies of reform,"[64] peace advocates greatly valued writing and publication as tools of persuasion, as much if not more so than other forms of personal activism (such as public speaking and interpersonal, face-to-face communication). Possibly because peace advocates may have felt morally and ideologically isolated from mainstream society, they may have found it easier to work for an unpopular cause through writing and publication, activities that could be carried on passionately and even anonymously. For instance, Massachusetts Peace Society founder Noah Worcester wrote for the *Friend of Peace* for many years under the pseudonym "Philo Pacificus"; however, he simply may have been following the tradition of impersonal journalism.

Peace advocates strove mightily to persuade through the written word. The *Messenger of Peace* stated that it was "filled with facts and arguments to prove that War is unchristian, inhuman and unnecessary."[65] Likewise, the *Friend of Peace* asserted in 1819, "It is in the power of the Editors of Newspapers to do much good with little labor and expense. A few well written remarks on the subject of war may occasion thousands to reflect, and eventually save thousands from untimely death by murderous hands."[66] Indeed, the *Friend of Peace* continued,

Among the numerous gifts of God for the advancement of our race, in knowledge, virtue, and happiness, the tongue, the pen, and the press hold a preeminent rank.... Had the tongue, the pen, and the press been always under the direction of wisdom and benevolence, duelling and war would never have been known among men; and even now, should all these gifts be henceforth duly consecrated to the purposes of love and peace, it is very certain that in *one year* from this day, war would be banished from the earth, never to return.[67]

Enlightenment rationality was a compelling factor in the formation of these ideas. Too, such sentiments are typical of what has been called the "genesis" stage in the life cycle of social movements, in which "the movement's initial leaders believe, often with remarkable naivete, that appropriate institutions will act if the movement can make institutional leaders and followers aware of the urgent problem and its solution."[68] However, this emphasis on writing and publication characterizes peace advocates not only shortly after the founding of the first peace organizations in 1815, but throughout the century.

Not surprisingly, the *Friend of Peace*'s sponsoring organization, the Massachusetts Peace Society, in its constitution singled out the role of the written word in encouraging "the formation of similar societies" both in the United States and abroad.[69] "We regard the *Advocate* [*of Peace*] as our main instrument," the American Peace Society stated in the pages of that periodical.[70] References to the press as "an engine of vast moral power" also appeared in the *Advocate*. The APS wished "to hear [the press's] ten thousand tongues speak on this subject, in the ear of all reading communities, through books, and pamphlets, and tracts, and newspapers, and every class of periodicals."[71] And the more radical *Voice of Peace*, while holding that "To live peace is better than to write it or speak it," still stressed the importance of sending forth the *Voice of Peace* "to be heard and heeded."[72]

Writers and editors frequently referred to their role as manipulators of public opinion. "The power of public opinion has become proverbial," wrote the *Advocate of Peace*. "It is the lever of the moral world."[73] In another issue, the *Advocate* stated, "Public opinion is our main instrument; and we would cast it in the mould of peace. It is the mistress of the world, and does more to control Christendom than all her fleets and armies."[74] Furthermore, the *Advocate* wrote, "We seek to effect such a change in public opinion as shall secure a right and universal application of the gospel to the intercourse of Christian nations."[75]

Such sentiments were echoed by the second Pennsylvania Peace Society, whose constitution stated its object was "to collect and disseminate information calculated to bring about a correct public opinion on the subject of *Peace* and *War*."[76] Similarly, the *Calumet* maintained, "Public opinion is yet to rule the world," and "by the simple process of *enlightening and influencing public opinion*...the war-spirit may be subdued."[77] The pages of the peace press contain many other such references to public opinion.[78] Perhaps the comparatively high education and socioeconomic class level of the movement's leaders contributed to their optimism about the efficacy of their written words to sway public opinion. Their belief that the press could influence public opinion directly and powerfully was shared by most other Americans of the time. This idea seems to have taken root after the Revolution and endured, occasionally challenged, into the 1880s.[79]

On the whole, the 19th-century peace press took itself seriously, perhaps in direct proportion to peace advocates' level of insecurity about society's acceptance of their message. As the *Bond of Peace* stated, "For ourselves rest assured we regard the cause as a life work, you will not find us to faltor [*sic*] for mere trifles."[80] The peace press tended toward a sober and serious style rather than one characterized by witty, entertaining invention. Reform and radical journalists have been perennially concerned that attempts to be entertaining would betray the gravity of their causes. This may be the result of sensing moral and ideological marginalization. The more one feels one's ideas are considered unacceptable or controversial by society, the more compelled one is to maintain a serious public demeanor, in order not to lose the precious amount of credibility already claimed.

So it is not surprising that in 1829 the *Harbinger* disavowed responsibility for some readers' complaints that it was "insipid and uninteresting," instead calling into question "the want of interest in the subject [of peace] itself." The *Harbinger* went on,

> We cannot make a novel of it. We cannot deal in fiction. We are bound to the truth. We cannot address the imagination; we can only appeal to the judgment and to the conscience, and what can we do with readers who have neither? Our object is not to *create* excitement, but to *allay* it."[81]

It is generally thought that until the brilliant, literary, and captivating radical periodical *Masses* (edited by Max Eastman) appeared in 1911, most advocacy journalists disavowed entertainment and literary craft for the safer path of staid content.[82] However, the 19th-century woman suffrage press "was not all suffrage and suffering," offering poetry, short stories, and essays on a variety of other subjects and even household hints in an attempt to attract more readers.[83] The temperance press, too, sought to offer varied, interesting content,[84] as did the antislavery press.[85]

Among peace movement publications, the *Herald of Peace* gave some thought to its attention-getting qualities. In the years following the Civil War, it chose not to devote its pages exclusively to peace, reasoning that the subject had limited audience appeal:

> The number of persons in the United States who would subscribe for a paper strictly devoted to the cause of peace, and pay their money for it cheerfully and promptly, and, what is more, read it with any degree of interest, we are sorry to say is very small.... [A] paper which presents one subject only, becomes dry and uninteresting to many.

Therefore, the *Herald* set out to offer not only content dealing specifically with peace, but on "all subjects which effect [*sic*] our interest as Christians.... We are truly convinced that peace will only be attained by a proper appreciation...of the peaceable requirements of the gospel." This meant that the *Herald*, while aiming to be "thoroughly acceptable to the Society of Friends," would "avoid a narrow sectarian character, and endeavor to maintain that charity and true catholic spirit which will make it a welcome visitor among thousands of every Christian name."[86]

Some Journalistic Strategies

Notwithstanding the *Harbinger of Peace*'s comment that it could not "address the imagination" of its readers, that it could "only appeal to the judgment and to the conscience," the peace press used a variety of strategies to communicate its message compellingly. A primary effort was to gather and publicize what Christina Phelps has called "'statistics of war'—facts which illustrate its conditions and its evils, which show its futility."[87] Such articles characterized war as inimical to civilization and culture. Frequently they decried the organized Christian churches' "war degeneracy."

Starting with the *Friend of Peace* before 1820, stories of the horrors of war were a staple, particularly among the earlier peace advocacy periodicals. Viewing "peace as health," and war as "a disease, in the body politic," the *Friend of Peace* and its later colleagues did not spare sensibilities in the accounting of war's human toll.[88] An article described the aftermath of the battle of Antietam during the recent Civil War in typically vivid terms. Men lay "dead, blackened, torn, disfigured, wounded; tended by no mother's hand, no sister's love.... As they rose they fell dead; some with cigars in their lips, others with bread in their hands, and some holding the miniatures of loved ones far away."[89]

The following is among the unforgettable scenes in the wake of one of Napoleon's battles:

a stout-looking man, and a beautiful young woman, with an infant, about seven months old, at the breast, all three frozen and dead. The mother had most certainly expired in the act of suckling her child; as with one breast exposed she lay upon the drifted snow, the milk, to all appearance, in a stream drawn from the nipple by the babe, and instantly congealed. The infant seemed as if its lips had but just then been disengaged, and it reposed its little head upon the mother's bosom, with an overflow of milk, frozen as it trickled from the mouth.[90]

Such a tableau offered war as an assault on women as the embodiment of the values of piety, purity, submissiveness, and domesticity.[91]

War's toll on women was also the focus of an article in the *Advocate of Peace*. The sufferings of compelling characters (a sergeant's wife, a "maniac mother") were detailed, to illustrate the point: "Women, being forced to part with lovers, husbands, sons, have often taken their own life in a frenzy of grief and despair, or fallen eventual victims to delirium, or some lingering disease that gnawed with fatal tooth on their vitals."[92]

Articles both described the appalling atrocities perpetuated by the soldier and characterized war from the abused soldier's perspective.[93] An example of the latter is "The Execution of a Deserter," an article published in the *American Advocate of Peace* about a father of three, who had left camp to make a brief visit to his wife and children nearby. Although "it was his intention to return [to camp]," he was declared a deserter. His story is related in considerable detail by the surgeon who was required to observe the sentence fully executed. At the "fatal spot," the surgeon reports, the deserter sees his coffin before him: "a box of rough pine boards—borne on the shoulders of two men." The narrative continues:

The prisoner stood, with his arms pinioned, between two clergymen—a white cotton gown, or winding sheet, reached to his feet. It was trimmed with black, and had attached to it, over the place of the real heart, the black image of a heart—the mark at which the executioners were to aim. On his head was a cap of white, also trimmed with black. His countenance was blanched to the hue of his winding sheet, and his frame trembled with agony.

The surgeon describes the execution in detail, down to the "[m]ingled fumes of burning cotton and burning hair" that emanated from the deserter's cap. It had ignited when "the serjeant [*sic*], from motives of humanity, held the muzzle of his musket near the head." The surgeon muses, "O war, dreadful even in thy tenderness—horrible even in thy compassion!" He concludes, "Do scenes such as this which I have described, enter the minds of those who have the chief agency in involving their respective countries in a war?"[94]

Such articles about executions, court-martials, and "brutal military punishments" are characteristic.[95] A particularly horrifying example is the *Advocate of Peace*'s "Sketches of War," in which an observer describes another execution of a deserter ("[N]othing remained but some blood and brains and a portion of his skull") and a monument made of human bones ("[T]hese walls, which I supposed to be built of marble, or white stone, were composed of regular rows of human skulls, bleached by the rain and sun, and cemented by a little sand and lime"). The military's excessive use of corporal punishment for minor infractions of discipline is also vividly described ("On the first lash, the blood spirted [*sic*] out some yards; and after he had received fifty, his back from the neck to the waist, was one continued stream of blood").[96]

Another antiwar rhetorical strategy was to appeal to the pocketbook, illustrating war's high financial cost as well as the body counts. "Stop and consider facts and figures—then judge of our cause," urged the *Herald of Peace*. "Within the past 14 years, there have been nearly 2,000,000 lives lost by war, sanctioned by professedly Christian nations." The *Herald* claimed that the recent Civil War "cost the loss of 600,000 of our young and strong men; and the actual cost and loss in money, not less than $8,000,000,000." Thus, war preparation was equated with economic weakness.[97]

Coverage of Other Reform Efforts

Finally, mention must be made of the peace advocacy press's wide-ranging coverage of other reform efforts. If the press was thought to be an "engine of vast moral power," perhaps it could also be deemed to drive the train of reform for other causes commanding significant moral weight. And so the peace press regularly featured articles on related reform efforts. The degree and range of advocacy was naturally a function of the ideology of the sponsoring publication or religion. For instance, besides peace, the Universal Peace Union in its organ the *Voice of Peace* backed a far-ranging set of reforms, pledging to be "just to all, irrespective of color, sex, race or condition." Military "taxes, schools, drills, pomp and preferment," as well as the restriction of the sale and use of deadly weapons, justice for Native Americans, and temperance were advocated.[98] Furthermore, educational reform was highlighted as a priority: "Petitioning governments to abolish war clauses is good; giving aid to men and women in overcoming evil passions is better," the *Voice* asserted,

but, to our mind, the best of all is to commence at the very foundation and teach the children of the rising generation in morality and good works. There are thousands of neglected children growing up with little or no instruction, save in the arts of wickedness, and by and by they will fill the ranks of those who carry on wars, murders and every immoral practice by which the world is cursed.[99]

Among this sample of the peace press, articles denouncing capital punishment were common, a not surprising correlation.[100] Also frequent, particularly after the Civil War, were articles advocating justice for Native Americans. The *Voice of Peace* even ran a regular "Indian Department."[101]

Reflecting the positions of their sponsoring organizations or religions, a few periodicals advocated varying degrees of equal treatment of women. For instance, the *Bond of Peace*, which "cordially invite[d] all to enroll...who are willing to labor irrespective of color[,] race[,] sex[,] or condition," wholeheartedly embraced equal rights for women. "In fact," stated the *Bond*, "it is useless for us to look on universal peace, while woman is kept back from having a voice in the council of the nation."[102]

In addition, occasional articles advocated temperance. The *Messenger of Peace* led the way, proposing in 1879 to increase the number of articles on this subject. "We regard intemperance as the handmaid, of war," the *Messenger* stated, "often having much to do in causing war, and leading to fearful sacrifices of men through the recklessness of officers under the influence of strong drink."[103] Articles in the peace press also denounced the use of tobacco. Anticipating by nearly one hundred years the U.S. Surgeon General's 1964 report, an article in an 1869 issue of the *Bond of Peace* condemned smoking, claiming it "conveys its poisonous influence into every part of the lungs."[104] Occasional articles also advocated just treatment of animals.[105] The *Herald of Peace* even suggested that the animal movement was "ill-directed," and that good treatment of animals would be insured when there was peace between human beings.[106]

Other articles backed a variety of other humanitarian reforms, among them antislavery, to which more coverage was given, of course, in the antebellum years;[107] gun control and the abolition of lynching;[108] and penal reform.[109] Some content also denounced children's war toys.[110]

During the antebellum period, of course, many individuals participated in not just one but several reform movements; for instance, membership in antislavery, women's rights, and peace associations was correlated. Thus movement publications naturally supported other, related causes. For example, in the 1880s and 1890s the temperance movement publication, the *Union Signal*, proselytized for a wide variety of reform causes, including woman suffrage and feminism.[111] Woman suffrage publications such as the *Lily* and the *Una* supported temperance,[112] while another, the *Revolution,* advocated a variety of reforms to help the poor and homeless, prisoners, and Native Americans.[113]

Still, the advocacy of many of the wide-ranging reforms noted above in the pages of the peace advocacy press (some of which were considered controversial) was probably not an effective strategy to help peace advocates win acceptance from the wider society. More research is needed to determine what, exactly, was going on. At the very least, this content suggests peace advocates' commitment to articulate the full breadth of their positions on even controversial issues, probably in the belief that the moral imperatives of their positions would be made apparent through the written word's persuasive powers. They firmly believed that the wide publication of their right thinking would change people's minds.

Conclusion

A picture emerges of a dynamic advocacy press sharing of the same characteristics and challenges of its more frequently studied contemporaries: the periodicals of abolitionists, evangelicals, temperance activists, and woman suffragists. Clearly, 19th-century peace advocates valued writing and publication as tools of persuasion to change public opinion, as much if not more than other forms of personal activism such as public speaking and interpersonal, face-to-face communication. They aimed their periodicals toward a dual audience of the converted and the not yet convinced. In their quest to publicize issues they believed the mainstream press ignored, peace advocates emphasized quality writing as an attention-getting strategy, in a manner not customarily seen among their advocacy contemporaries. They saw style and substance as a symbiotic, persuasive partnership.

Many questions remain to guide further research about the 19th-century U.S. peace advocacy press. For instance, how did its editors' and writers' backgrounds and training compare to that of other advocacy press personnel of the time, and to mainstream journalists'? How did peace advocacy editors regard other journalism, both advocacy and mainstream, in comparison to their own? In short, what was their consciousness of journalism? Answers to these and other questions will provide a more complete profile of this press.

Appendix
A Taxonomy of 19th-Century Peace Advocacy and Its Periodicals

Note: A wide variation in peace positions existed, from radical to reformist—from absolute pacifism, including Christian anarchism and nonresistance, to comparatively conservative peace advocacy which allowed for "defensive" war.

A. Nonsectarian
   1. State and regional peace societies, e.g., New York Peace Society (founded 1815); Massachusetts Peace Society (founded 1815, published *Friend of Peace*, Boston and Cambridge, Mass., 1815–27); Pennsylvania Peace Society (founded 1822, published *Advocate of Peace and Christian Patriot*, Philadelphia, Sept. 1828–June 1829); Connecticut Peace Society (founded 1831, published *American Advocate of Peace*, Hartford, Conn., 1834–36).

2. American Peace Society (founded 1828, published *Angel of Peace* for children, Boston, started 1872; *A.P.S. Bulletin*, Washington, D.C., irregular; *Harbinger of Peace*, New York, 1828–31; *Calumet*, New York, N.Y., 1831–35; *Advocate of Peace*, Boston, 1837–45, Worcester, Mass., 1846, Boston, 1846–1910, continued in 1910 in Washington, D.C., as *World Affairs*).

3. New England Non-Resistance Society (founded 1838, published *Journal of the Times*, Boston, antebellum period, irregular; *Liberator*, Boston, 1831-1865; *Non-Resistant*, Boston, 1839–1845).

4. League of Universal Brotherhood (founded 1846, published *Burritt's Christian Citizen*, Worcester, Mass., 1844–1851; *Bond of Brotherhood*, London and Worcester, Mass., 1846–1867).

5. Universal Peace Union (founded 1866 as Universal Peace Society, published *Bond of Peace*, Philadelphia, 1868–1874; *Voice of Peace*, Philadelphia, 1874–1882); *Peacemaker*, Philadelphia, 1883–1913).

B. Sectarian

1. Members of the historic peace churches

   a. Brethren (or dunkers) and other Anabaptist remnants, many located in Pennsylvania (Brethren publications include *Gospel Visitor,* Covington and later Columbiana, Ohio, 1851–73; *Christian Family Companion*, Tyrone, Pa., 1865–1873; *Primitive Christian*, Meyersdale and Huntingdon, Pa., 1873–83; *Progressive Christian*, Berlin, Pa., and later Ashland, Ohio, 1878–88; *Gospel Messenger*, Mount Morris and later Elgin, Ill., started 1883)

   b. Mennonites (publications include *Herald of Truth*, Chicago, Ill., 1864–67 and Elkhart, Ind., 1867–1908; *Family Almanac*, Elkhart, Ind., 1870–1908 and Scottdale, Pa., 1908–40)

   c. Quakers (publications include *Moral Advocate*, Mount Pleasant, Ohio, 1821–24; *Friends' Intelligencer*, Hicksite branch, Philadelphia, 1844–1955; *Friends' Review*, evangelical wing in Orthodox branch, Philadelphia, 1847–94; *Herald of Peace*, Chicago, 1868–89; *Messenger of Peace*, Peace Association of Friends in America, New Vienna, Ohio, 1870–87, Richmond, Ind., 1887–90, Philadelphia, 1890–1943; *Christian Worker*, orthodox branch, New Vienna, Ohio, 1871–94; *American Friend*, Richmond, Ind., 1894–1960)

2. Communitarian-utopian groups emphasizing peace among their tenets

a. Harmonists (or Rappists) (*New Harmony Gazette/Free Enquirer*, New Harmony, Ind., 1825–35)
b. Hopedale Community members (*Practical Christian*, Milford, Mass., 1840–60)
c. Inspirationists (of Amana), publications unknown
d. Oneida Community members (publications include *Witness*, Putney, Vt., 1837–46; *American Socialist*, Oneida, N.Y., 1876–79; *Circular* [title varies], Brooklyn, N.Y., Oneida, N.Y., Wallingford, Conn., 1851–76)
e. Shakers (*Shaker Manifesto* [title varies], Shakers, N.Y., Mount Lebanon, N.Y., Shaker Village, N.H., East Canterbury, N.H., 1871–99)
3. Others
a. Adventists (*Advent Shield and Review*, Boston, 1844–45; *Advent Christian Times*, Buchanan, Mich.; *Advent Review and Sabbath Herald*, Paris, Maine., Saratoga Springs, N.Y, Rochester, N.Y., Battle Creek, Mich., started 1850; *World's Crisis*, Boston, 1854–92)
b. Christadelphians, publications unknown
c. Disciples of Christ (publications include *Christian Baptist*, Buffaloe [Bethany], Brooke County, Va. [W.Va.], 1823–30; *Millennial Harbinger*, Bethany, Va. [W. Va.], 1830–70; *Western Reformer*, Milton, Ind., 1843–49; *Proclamation and Reformer*, Milton, Ind., 1850–51; *American Christian Review*, Indianapolis, Ind., started 1856; *Disciples of Christ*, Cincinnati, 1884–87)
d. Osgoodites, publications unknown
e. Rogerenes, publications unknown

Notes

The author wishes to thank Jean Ward of the University of Minnesota for commenting on an early draft of this article, the staff of the Swarthmore College Peace Collection for their assistance, and the University of Minnesota Graduate School and the American Philosophical Society for research funding.

1. "Correspondence," *Messenger of Peace* 9, no. 1 (January 1879), 1; *Friend of Peace* 1, no. 11 (1 February 1816), 40.

2. Charles DeBenedetti, *The Peace Reform in American History* (Bloomington: Indiana University Press, 1980), xi; also supported by these key peace histories: Peter Brock, *Freedom from Violence: Sectarian Nonresistance from the Middle Ages to the Great War* (Toronto: University of Toronto Press,

1991); Brock, *Pacifism in the United States: From the Colonial Era to the First World War* (Princeton: Princeton University Press, 1968); Charles Chatfield, *For Peace and Justice: Pacifism in America, 1914–1941* (Knoxville: University of Tennessee Press, 1971); Merle Curti, *The American Peace Crusade, 1815–1860* (Durham, N.C.: Duke University Press, 1929); Curti, *Peace or War: The American Struggle, 1636–1936* (New York: Norton, 1936); DeBenedetti, assisted by Charles Chatfield, *An American Ordeal: The Antiwar Movement of the Vietnam Era* (Syracuse: Syracuse University Press, 1990); Lawrence S. Wittner, *Rebels Against War: The American Peace Movement, 1933–1983* (New York: Columbia University Press, 1969; rev. ed., Philadelphia: Temple University Press, 1984); Valarie H. Ziegler, *The Advocates of Peace in Antebellum America* (Bloomington: Indiana University Press, 1992). Additional sources are listed in Charles F. Howlett, *The American Peace Movement: References and Resources* (Boston: G.K. Hall, 1991).

3. The only works by historians of the peace movement that focus on the peace press are the introductions to the microfiche reproductions of selected 19th-century peace periodicals published by Clearwater Publishing, as part of the Library of World Peace Studies, by these authors: Warren F. Kuehl and David C. Lawson, *Advocate of Peace* (1979); David C. Lawson, *American Advocate of Peace* (1978); *Calumet* (1978); *Friend of Peace* (1978); *Harbinger of Peace* (1978); David S. Patterson, *Peacemaker and Court of Arbitration* (1979).

4. David Paul Nord, "The Evangelical Origins of Mass Media in America," *Journalism Monographs* 88 (May 1984).

5. For example, Karlyn Kohrs Campbell, *Man Cannot Speak for Her: A Critical Study of Early Feminist Rhetoric*, 2 vols. (New York: Praeger, 1989); Lana F. Rakow and Cheris Kramarae, eds., *The Revolution in Words: Righting Women 1868–1871* (New York: Routledge, 1990); Ann Russo and Cheris Kramarae, eds., *The Radical Women's Press of the 1850s* (New York: Routledge 1991); Martha M. Solomon, ed., *A Voice of Their Own: The Woman Suffrage Press, 1840–1910* (Tuscaloosa: University of Alabama Press, 1991); Linda Steiner, "Finding Community in Nineteenth-Century Suffrage Periodicals," *American Journalism* 1, no. 1 (summer 1983), 1-15.

6. Merton L. Dillon, *Elijah P. Lovejoy, Abolitionist Editor* (Urbana: University of Illinois Press, 1961); Asa Earl Martin, "Pioneer Anti-Slavery Press," *Mississippi Valley Historical Review* 2, no. 4 (March 1916), 509-28; Russel B. Nye, *Fettered Freedom: Civil Liberties and the Slavery Controversy, 1830-1860* (East Lansing: Michigan State University Press, 1963), chap. 7; Roland E. Wolseley, *The Black Press, U.S.A.*, 2nd ed. (Ames: Iowa State University Press, 1990), chap. 2.

7. For example, Ruth Bordin, *Woman and Temperance: The Quest for Power and Liberty, 1873–1900* (Philadelphia: Temple University Press, 1981), chap. 5.

8. Ronald G. Walters, *American Reformers, 1815–1860* (New York: Hill and Wang, 1978), 101.

9. See Curti, *The American Peace Crusade, 1815–1860*, 3-41; W. Freeman Galpin, *Pioneering for Peace: A Study of American Peace Efforts to 1846* (Syracuse, N.Y.: Bardeen Press, 1933), 1-34; Ziegler, *The Advocates of Peace in Antebellum America.*

10. Charles Chatfield, ed., *Peace Movements in America* (New York: Schocken Books, 1973); Curti, *The American Peace Crusade, 1815–1860*, 18-19.

11. Brock, *Pacifism in the United States*, 16-17.

12. DeBenedetti, *The Peace Reform in American History*, 32, 34; Brock, *Pacifism in the United States*, 479.

13. Brock, *Pacifism in the United States*, 459; Curti, *The American Peace Crusade, 1815–1860*, 8. It was absolutely pacifist, opposing all warfare, and aiming "not to form a popular society, but to depend, under God, upon individual personal effort, by conversation and circulating essays" to win a hearing for peace ideas through the churches. (*Memorial of Mr. David L. Dodge, Consisting of an Autobiography Prepared at the Request for the Use of His Children, with a Few Selections from His Writings* [Boston: S.K. Whipple, 1854], 90, as quoted by DeBenedetti, *The Peace Reform in American History*, 33.)

14. The MPS's founder, Noah Worcester (1758–1837), a Unitarian minister, served as the corresponding secretary, and he edited the society's first periodical, the *Friend of Peace*. The ecumenical MPS welcomed a much broader peace constituency than did the NYPS. It grew fairly quickly, eventually emerging as the more vital and important of the two organizations. At the end of the Society's first year, it reported 185 members (of whom 58 were ministers), and claimed to have distributed 4,820 tracts. Also, 925 numbers of the *Friend of Peace* were distributed, including those sent to members of the Massachusetts Peace Society. (*Friend of Peace* 1, no. 7 [1817]), 39; *Friend of Peace* 2, no. 7 [January 1820], 9; "First Annual Report of the Massachusetts Peace Society," *Friend of Peace* 1, no. 7 [1817], 31.)

At the end of 1817, the Society reported a total of 304 members and the distribution of 5,370 tracts. In 1818, the Society's third year, it claimed "upwards of 500" members (Brock claims 1,000), with six branch societies. ("Fourth Annual Report of the Massachusetts Peace Society," *Friend of Peace* 2, no. 7 [1820]), 9, 10; Brock, *Pacifism in the United States*, 473.) It distributed 8,298 tracts, of which 4,785 were copies of the *Friend of Peace*. In 1819, this figure jumped to 16,149 tracts, of which 7,360 were copies of the *Friend of Peace*. (*Friend of Peace* 2, no. 7 [1820], 9-10; "Third Annual Report of the Massachusetts Peace Society, Made at the Annual Meeting in Boston, December 25, 1918," Swarthmore College Peace Collection, Swarthmore, Pa.)

Total membership for that year was put at 882, including 335 members in the twelve branch societies. ("Fourth Annual Report of the Massachusetts Peace Society," *Friend of Peace* 2, no. 7 [1820], 9, 10.) In 1819, the *Friend of Peace* reported that its first three numbers had passed through seven editions in the United States, with the seventh edition of no. 4 currently in press. Also, several other numbers had gone through "5 or 6 editions." (*Friend of Peace* 2, no. 3 [1819], 40.)

15. DeBenedetti, *The Peace Reform in American History*, 33.

16. In addition, 2,860 were sold during that year. Five hundred copies of the *Friend of Peace* were sent to "foreign states and countries," including Great Britain, France, Germany, Russia, India, and Ceylon. ("Fourth Annual Report of the Massachusetts Peace Society," *Friend of Peace* 2, no. 11 [1821], 12.)

17. See Edson L. Whitney, *The American Peace Society: A Centennial History* (Washington, D.C.: American Peace Society, 1928); Ziegler, *Advocates of Peace in Antebellum America*.

18. C. Wendell King, *Social Movements in the United States* (New York: Random House, 1956), 27.

19. Alexis de Tocqueville, *Democracy in America*, vol. 2, ed. Phillips Bradley (1835; New York: Alfred A. Knopf, 1948), 111, 112, quoted in Richard B. Kielbowicz and Clifford Scherer, "The Role of the Press in the Dynamics of Social Movements," *Research in Social Movements, Conflicts and Change* 9 (1986), 71.

20. "Address to the Friends of Peace," *Advocate of Peace* 1, no. 1 (June 1837), 11.

21. Love wrote a series of articles for the *Voice of Peace* which detailed the genesis of that organization. See, for example: "History of the Organization of the Universal Peace Union," *Voice of Peace* 2, no. 1 (January 1873): 1-3, and the conclusion, 2, no. 2 (February1873): 1-3.

22. Brock, *Pacifism in the United States*: 478-79, 375-88.

23. DeBenedetti, *The Peace Reform in American History,* 59-78.

24. Phelps, *The Anglo-American Peace Movement in the Mid-Nineteenth Century*, 68.

25. Nord, "The Evangelical Origins of Mass Media in America," 1, 2.

26. Curti, *The American Peace Crusade*, 232.

27. For an overview of the peace advocacy press, see Nancy L. Roberts, *American Peace Writers, Editors, and Periodicals: A Dictionary* (Westport: Greenwood Press, 1991): xv-xvii.

28. Brock, *Pacifism in the United States*, 389.

29. Brock, *Pacifism in the United States*, 366, 367, 375-76, 377.

30. Brock, *Pacifism in the United States*, 405.

31. The information about these periodicals presented in this section is based upon my own examination of the files at the Swarthmore College Peace

Collection, Swarthmore, Pa., supplemented by these secondary sources: Curti, *The American Peace Crusade*, 232-33; Frank Luther Mott, *A History of American Magazines:* vol. 1 (New York and London: D. Appleton, 1930), vols. 2–5 (Cambridge, Mass.: Harvard University Press, 1938–68); and the *National Union Catalogue* (Pre-1956 Imprints).

32. There the *American Advocate of Peace*, as it was known, was edited by the Rev. Caleb Sprague Henry (1834-35) and by Francis Fellowes (1835–36). The *American Advocate of Peace* (averaging about 48 pages) absorbed the *Calumet* in June 1835. The *American Advocate of Peace* published its last number in November 1836 and was succeeded by a new series, the *Advocate of Peace*. The latter was variously a monthly, a bimonthly, and a quarterly; its editors included Rev. George Beckwith and Elihu Burritt. (During Burritt's 1846 editorship, the periodical was renamed the *Advocate of Peace and Universal Brotherhood*.) The *Advocate of Peace* moved to Washington, D.C., in 1910, and later changed its title to *World Affairs*.

33. Editors included Thomas W. Stuckey and Alfred H. Love.

34. Quakers had always opposed war, but in 1867 the Peace Association of Friends was formed by seven of the American Yearly Meetings, "for the purpose of bringing this important subject more promptly to the notice of Christian purposes, and to the world at large, than had hitherto been done, and to labor for the spread of this very important feature of the Gospel" (*Messenger of Peace* 2, no. 5 [1 February 1872], 65).

35. Solomon, ed., *A Voice of Their Own*, 15, 29.

36. Thus, for instance, the *Advocate of Peace* aimed to reach "*every class* of readers" (*Advocate of Peace* 2, no. 5 [June 1838], 10). And the *Friend of Peace* sometimes found it difficult to address simultaneously its dual audience of readers in the United States and abroad; for instance, it had considered listing duels under a regular column called "Disgraceful Occurrences." But this was deemed not a good idea, because, "recollecting that the circulation of this work is not confined to the United States, we are unwilling to be the instruments of extending to other countries a detail of such barbarous occurrences in our own" ("Disgraceful Occurrences," *Friend of Peace* 2, no. 5 [August 1819], 39).

37. "First Annual Report of the Massachusetts Peace Society," *Friend of Peace* 1, no. 7 (1816), 30, 31.

38. "While correcting the last proof, we received the pleasing intelligence from Maine, that at Minot, July 9th, a READING PEACE SOCIETY was organized, consisting of seventy-nine members" ("Auspicious Occurrences," *Friend of Peace* 4, no. 1 [July 1824], 32). See also, for example: "Auspicious Occurrences," *Friend of Peace* 2, no. 3 (1819), 39-40.

39. "Auspicious Occurrences," *Friend of Peace*, Appendix, no. 3 (July 1828), 96; "Auspicious Occurrences," *Friend of Peace* 2, no. 5 (August 1819), 35. Also see: "Intelligence from Peace Societies," *Friend of Peace* 1, no. 9

(August 1816), 40; "Peace Societies in Great Britain," *Friend of Peace* 2, no. 5 (August 1819), 31-32; "Raleigh Peace Society," *Friend of Peace* 2, no. 5 (August 1819), 32-33; "Rhode-Island and Providence Plantations Peace Society," *Friend of Peace* 2, no. 5 (August 1819), 34; "Interesting Facts," *Friend of Peace* 1, no. 12 (1 May 1818): 38-39.

40. "Auspicious Movements," *Advocate of Peace* 1, no. 3 (Dec. 1837).

41. For example, "New Peace Societies," *Harbinger of Peace* 1, no. 12 (April 1829), 283; "Intelligence: Peace Societies—Resolutions, & c.," *American Advocate of Peace* 1, no. 7 (December 1835), 340-42; "Report of Kindred Movements," *Bond of Peace* 2, no. 8 (August 1869), 66; "Iowa Peace Society," *Messenger of Peace* 4, no. 2 (Nov. 1873), 26; "An Earnest Peace Movement in England," *Voice of Peace* 5, no. 9 (December 1878), 129-31; "Woman's Peace Movement in England," *Voice of Peace* 1, no. 6 (September 1874), 96.

42. For example, "Influence of Peace Reading—of the Advocate," *Advocate of Peace* 5, no. 2 (February 1843), 20.

43. *Friend of Peace* 1, no. 11 (1 February 1816), 40.

44. "Exposition of the American Peace Society," *Advocate of Peace* 2, no. 13 (Feb. 1839), 199.

45. *Harbinger of Peace* 1, no. 12 (April 1829), 286.

46. "Annual Report of the American Peace Society," *Calumet* 1, no. 7 (May–June 1832), 198. The *Friend of Peace* measured its journalistic impact by the growth of regional peace societies, and by the Convention of Congregational Ministers' voted official approval of the Massachusetts Peace Society. ("First Annual Report of the Massachusetts Peace Society," *Friend of Peace* 1, no. 7 [1817], 32).

47. *American Advocate of Peace* 2, no. 11 (December 1836), back cover.

48. "Explanatory & Salutatory," *Voice of Peace* 1, no. 1 (June 1872), 6. Note: similarly, the first Pennsylvania Peace Society's *Advocate of Peace* pledged that "being devoted to the cause of peace and brotherly love…[it would] never exhibit its columns disgraced by unprofitable altercation…. Well digested arguments; deductions from certain data; abstracts of Missionary news; reflections on existing abuses relative to our subject; reports of other similar societies; extracts of a useful and entertaining nature; and whatever may tend to promote 'peace on earth,' will be considered matter germain [*sic*] to our purpose" (*Advocate of Peace* 1, no. 1 [Philadelphia: Pennsylvania Peace Society, 1823], 7).

49. *Messenger of Peace* 9, no. 3 (March 1879), 1, 34-35; J.J. Copp, *Voice of Peace* 2, no. 4 (April 1873), 10-12; William M. Holland, *American Advocate of Peace* 2, no. 11 (December 1836), 107-14.

50. For example, "Hymn to Peace," *Harbinger of Peace* 2, no. 5 (September 1829), 120; "What the Winds Bring," *Herald of Peace* 3, no. 7

(1 May 1869), 87; Bernard Barton, "Power and Gentleness," *Bond of Peace*, new ser., 1, no. 1 (January 1871), 11; "The Star of Peace," *Voice of Peace* 1, no. 1 (June 1872), 1; "Horrors of War," *Messenger of Peace* 10, no. 2 (February 1880), 1; Milton Belden, "The Brotherhood of Man," *Peacemaker* 1, no. 1 (July 1882), 7.

51. For example, "Harry's Mittens," *Voice of Peace* 2, no. 1 (January 1873), 7; "Joe Benton's Coal Yard," *Messenger of Peace* 9, no. 3 (March 1879), 37-38.

52. Lynne Masel-Walters, "Their Rights and Nothing More: A History of *The Revolution*, 1868-70," *Journalism Quarterly* 53 (summer 1976), 249; Solomon, ed., *A Voice of Their Own*, 50-51; Bordin, *Woman and Temperance*, 91-93; Nye, *Fettered Freedom*, 122.

53. For example, "Our Little Folks' Corner, " *Bond of Peace*, new ser., 1, no. 1 (January 1871), 11, and no. 4 (April 1871), 57; "Children's Department," *Herald of Peace* 3, no. 5 (1 April 1869), 58-59 and 3, no. 7 (1 May 1869), 86-87; "Children's Department," *Voice of Peace* 6, no. 4 (July 1879), 61-64; "For Young Readers," *Peacemaker* 1, no. 1 (July 1882), 14-16.

In some cases, a separate publication evolved for children, such as the American Peace Society's *Angel of Peace* and the Universal Peace Union's *Leaflets of Peace for Children* (which, although a separate monthly publication, was apparently appended to monthly issues of the *Voice of Peace*).

Sometimes the children's publication replaced the special children's section within the adult periodical. Thus, the *Herald of Peace* dropped its children's section with the publication by the Herald Company, starting in January 1869, of the *Guiding* Star ("Announcement," *Herald of Peace* 2, no. 5 [1 October 1868], 74).

54. Bordin, *Woman and Temperance*, 92-93.

55. Bordin, *Woman and Temperance*, 93.

56. According to Frank Luther Mott, magazine subscription prices were rather variable in the 1741–1850 period, with reviews (such as the *Knicker-bocker*, the *Southern Literary Messenger*, and the *Democratic*) each charging $5 per year. During this period, "Three dollars a year came the nearest to being a standard rate; that was the subscription price of the leading women's magazines, of the *New World* and *Brother Jonathan*, of *Graham's* and many others. The number of dollar magazines is surprisingly large, however" (*A History of American Magazines*, 1:513-14).

57. See, for example, *Friend of Peace* 1, no. 8 (1817), 40; *Calumet* 2, no. 4 (November-December 1834), 97; *Advocate of Peace* 1, no. 2 (September 1837), 96; *Herald of Peace* 4, no. 2 (15 August 1869), 5; *Bond of Peace*, new ser., 1, no. 12 (December 1871), 182.

58. *Harbinger of Peace* 1, no. 10 (February 1829), 220; and 2, no. 5 (September 1829), back cover. "Whenever the society can afford to *pay* an

editor, a more able one will be procured; but it will be difficult to find an editor who will do the work for nothing, and take all the trouble and risk on himself besides, as we have done" (*Harbinger of Peace* 1, no. 12 [April 1829], 287; Lawson, "Introduction," microfiche reproduction of *Calumet,* 2).

59. For example, *Calumet* 2, no. 1 (May-June 1834), 31-32; *Advocate of Peace* 3, no. 18 (August 1839), 48; *Advocate of Peace* 3, no. 19 (October 1839), 72; *Bond of Peace* 1, no. 5 (May 1868), 2; *Voice of Peace* 5, no. 10 (January 1879), 156; *Peacemaker* 4, no. 1 (July 1885), 16.

60. J.G.C. Kennedy, *Catalogue of the Newspapers and Periodicals Published in the United States. Compiled from the Census of 1850* (New York: J. Livingston, 1852), 19. One of the few additional sources for this period is Daniel J. Kenny, *The American Newspaper Directory and Record of the Press* (New York: Watson, 1861).

The more available but self-reported circulation data indicates, for example, that in 1831, the *Harbinger of Peace* printed about 18,500 copies and that in 1840 the *Advocate of Peace*, a bimonthly, was being issued in quantities from 2,000 to 2,700 ("Third Report of the American Peace Society," *Calumet* 1, no. 1 [May-June 1831], 8; *Advocate of Peace* 3, no. 23 [June 1840], 153). The *Messenger of Peace* announced that in 1878, 214,600 pages of tracts were distributed, and 169 volumes, "while the matter contained in the *Messenger of Peace* has been equal to 1,404,000 pages of tracts" (*Messenger of Peace* 9, no. 10 [Oct. 1879], 149).

61. See, for example, Mott, *A History of American Magazines,* 1:514; 2:10; 3:6, 7; 4:16, 17.

62. DeBenedetti, *The Peace Reform in American History,* 32; Brock, *Pacifism in the United States,* 3, 17.

63. "Annual Report of the American Peace Society," *Calumet* 1, no. 7 (May-June 1832), 198.

64. American Anti-Slavery Society, *First Annual Report,* 1834, 41, quoted in Savage, *The Controversy over the Distribution of Abolition Literature 1830–1860,* 9.

65. *Messenger of Peace* 2, no. 5 (1 February 1872), 72.

66. "Peace Societies in Great Britain," *Friend of Peace* 2, no. 5 (August 1819), 32.

67. "The Tongue, the Pen and the Press," *Friend of Peace,* Appendix, no. 3 (July 1828), 90-94.

68. Charles Stewart, Craig Smith, and Robert E. Denton, Jr., *Persuasion and Social Movements* (Prospect Heights, Ill.: Waveland Press, 1984), 38.

69. *Friend of Peace* 1, no. 4 (1815), 38.

70. "Twelfth Annual Report," *Advocate of Peace* 3, no. 23 (June 1840), 153.

71. "Address to the Friends of Peace," *Advocate of Peace* 1, no. 1 (June 1837), 11; "Exposition of the American Peace Society," *Advocate of Peace* 2, no. 13 (February 1839), 201-02.

72. "Explanatory & Salutatory," *Voice of Peace* 1, no. 1 (June 1872), 6.

73. "Public Opinion Against War," *Advocate of Peace* 1, no. 2 (September 1837), 7.

74. "Tenth Annual Report of the American Peace Society," *Advocate of Peace* 2, no. 5 (June 1838), 9.

75. "Address to the Friends of Peace," *Advocate of Peace* 1, no. 1 (June 1837), 11.

76. "Proceedings of the Convention of the Friends of Peace, of the State of Pennsylvania, Held at Philadelphia, on Thursday, April 4th, 1850" (Philadelphia: Joseph Rakestraw, 1850), 6.

77. "Report of the Connecticut Peace Society," *Calumet* 1, no. 14 (May-June 1833), 418.

78. For instance, "Report of the Rev. George C. Beckwith's Agency in Behalf of the American Peace Society," *Advocate of Peace* 1, no. 1 (June 1837), 31; "The Ninth Annual Report of the American Peace Society," *Advocate of Peace* 1, no. 1 (June 1837), 19-20; *Advocate of Peace and Universal Brotherhood* 1, no. 1 (January 1846), 11; "Close of Volume VIII," *Voice of Peace* 8, supplement to no. 12 (April 1882), 197.

79. Hazel Dicken-Garcia, *Journalistic Standards in Nineteenth-Century America* (Madison: University of Wisconsin Press, 1989), 47-48.

80. *Bond of Peace* 2, no. 3 (Mar. 1869), 20.

81. *Harbinger of Peace* 1, no. 12 (Apr. 1829), 285.

82. Laurence Leamer, *The Paper Revolutionaries: The Rise of the Underground Press* (New York: Simon and Schuster, 1972), 16-17.

83. Masel-Walters, "Their Rights and Nothing More," 249; Solomon, ed., *A Voice of Their Own,* 14-15, 50-51.

84. Bordin, *Woman and Temperance,* 93-93.

85. John Tebbel and Mary Ellen Zuckerman, *The Magazine in America, 1741–1990* (New York: Oxford University Press, 1991), 14-17.

86. "A Peace Paper," *Herald of Peace* 3, no. 5 (1 April 1869), 54.

87. Phelps, *The Anglo-American Peace Movement in the Mid-Nineteenth Century,* 62.

88. "Imperial Policy," *Friend of Peace* 1, no. 12 (1 May 1818), 39.

89. "War Scenes and Expenses," *Voice of Peace* 6, no. 5 (August 1879), 67.

90. "Sketches of War," *Advocate of Peace* 1, no. 2 (September 1837), 80, 81.

91. Barbara Welter, "The Cult of True Womanhood, 1820–1860," *American Quarterly* 18 (summer 1966), 151-74.

92. "War and the Social Affections: The Maniac Mother," *Advocate of Peace* 2, no. 9 (October 1838), 111.

93. "British Atrocities in South Africa," *Messenger of Peace* 9, no. 8 (August 1879), 115; "A Doomed Army," *Messenger of Peace* 9, no. 8 (August 1879), 124.

94. "The Execution of a Deserter," *American Advocate of Peace* 1, no. 7 (December 1835), 312, 314, 315.

95. Phelps, *The Anglo-American Peace Movement in the Mid-Nineteenth Century*, 77.

96. "Corporal Punishment," *Harbinger of Peace* 1, no. 12 (April 1829), 280. See also: "Treatment of Soldiers," *Advocate of Peace* 3, no. 19 (October 1839), 68-69.

97. John H. Douglass, "Consideration of the Question of Peace," *Herald of Peace* 1, no. 12 (15 July 1868), 1.

98. "A Plain Statement," *Voice of Peace* 1, no. 1 (June 1872), 11.

99. "To the U. Peace Union," *Voice of Peace* 2, no. 4 (Apr. 1873), 5.

100. For example, "On the Infliction of Death as a Punishment," *Advocate of Peace* 1, no. 4 (March 1835), 17; "Nature and Object of Punishment" and "The Prison a Sphere for Womans' [sic] Labor," *Herald of Peace* 2, no. 1 (1 August 1868), 1; "The Death Penalty," *Bond of Peace* 1, no. 11 (November 1868), 3-4; "Capital Punishment," *Bond of Peace* 2, no. 1 (January 1869), 4; Charles Williams, "Capital Punishment," *Bond of Peace*, new ser., 1, no. 1 (January 1871), 1; J.P. Haines, "Capital Punishment," *Messenger of Peace* 2, no. 6 (1 March 1872), 73 (cover page), 74; "Universal Peace Union and Capital Punishment," *Peacemaker* 1, no. 1 (July 1882), 11; "Gallows Fruits," *Peacemaker* 1, no. 1 (July 1882), 11. Note: the *Advocate of Peace* discussed why the American Peace Society did not wish to debate the capital punishment issue ("Ninth Annual Report of the American Peace Society," *Advocate of Peace* 1, no. 1 [June 1837], 27).

101. For example, "Auspicious Occurrences," *Friend of Peace* 2, no. 3 (1819), 39; "Fourth Annual Report of the Massachusetts Peace Society," *Friend of Peace* 2, no. 7 (January 1820), 44; "Report of the Committee on Indian Affairs," *Friend of Peace* 4, no. 2 (October 1824), 45-47; "The Indians," *Bond of Peace* 1, no. 11 (November 1868), 4, 6-7; "Our Memorial in Behalf of the Indians" and "The Late Indian Massacre," *Bond of Peace* 2, no. 1 (January 1869), 4; "Universal Peace Union," *Bond of Peace* 2, no. 3 (March 1869), 21; "Our Indian Interest," *Bond of Peace* 2, no. 8 (August 1869), 64; "Letter to the Ojibway Indians," *Voice of Peace* 1, no. 1 (June 1872), 3-4; "Indian Affairs," *Voice of Peace* 1, no. 5 (October 1872), 12; "The Modoc Indians," *Voice of Peace* 2, no. 4 (April 1873), 9; "The Condemned Modocs," *Voice of Peace* 2, no. 10 (October 1873), 2; "Christian and Savage Warfare," *Messenger of Peace* 4, no. 2 (November 1873), 1; "Indian Department—Indians and Negroes,"

Voice of Peace 1, no. 6 (September 1874), 84-85; "Of Indians Who Were Once Our Guests in Philadelphia," *Voice of Peace* 1, no. 6 (September 1874), 85; "Civilization Amongst the Indians," *Voice of Peace* 1, no. 6 (September 1874), 86-88; "Official Report of the Twelfth Annual Meeting of the Pennsylvania Peace Society," *Voice of Peace* 5, no. 10 (January 1879), 149, 152-53; "Indian Department," *Voice of Peace* 8, no. 1 (April 1881), 4-6; "Greeting of Indian Children and Baltimore Children to the Peace Girls and Boys," *Voice of Peace* 8, no. 4 (July 1881), part of the children's section (*Leaflets of Peace for Children*), 62-64; "Indian Subject," *Peacemaker* 4, no. 1 (July 1885), 10.

"To the Readers of the Philadelphia Tribune," *Bond of Peace* 1, no. 2 (February 1868), 4. See also: "Woman," *Bond of Peace* 2, no. 1 (January 1869), 5; "The Woman Movement," *Bond of Peace* 2, no. 3 (March 1869), 20; "Does the Peace Movement Comprehend Woman Suffrage," *Bond of Peace* 2, no. 7 (July 1869), 51; "Sojourner Truth," *Bond of Peace* 3, no. 1 (Jan. 1870), 4; "The Iowa Idea of Woman's Rights," *Messenger of Peace* 9, no. 3 (March 1879), 44; "Woman Suffrage to Secure Peace," *Voice of Peace* 7, no. 8 (Nov. 1880), 128; "Official Report of the Fifteenth Anniversary of the Universal Peace Union, Held in New York City, May 27th, 28th and 29th, 1881," *Voice of Peace* 8, no. 4 (July 1881), 55-56; "A Girl's Work at Home," *Messenger of Peace* 12, no. 2 (February 1882), 30-31. Note: in keeping with its editorial philosophy, the *Bond of Peace* published an advertisement for the *Women's Advocate*, a reform magazine (2, no. 6 [June 1869], page 4 of the advertising supplement following page 44).

103. *Messenger of Peace* 9, no. 7 (July 1879), 104. See also "Temperance," *Herald of Peace* 3, no. 5 (Apr. 1869), 60; H.J. Smith, "Intemperance," *Herald of Peace* 3, no. 7 (1 May 1869), 75; "Intemperance versus Peace," *Voice of Peace* 2, no. 4 (Apr. 1873), 12-13; "Anti-Treating Pledge," *Messenger of Peace* 9, no. 3 (March 1879), 43; "Temperance Tidbits," *Messenger of Peace* 9, no. 8 (August 1879), 125; "A Cruel King," *Messenger of Peace* 9, no. 11 (November 1879), 168.

104. "The Smoker," *Bond of Peace* 2, no. 7 (July 1869), 54. See also, for example, "A Smoking Clergyman," *Bond of Peace* 2, no. 8 (August 1869), 64; "Mental Effects of Tobacco," *Messenger of Peace* 15, no. 9 (September 1885), 138-39; "A Little Boy's Resolve," *Messenger of Peace* 15, no. 9 (September 1885), 139.

105. For example, "Animals Versus Men," *Bond of Peace* 2, no. 3 (March 1869), 20, 24; J. Murray Spear, "Treatment of Dumb Animals," *Voice of Peace* 2, no. 13 (January 1874), 1, 2; "No Peace where there is Cruelty to Animals," *Voice of Peace* 1, no. 5 (August 1874), 76; "Kindness to Animals," *Messenger of Peace* 9, no. 10 (October 1879), 151.

106. "Cruelty to Animals," *Herald of Peace* 2, no. 2 (15 August 1868), 19.

107. "An Estimate of Human Sacrifices in the Russian Campaign," *Friend of Peace* 1, no. 3 (1815), 25; "War and Slavery—Their Abolition," *Herald of Peace* 3, no. 5 (1 Apr. 1869), 50. Note: along with women's rights, abolition was the most common companion movement in which antebellum peace advocates were involved. The small number of articles opposing slavery in this sample undoubtedly is a function in part of the time period of the publications sampled.

108. For example., "Carrying Concealed Deadly Weapons," *Voice of Peace* 2, no. 1 (Jan. 1873), 5; "Boys and Pistols," *Messenger of Peace* 9, no. 2 (February 1879), 22; "Official Report of the Fifteenth Anniversary of the Universal Peace Union, Held in New York City, May 27th, 28th and 29th, 1881," *Voice of Peace* 8, no. 4 (July 1881), 56; "Lynch Law," *Herald of Peace* 2, no. 2 (15 August 1868), 1.

109. For example, "Prison Discipline," *Herald of Peace* 1, no. 12 (15 July 1868), 1; "Term Sentences," *Herald of Peace* 2, no. 3 (1 September 1868), 1; "Efforts Against the Whipping Post," *Voice of Peace* 8, no. 1 (April 1881), 3-4.

110. "American Peace Society. Proceedings of the Fifth Anniversary," *Calumet* 1, no. 13 (May-June 1833), 387; "Boys and Pistols," *Messenger of Peace* 9, no. 2 (February 1879), 22.

111. Bordin, *Woman and Temperance,* 91-92.

112. Solomon, ed., *A Voice of Their Own,* 37, 57.

113. Masel-Walters, "Their Rights and Nothing More," 249.

Contributors

Sherilyn Cox Bennion is a professor of journalism at Humboldt State University, Arcata, California, and the author of *Equal to the Occasion: Women Editors of the Nineteenth-Century West*. She also has published many articles, primarily on women in journalism history, in professional and historical periodicals. She received a B.A. degree from the University of Utah in journalism and M.S. and Ph.D. degrees from Syracuse University in mass communication. A recipient of the annual Service to Journalism Award from the University of Utah, she also is a two-time winner of the Mormon History Association's prize for best article in women's studies. She recently served a three-year term on the board of the American Journalism Historians Association.

David A. Copeland is the author of the forthcoming *Colonial American Newspapers: Character and Content* and articles and reviews on media history. He received his Ph.D. from the University of North Carolina at Chapel Hill in mass communication research and also holds a Th.M. degree in church history from Southeastern Baptist Theological Seminary. His research has earned numerous awards from the American Journalism Historians Association and the Association for Education in Journalism and Mass Communication. He is an assistant professor of mass communication at Emory & Henry College. As a journalist, Copeland has worked as an editor, writer, and photographer on both daily and weekly newspapers and has been recognized for investigative journalism and writing.

John M. Coward is an assistant professor of communication at the University of Tulsa, where he teaches both journalism skills and media theory courses. A former newspaper reporter and editor in Tennessee, he received his Ph.D. in communication from the University of Texas at Austin in 1989. His primary research interest is in media representations of Native Americans. He has contributed chapters on Native American images to *Media/Reader* and *Pluralizing Journalism Education* and has published articles in *Journalism Quarterly* and *Journalism History*. He is currently completing a book on Native American identity in the 19th-century press called *The Newspaper Indian*.

Victoria Goff is an assistant professor in journalism and history at the University of Wisconsin, Green Bay. Professor Goff has worked as a newspaper and magazine journalist and has written two trade books. Her academic research has included international mass media, ethnic and immigrant press, women's consumer magazines, and women journalists. She has been published in several journals and books and is the editor of *Voyageur*, a history journal. She was also the recipient of the Top Research Paper Award at the American Journalism Historians Association Convention in 1990 and has served for three years as the chair of the Women's Interest Group of the same organization.

William E. Huntzicker, a former reporter for The Associated Press in Minneapolis, Minnesota, and the Miles City Star in Montana, teaches journalism at the University of Minnesota. He holds a bachelor's degree in history from Montana State University and a master's and doctorate in American studies from the University of Minnesota and has published academic articles on American frontier newspapers and the 19th-century illustrated magazines.

Frankie Hutton worked her way through North Carolina A&T University as a copyperson and intern at the *Greensboro Daily News*. She was also managing editor of the *A&T Register*, the campus newspaper. She earned the master's degree in journalism at the University of South Carolina, Columbia, in 1971 and has since worked in industry and in journalism academe. For WBTV in Charlotte, North Carolina, she produced a pilot minority affairs program. From 1988 to 1991 she served a gubernatorial appointment as a member of the Commission on Sex Discrimination in the New Jersey Statutes. Dr. Hutton has taught journalism at Hampton University, the University of Virginia, and at Lehigh University. She was awarded the doctorate in American history at Rutgers University in 1990 and is the author of *The Early Black Press in America, 1827–1860,* scholarly articles, and reviews.

Barbara F. Luebke, who has been teaching journalism since 1974, is professor of journalism and women's studies and chairwoman of the Department of Journalism at the University of Rhode Island. She holds a Ph.D. in journalism from the University of Missouri. She has been interested in journalism's "outsiders" since participating in the late Leslie D. Polk's groundbreaking course, "The Minority Press in America," in 1970 at the University of Wisconsin, Eau Claire. Her essay is adapted from her 1981 dissertation, "Elias Boudinot, Cherokee Editor: The Father of American Indian Journalism." Dr. Luebke's recent research and writing have focused on images of women in the media. She is co-author with Mary Ellen Reilly of *Women's Studies Graduates: the First Generation.*

Catherine C. Mitchell is professor of mass communication and chair of the Department of Mass Communication at the University of North Carolina at Asheville. She received her Ph.D. in communications in 1987 from the University of Tennessee. She has written three books: *Margaret Fuller's New York Journalism: A Bibliographical Essay and Key Writings*; *The Light on Synanon* (with David Mitchell and Richard Ofshe); and *The Newswriting Formula* (with Mark West) (forthcoming). She teaches newspaper skills courses and media history with a specialization in 19th-century newspaper women. In 1979 she shared a Pulitzer Prize for public service awarded to the *Point Reyes (Calif.) Light.*

Barbara Straus Reed is an associate professor of journalism and mass media at Rutgers University, New Brunswick, New Jersey, having received her Ph.D. in mass communication from the Scripps School of Journalism, Ohio University, Athens. She has also taught at California State University, Los Angeles, and at Ohio University. She has worked for the Associated Press, Young & Rubicam, KCET-TV, and *Journalism Quarterly*. In addition, Dr. Reed did public relations for the first national conference on children and edited another book, *About Elaine*. A contributor to the major academic journals in the field, she received a post-doctoral fellowship to the American Jewish Archives in Cincinnati.

Nancy L. Roberts is an associate professor in the School of Journalism and Mass Communication and an adjunct faculty member in the Program in American Studies at the University of Minnesota, Twin Cities. Her books include *American Catholic Pacifism* (with Anne Klejment), *American Peace Writers, Editors, and Periodicals: A Dictionary*, and *Dorothy Day and the "Catholic Worker."* She has chaired the History Division, Association for Education in Journalism and Mass Communication, and served as president of the American Journalism Historians Association. She holds a B.A. in history from Swarthmore College, an M.A. in American studies from Brown University, and an M.A. and Ph.D. in mass communication from the University of Minnesota.

Index

abolitionists, 225

*Advocate, see Advocate of Peace,
Cherokee Advocate*

Advocate of Peace, 211, 218-19, 221, 222

Advocate of Peace and Christian Patriot,
212

African-American, *see also* black press
3, 5-6, 159, 160, 163

Aguacero, El, 60, 65

Aliened American, 9

Alki, 174, 175 180

Amendments, U.S. Constitution
1st Amendment, 4, 187, 188, 192, 193
193, 195, 203
13th Amendment, 15
14th Amendment, 15, 159
15th Amendment, 15, 159

American Anti-Slavery Society, 15

*American and Chinese Commercial
Newspaper*, 85

American Colonization Society, 11

American Israelite, 43

American Moral Reform Society, 12

American Advocate of Peace, 212, 216,
217, 222

American Peace Society, 210, 211-12

American Revolution, 7, 8, 21

American Society for Meliorating the
Condition of the Jew, 21-26, 29, 32, 44

Amigo del Pueblo, El, 60, 64

Anglo-African Magazine, 13

Anglo-Spanish Merchant, 61

Anthony, Susan B., 159, 162, 163-64

Anti-Semitism, 35-37, 48

Arts, Hispanic press, 66

Asmonean, 39, 40-43

assimilation, 155
Hispanic press, 57, 67
Jews, 30, 48

Atlanta Daily Constitution, 194, 196

Azusa Valley News, 60, 66, 67

Bailyn, Bernard, 8

Bandera Mexicana, La, 61, 65

Baptist Society for Evangelization of the
Jew, 21

Barbareño, El, 61, 66

Barlow, William, 5, 17

Bell, Philip, 12

Bennett, James Gordon, 47, 101

Berlin, Ira, 8, 18

bilingual newspapers, 58, 59, 61-62

Bitter Creek, 95

black press, 1, 2, 3, 7, 10, 13, 20

Bloomer, Amelia, 162

blue laws, *see* Sunday "blue" laws

Board of Delegates of American
Israelites, 38

Bond of Peace, 216, 219, 223, 224

Boudinot, Elias, 115-41, 147-48, 151, 152,
153

Brown, Elsa Barkley, 160

Burlingame Treaty, 108

Bush, Isidor, 40

California, 71, 74, 77, 78, 93, 99, 101,
102, 103, 108, 109

Californian, 58, 61-62

Calumet, 211, 217

Campbell, E.L. (Mrs. Schlachtfeld),
175-76

Canada West, 9

Canton, 75, 81

Castillo, Guadelupe, 59-60

Celestial Empire, 102, 108, 111

Cherokee Advocate, 146, 147, 149, 151, 152, 153, 154

Cherokee Nation, 118, 120, 122, 126, 129, 130, 132, 134, 136

Cherokee Phoenix, see *Cherokee Phoenix and Indians' Advocate*

Cherokee Phoenix and Indians' Advocate, 115-17, 121, 123-24, 125, 128-29, 131, 132, 134, 135, 136, 137, 138, 139, 141

Chicago Tribune, 194, 198, 199

China, 72-77, 82, 83, 87, 94, 96, 99-100, 102-06, 109, 111

Chinese American, 85

Chinese dialect, 73-74

printing, 86

Chinese Exclusion Act of 1882, 72, 98, 99, 102, 108

Chinese Newspaper, 84-85

Chinese Record, 78

Chinese Repository, 75-76

Chinese World, 86-87

Ch'ng Dynasty, 73

Christian History, 29

Churchill, Caroline, 173, 174

Active Footsteps, 173

civil rights, 97

Civil War, 5, 6, 7, 8, 9, 10, 15, 16, 17

Clamor Público, El, 60, 64, 66, 67

Clarion, 13

Cleveland, Grover, 95, 102

colonization movement, 10

Colorado Antelope, 173

Colored American, 6, 7, 11, 12

Colored Patriot, 16

Colton, Reverend Walter, 62

Coming Century, 172, 181

Confucius, 82

conversion, 21, 48

coolie labor, 99, 100

Cornish, Samuel, 7, 11, 12, 15

Correspondencia, La, 61

Cortés, Carlos E., 59

Crespusculo, El, 61, 65

Crónica, La (Los Angeles), 60, 65

Crónica, La (San Francisco), 59, 61, 63

Cronista, La, 61

Cuba, 83, 100

Cult of True Womanhood, 162-63

culture, 162

Hispanic, 3, 57, 58

Cummings, C.O., 71, 72

Curti, Merle, 10

Custer, legend and myth, 145

Daily Constitution, 197, 198

Damascus affair, 31

Dates, Jannette, 5, 17

Davis, Angela, 160

Davis, Paulina Wright, 162

Day, William Howard, 9

Declaration of Independence, 7, 8, 11

defense of Judaism, 22, 23, 35, 44

Demócrata, El, 60, 66

democratic idealism, 7, 8, 9, 10, 13, 16, 17

Diario de México, El, 60, 62

diversity, 1, 2, 16, 31, 56, 160; *see also* ethnic, multicultural

Don Clarito, 61, 65

Dos Repúblicas, Las, 60, 66

Douglass, Frederick, 7, 13-15

Duniway, Abigail S., 171, 172, 173, 174, 177, 178, 179, 180, 181, 182-83

Path-Breaking, 171

Dunlap, T., Jr., 64

Echo du Pacifique, L', 61, 64

Eco de la Patria, El, 56, 60, 65

Eco de la Puerta, El, 60, 65

Eco de la Raza Latina, El, 56, 61, 65

Eco del Pacífico, El, 58, 60, 61, 64

Eco Mexicano, El, 60
editorial
    black, 7, 8-10, 11, 12, 17
    Chinese, 72, 76-77, 81, 82, 84, 87,
        96-97, 99-102, 104, 105, 108, 111
    Hispanic, 65, 66
    Jewish, 34, 35-37, 39, 41-42, 43-44, 45
    Mormon, 188, 192, 194, 195, 197-199
    Native American, 120, 123, 124, 129-
        30, 132, 135, 146, 148, 151-53,
        154, 188
    peace advocacy, 216-17, 219
    response, 151, 153, 155
    risk, 151
education, 48-49
    Jewish, 36, 38
    language, 36
    religious, 36, 38
Estrella, La, 60, 63, 64
ethnic, 55, 57, 58, 79; *see also* diversity,
    multicultural

Fairbank, John K., 75
Fe en la Democratia, La, 60
Feminism, 169-85
    natural rights, 178
    personal, 178, 181
    social, 178
Five Civilized Tribes, 148, 152
Foner, Eric, 15
Fortune, Timothy Thomas, 7, 16
Frank Leslie's Illustrated Newspaper,
    94, 95, 103-11
Frederick Douglass' Paper, 15
Freedom's Journal, 5, 6, 11
Friend, 213
Friend of Peace, 211, 212, 217, 218, 221
Fugitive Slave Law, 10

Gaceta, La (Texas), 62
Gaceta de México, La, 62
Garnet, Henry Highland, 13, 15

Garrison, William Lloyd, 14, 211
Garvey, Marcus, 16
Gazette, 61, 64
Georgia, 116-17, 118-19, 121, 126-35,
    137, 138
    Georgia Acts, 121-22, 139
    Georgia Guard, 125, 129, 130-34, 137
Germans, 97
Gilmer, Governor George R., 125
Gold Hill News, 77, 78
Golden Hill News, 77, 78
Golden Mountain News, 77, 78
Grant's order, 38
Gray, Reverend W., 28
Great Awakening, 29
Greene, Louisa Lula, 176
Grievances, Hispanic press, 58, 66
Gutiérrez, Félix, 1, 59

Herald, see Herald of Peace
Herald of Peace, 216, 217, 220, 223, 224
Harbinger, see Harbinger of Peace
Harbinger of Peace, 211, 212, 213, 220,
    221
Harper's Weekly, 94, 95-97
Hebrew fonts, 22
hojas volantes, 62

idealism, democratic black, 5-20
ideology
    of race and progress, 146
    progressive, 155
Indian Herald, 146
Indian Journal, 146, 147, 149, 150, 155
Indian removal, 131, 139
Indian Removal Bill, 124
Indian-white relations, 146, 151
Intermarriage, 37
Irish, 97, 109
Israel's Advocate, 21, 22, 23, 25, 26, 28
Israel's Herold, 40

Jackson, Andrew, 116-17, 118, 124, 128, 137, 138
Jackson, Solomon Henry, 21-27, 47
Jew, 22-29
Jew Indeed, 29
Jewish burial grounds, 45
Jewish Chronicle, 32
Jewish
   community, 31
   education, 36
   the *Jew,* 27
   rights, 32
   unity, 33, 36, 37, 41, 44, 45
Jim Crow laws, 5
Joffre, J., 63
Journal, see *Indian Journal*
Joven, El, 56, 60, 65

Kemble, Edward C., 58, 77, 78
Knights of Labor, 95, 96, 97
Know-Nothingism, 42

Lafuente, J.T., 63
land rights, 148, 149, 151
language
   Chinese, 3, 73, 76, 78, 86
   Spanish, 3
League of Universal Brotherhood, 210
Leeser, Isaac, 30, 31, 47
Lemaitre, Reverend Cure 15-16
Liberator, 14
"Liberty of the Press" columns, 132, 133
Lilienthal, Rabbi Max, 43
Lily, 162, 165, 170, 224
Little Bighorn battle, 150, 154
London Society for Promoting
   Christianity Among the Jews, 21, 44
Los Angeles Star, 63, 67
loyalty oath, 130, 131
Lyon, Robert, 39, 40

magazines, 29-30, 32, 39-40; *see also*
   publications
mainstream publications, 1, 2, 3, 6-7, 14, 81, 86, 87, 145, 170, 203
   Atlanta Daily Constitution, 194, 196
   Californian, 58, 61-62
   Chicago Tribune, 194, 198, 199
   Denver Mirror, 152
   Frank Leslie's Illustrated
      Newspaper, 94, 95, 103-11
   Harper's Weekly, 94, 95-97
   Los Angeles Star, 63, 67
   New York Sun, 153
   New York Times, 194, 195, 198, 199, 200, 201, 202
   New York World, 87, 109
   Oklahoma Star, 146
   Overland Monthly, 100
   Rock Springs Independent, 93, 95, 97
   Rocky Mountain News, 175
   San Francisco Chronicle, 193, 195, 198, 199, 200, 202
   Weekly Advocate, 11
   Weekly Anglo-African, 12, 13, 15
   Woman's Exponent, 176
   Woman's Herald of History and
      Social Science Co-operator, 176
   Woman's Journal, 162
   Woman's Pacific Coast Journal, 176
   Women's Tribune, 174
   World, 87
Marshall, Chief Justice John, 127, 136
Martin, Waldo, 14
Massachusetts 54th, 16
Massachusetts Peace Society, 210-11
McKenney, Thomas L., 136
McLeod, Reverend Alexander, 25-26
Mennonite press, 213
Messenger of Peace, 216, 217, 224
Mexican-American press, 56, 59
Mexicano, El, 62
Micheltorana, Governor Manuel, 63

Misisipi, El, 62
missionaries, 22, 23, 24-26, 27, 28, 48,
     72-79, 88, 101, 102, 108, 130, 131,
     139, 197
Monitor, El, 60, 66
Monitor Mexicano, El, 61, 65
Mormonism, 188-89, 194
Morrill Act, 190
Mortara case, 38
multicultural, 11-12, 27, 31, 32, 35, 45,
     57, 59-60, 63, 67, 155, 160, 223; *see
     also* ethnic, diversity

National Equal Rights, 176
National Equal Rights Party, 176
National Reformer, 7, 12
National Watchman, 13
National Woman Suffrage Association,
     164; *see also* suffrage
Native Americans, 3, 99, 102-03
negative images, 6
Nelson, Colonel C.H., 132, 133, 134
Nevada Citizen, 175, 178, 180
New Northwest, 171-72
New York Age, 16
New York Herald, 76, 101-02
New York Peace Society, 210, 218
New York Times, 194, 195, 198, 199,
     200, 201, 202
New York World, 87, 109
newspapers, *see* publications
Noah, Mordecai Manuel, 47
North, S.N.D., 79
North Star, 12, 14
Nuevo Mundo, El, 61, 64-65

Occident, 30, 32-37, 39, 40
Occident and American Jewish Advocate,
     see Occident
Oklahoma Star, 146
Omaha, 104
opium, 102

Opium War, 76, 101
Oriental, 77, 78, 79
Oriental Chinese Newspaper, see Oriental
outside commentary, 154
outsider, 2-3, 6, 21, 27, 32, 48, 116, 128,
     137, 170, 188
Overland Monthly, 100

Pacific Empire, 172, 173
Pacific Journal of Health, 176
patriotism, 8, 15, 16, 17
peace advocacy press, 209-13
     Swarthmore College Peace
          Collection, 213-14
Peacemaker, 216
Pennington, J.W.C., 9
Penny Press, 6,18n3
periodicals, 30; *see also* publications
     Western, 170, 177, 178
          aims, 171, 172, 173, 174, 175, 176
          contents, 171, 172, 173, 174, 175,
               176
          dissidents, 169, 170
          dress reform, 175
          obstacles, 179, 180, 181
          suffrage, 177, 178, 179, 181, 183
          temperance, 176, 180
Phillips, Wendell, 149
Philo Pacificus, *see* Worcester, Noah
Pioneer, 171, 178
pioneer publication, 27
Pitts-Stevens, Emily, 170, 171, 178, 179
polygamy, 189-192, 193, 194, 195, 196,
     200, 201-02, 203
Prensa Mexicana, La, 61, 65
press
     abolitionist, 14-15
     activism, 209
     antiwar, 222
     audience, 214-15
     content, 216
     credibility, 219-20

Mexican-American, 56-57
peace advocacy, 209, 213
Sketches of War, 222
strategies, 221-23
Pride, Armistead, 6
printing press, California, 62
privilege, 159-60, 161-62, 164-65
  African-American, 159, 163, 164
  woman's rights press, 163
  women, 159
progress, 99
  "civilized," 146
  Indian, 146, 147
Progresso, El, 61, 65
Promontory Point, 104
prostitution, 83, 84, 100, 110, 111
public opinion, 209, 219
public relations
  role, 146
  strategies, 146, 149
publications
  Advocate, see Advocate of Peace,
    Cherokee Advocate
  Advocate of Peace, 211, 218-19,
    221, 222
  Advocate of Peace and Christian
    Patriot, 212
  Aguacero, El, 60, 65
  Aliened American, 9
  Alki, 174, 175, 180
  American Advocate of Peace, 212,
    217, 222
  American and Chinese Commercial
    Newspaper, 85
  American Israelite, 43
  Amigo del Pueblo, El, 60, 64
  Anglo-African Magazine, 13
  Anglo-Spanish Merchant, 61
  Asmonean, 39, 40-43
  Atlanta Daily Constitution, 194, 196
  Azusa Valley News, 60, 66, 67
  Bandera Mexicana, La, 61, 65

Barbareño, El, 61, 66
Bond of Peace, 216, 219, 223, 224
Californian, 58, 61-62
Calumet, 211, 217
Cherokee Advocate, 146, 147, 149,
  150, 153, 154, 155
Cherokee Phoenix,
  see *Cherokee Phoenix and*
    Indians' Advocate
Cherokee Phoenix and Indians'
  Advocate, 115-117, 121, 123-24,
  125, 128, 129, 131, 132, 134,
  135, 136, 137, 138, 139, 141
Chicago Tribune, 194, 198, 199
Chinese American, 85
Chinese-English Newspaper, 79
Chinese Newspaper, 84-85
Chinese Record, 78
Chinese Repository, 75-76
Chinese World, 87
Christian History, 28
Clamor Público, El, 60, 64, 66, 67
Clarion, 13
Colorado Antelope, 173
Colored American, 6, 7, 11, 12
Colored Patriot, 16
Coming Century, 172, 181
Correspondencia, La, 61
Crespusculo, El, 61, 65
Crónica, La (Los Angeles), 60, 65
Crónica, La (San Francisco), 59
  61, 63
Cronista, La, 61
Daily Constitution, 197, 198
Demócrata, El, 60, 66
Denver Mirror, 152
Diario de México, El, 60, 62
Don Clarito, 61, 65
Dos Repúblicas, Las, 60, 66
Echo du Pacifique, L', 61, 64
Eco de la Patria, El, 56, 61, 64
Eco de la Puerta, El, 60, 65

Eco de la Raza Latina, El, 56, 61, 65
Eco del Pacífico, El, 58, 60, 61, 64
Eco Mexicano, El, 60
Estrella, La, 60, 63, 64
Fe en la Democratia, La, 60
Frank Leslie's Illustrated Newspaper, 94, 95, 103-11
Frederick Douglass' Paper, 15
Freedom's Journal, 5, 6, 11
Friend, 213
Friend of Peace, 211, 212, 217, 218, 221
Gaceta, La (Texas), 62
Gaceta de México, La, 62
Gazette, 61, 64
Gold Hill News, 77, 78
Golden Hill News, 77, 78
Golden Mountain News, 77, 78
Harbinger, see Harbinger of Peace
Harbinger of Peace, 211, 212, 213, 220, 221
Harper's Weekly, 94, 95-97
Herald, see Herald of Peace
Herald of Peace, 216, 217, 220, 223, 224
Hispanic listing, 60-61
Indian Herald, 146
Indian Journal, 146, 147, 149, 150, 155
Israel's Advocate, 21, 22, 23, 25, 26, 28
Israel's Herold, 40
Jew, 22-29
Jew Indeed, 29
Jewish Chronicle, 32
Journal, see Indian Journal
Joven, El, 56, 60, 65
Liberator, 14
Lily, 162, 165, 170, 224
Los Angeles Star, 63, 67
Messenger of Peace, 216, 217, 224
Mexicano, El, 62
Misisipi, El, 62

Monitor, El, 60, 66
Monitor Mexicano, El, 61, 65
National Equal Rights, 176
National Reformer, 7, 12
National Watchman, 13
Nevada Citizen, 175, 178, 180
New Northwest, 171-72
New York Age, 16
New York Herald, 76, 101-02
New York Sun, 153
New York Times, 194, 195, 198, 199, 200, 201, 202
New York World, 87, 109
North Star, 12, 14
Nuevo Mundo, El, 61, 64-65
Occident, 30, 32-37, 39, 40
Occident and American Jewish Advocate, see Occident
Oklahoma Star, 146
Orient, Der, 32
Oriental, 77, 78, 79
Oriental Chinese Newspaper, see Oriental
Overland Monthly, 100
Pacific Empire, 172, 173
Pacific Journal of Health, 176
Peacemaker, 216
Pioneer, 171, 178
Progresso, El, 61, 65
Queen Bee, 173
Reforma, La, 60, 65
República, La, 61, 65
Republicano, El, 61, 65
Revista Hispano-Americano, 60
Revista Latino-Americano, 60, 66
Revolution, 159, 161, 163-64, 165
Rights of All, 11
Rock Springs Independent, 93, 95, 97
Rocky Mountain News, 175
San Francisco China News, 74, 79-83
San Francisco Chinese Newspaper, 84
San Francisco Chronicle, 193, 195,

198, 199, 200, 202
Sociedad, El, 56, 61, 65
Sud Americano, 61, 64
Tecolote, El, 56, 60, 61, 65
Tiempo, El, 61, 65
Tong Fan San Bo, see Chinese-English Newspaper
Una, 162, 165, 224
Union, L', 15, 16
Union, La, 60, 65
Union Signal, 217, 224
Vindicator, 146
Voice of Peace, 216, 219, 223
Voz de Chile, La, 61
Voz de la Justicia, La, 60, 65
Voz de México, La, 61, 65
Voz del Nuevo Mundo, La, 56, 61, 65
Wah Kee, see Oriental
Watsonville Pajaronian, 71
Weekly Advocate, 11
Weekly Anglo-African, 12, 13, 15
Woman's Exponent, 176
Woman's Herald of Industry and Social Science Co-operator, 176
Woman's Journal, 162
Woman's Pacific Coast Journal, 176
Women's Tribune, 174
World, 86-87

Qing Dynasty, 73
Quaker press, 213
Queen Bee, 173

racial solidarity, 149, 150
racial tolerance, 149
railroads, 84, 93-98, 102, 104, 109
Ramírez, Francisco, 64, 67
Ray, Charles, 12
reform, 223-24
Reforma, La, 60, 65
República, La, 61, 65
Republicano, El, 61, 65

revisionism
  cultural history, 161
  multiculturalism, 160
  women's history, 160
Revista Hispano-Americano, 60
Revista Latino-Americano, 60, 66
Revolution, 159, 161, 163-64, 165
Reynolds *v.* United States, 187-88, 190-92, 194, 195, 196, 199, 202
Rights of All, 11
Rios, Herminio, 59-60
Rock Springs Independent, 93, 95, 97
Rock Springs, Wyoming Territory, 93-99
Rocky Mountain News, 175
Ross, Principal Chief John, 137, 140, 141
Ross, William Potter, 147, 148, 149, 150, 151
Russwurm, John Brown, 7, 11

San Francisco, 97, 81, 100
San Francisco China News, 74, 79-83
San Francisco Chinese Newspaper, 84
San Francisco Chronicle, 193, 195, 198, 199, 200, 202
"savagism," 146
Scandinavians, 93
Schlachtfeld, Mrs. (E.L. Campbell), 175-76
Semple, George, 62
Sioux campaign, 3, 149, 150, 153
  and Cheyenne, 3, 154-55
Six Companies, 73, 77, 108, 111
Sketches of War, 222
slavery, 5, 6, 7, 8, 10, 12, 14, 15, 83, 100, 110
slaves, 98, 99, 100
Smith, James McCune, 12
Smith, Page, 10
Sociedad, El, 56, 61, 65
sojourners, 72, 74-75, 99, 101
Solomon, Martha, 161
Standing, Joseph, 197, 198

Stansell, Christine, 160
Stanton, Elizabeth Cady, 159, 162, 163-64
status, Hispanic, 57
stereotypes, Chinese, 99-101, 102, 103-09
Stone, Lucy, 162
Stow, Marietta L., 176
Sud Americano, 61, 64
suffrage, 3, 225
    African-Americans, 159, 163-64
    ideology, 177, 178-79
    National Woman Suffrage
        Association, 164
    temperance and, 180, 225
    white women, 159, 163-64
    woman, 169, 170, 171, 175, 176, 177,
        178, 179, 181, 183
Sunday "blue" laws, 35, 45, 48
Swarthmore College Peace Collection,
    213-14
Swiss Treaty, 46

Tammany Hall, 42
Tecolote, El, 56, 60, 61, 65
temperance, 180
Thanksgiving Day proclamations,
    36, 45, 48
Tiempo, El, 61, 65
Tocqueville, Alexis de, 211
*Tong Fan San Bo, see Chinese-English
    Newspaper*
Twain, Mark, 71, 72

Una, 162, 165, 224
Underground Railroad, 12
Union, L', 15, 16
Union, La, 60, 65
Union Signal, 217, 224
United States Constitution, 7, 8, 14, 15
United States Supreme Court, 126, 127,
    128, 129, 136, 137, 140
Universal Peace Union, 210, 212
Us *vs.* them thinking, 150

Vindicator, 146
Voice of Peace, 216, 219, 223
Voz de Chile, La, 61
Voz de la Justicia, La, 60, 65
Voz de México, La, 61, 65
Voz del Nuevo Mundo, La, 56, 61, 65

Wah Kee, see Oriental
Waite, Chief Justice, 191, 192
Walker, Alice, 160
Walker, Clarence, 8, 21
War Department, 119, 121
Ward, Samuel Ringgold, 9, 10
Watsonville Pajaronian, 71
Weekly Advocate, 11
Weekly Anglo-African, 12, 13, 15
Wells, Emmeline B., 176
Wells, Ida B., 17
Whipper, William, 7, 12, 15, 18 n 6
white sympathizers, 149
Williams, Reverend Samuel Wells, 73
Wise, Rabbi Isaac Mayer, 43
womanist, 160
Woman's Exponent, 176
*Woman's Herald of History and Social
    Science Co-operator*, 176
Woman's Journal, 162
Woman's Pacific Coast Journal, 176
woman's rights
    editors, 162
    press, 161, 162, 163
women, 75, 83, 100, 110, 111
Women's Tribune, 174
Worcester, Noah, 217, 218
Worcester, Reverend Samuel, 130, 131, 132
World, 86-87
Workingman's Party, 111

Young, Brigham, 189, 190
Young, Carrie Fisher, 176
Young, John, 58

Zamorano, Augustín, 62